William Beamont

A history of the castle of Halton and the priory or abbey of Norton

With an account of the barons of Halton

William Beamont

A history of the castle of Halton and the priory or abbey of Norton
With an account of the barons of Halton

ISBN/EAN: 9783337161798

Printed in Europe, USA, Canada, Australia, Japan

Cover: Foto ©ninafisch / pixelio.de

More available books at **www.hansebooks.com**

A HISTORY

OF THE

CASTLE OF HALTON

AND THE

PRIORY OR ABBEY OF NORTON

WITH AN ACCOUNT OF THE

Barons of Halton, the Priors and Abbots of Norton

AND AN ACCOUNT OF

Rock Savage and Daresbury Church

WITH NOTICES OF THE HISTORIC EVENTS OF THE NEIGHBOURHOOD

ILLUSTRATED WITH VIEWS AND OTHER ILLUSTRATIONS

IN TWO PARTS.

I.—HALTON.   II.—NORTON.

By WILLIAM BEAMONT, Esq.

WARRINGTON
PERCIVAL PEARSE, 8 SANKEY STREET
1873

Printed by R. & R. CLARK, *Edinburgh.*

TO

SIR RICHARD BROOKE, Baronet,

Descended of a time-honoured Cheshire house, which he worthily represents, and to whom the artist, the architect, and the archæologist owe a large debt for the taste and judgment he has exhibited in revealing, after they had been so long hidden from view, the beautiful arches of the ancient Priory or Abbey within his domain of Norton, this account of that place, and of the Castle of Halton, *once* a protection and *now* a picturesque ornament of the neighbourhood, is, with much esteem and respect, and every good wish, inscribed by the Author.

LIST OF ILLUSTRATIONS.

PART I.

HALTON CASTLE	*Frontispiece to the Volume.*
SITE OF ELFLEDA'S CASTLE AT RUNCORN	*To face* p. 4
SEAL OF HENRY V. WHEN PRINCE OF WALES, CORBEL AND WINDOW AT HALTON, AND SEAL OF HALTON COURT	„ 90
ROCK SAVAGE	„ 107

PART II.

VIEW OF NORTON PRIORY, reduced from Buck's Engraving	*Frontispiece to Part II.*
NORMAN DOORWAY AT NORTON	*To face* p. 151
SEPULCHRAL SLABS FROM NORTON	„ 153
SLABS AND TILES FROM DARESBURY	„ 156
STATUE OF ST. CHRISTOPHER	„ 161
TILES AND RELICS FROM NORTON	163

PREFACE.

The day is past of fight and feud,
The spear has lost its sullen food;
No more the chieftain in his hall
Starts at the warder's trumpet call.
The moat is filled, the umber'd tower
Is curtain'd with the woodbine's flower.
The lilies round the portal shield
Veil the rich spoils of flood and field.

HALTON and BEESTON, the only two Norman castles of Cheshire which stand on commanding isolated eminences, were built with the same design of checking marauders, and strengthening the law when it was too weak to assert itself, and needed to call the sword to its aid. Halton looked to control the danger that might cross the Mersey from Lancashire, and Beeston to guard the rich plains of Cheshire from the attacks of the half-subdued mountaineers of Wales. Halton, the older fortress, was built by Nigel, or his son, the contemporaries of Hugh Lupus, and two of his palatine barons; but Beeston, the later structure, was the work of Randle Blundeville, one of the last but not the least of the palatine earls, and, as we might naturally expect, was the stronger and the grander place. Of the architecture of Halton—though it was undoubtedly Norman, as we have few of its remains to appeal to—we are unable to give a precise account; some old vaultings and a well in the cellar, a winding staircase in ruins, with an arched window, a few frag-

Preface.

ments of tracery, and some mouldering walls extending round the greatest part of the area, being all that now remain of its former self,—the gatehouse, its best feature, having been removed, with little regard to taste, in the year 1738 ; but as to the architecture of Beeston we are left in no doubt, for tradition says, and its large remains confirm her story, that its builder, on returning from the east about the year 1220, took for his model the walls of Constantinople ; and if we are to ascribe to him, who was certainly a man in advance of his age, the plan and design of the great gateway at Beeston, to which no similar work, not even the grand gateway at Arques, is at all to be compared, he possessed a taste very uncommon in his own age, and which is to be envied even now. Beeston probably formed the model of the Edwardian castles afterwards built in Wales. But our business is more immediately with the castle at Halton, and the priory or abbey of Norton,—the two parts into which this work is divided. It will be seen in the following pages, that, besides the castle at Halton, its lords, in regular series, have been brought before the reader ; and it has been shown how, from being originally simple barons, they became first earls, then dukes, and finally wore the imperial crown of England. Of the knightly lords of Norton, since its abbey fell, having had no opportunity of treating in the following work, we propose to supply that deficiency in this place.

Sir RICHARD BROOKE, the purchaser of the abbey after the dissolution, sprang from a family who had been long settled at Leighton, in the hundred of Nantwich, one of whom, the lord of that place, in the time of Henry III., was called William de la Brook de Leighton. In that age, however, when names were often changed very capriciously, his son called himself Richard de Doito, that is of the brook, for Douit or Doit in Norman-French answers to the English for a duct or channel, and means a brook, and this new name was suggested to Richard by the streamlet running by his manor-house of Leighton.

Preface.   xi

RICHARD, the purchaser of Norton, who was a younger son of Thomas Brooke of Leighton, about the time of Henry VII. adopted the profession of arms, and cast in his lot with the order of knights, who were called successively hospitallers of St. John of Jerusalem, of Rhodes, and of Malta, and became Sir Richard Brooke, knight of Rhodes, which order, in consequence of Henry VII. having been made its protector in the year 1500, had become very popular in England.[1] Like very many things that are great, the origin of the order had been humble. Touched with compassion for the hardships to which pilgrims visiting the holy places of the East were exposed, a simple merchant of Amalfi, in the year 1048, built them a house at Jerusalem, where its remains still attest its western origin. The keepers of this house or hospital, who in 1092 became a monastic body, and in 1118 a military order, rose to be a great power, which was able for a time to check the advancing surges of Eastern barbarism, and sustain the fortunes of Godfrey and the glories of the Latin kingdom, and which only withdrew from Palestine when longer resistance was hopeless. They retired first to Margat, then to Acre, and when neither of these places was any longer tenable, they established themselves in Cyprus, where the best wine of the island, which they taught the inhabitants to make, and which from them is called "Commanderia," still retains their memory. In 1307 the Order, under their grand master Sir Fulk de Villaret, besieged and took Rhodes, where, in spite of many a vigorous onslaught made on them by their powerful neighbours, they remained masters of the island for two hundred years, to the great advantage both of the place and its inhabitants. Justly proud that they had so long held the island of Rhodes against so many powerful enemies, the knights, in memory of it, chose for their motto these four letters, F. E. R. T. Mottoes are not always translateable, but this even requires an Œdipus to read it into "Fortitudo ejus Rhodum tenuit." In 1522, however, after a glorious defence, and a capitulation if possible yet more glorious, the island fell under the Ottoman power, when the skill

[1] Hume's Hist. Eng. iii. 385.

and valour of the grand-master Vilars de l'Isle Adam extorted from Suleiman II. such admiration, that he could not help exclaiming to his vizier—" It grieves me to turn this aged Christian out of the home he has defended so well." From Rhodes the Order retired to Candia, then to Sicily, afterwards to Viterbo, and lastly to Malta, which in 1530 was given them by the Emperor Charles V. In their new abode they lost none of the reputation which they had gained by their skill and conduct in their previous homes.

To this semi-military and religious order Sir Richard Brooke was admitted in 1531, the year after they had been domiciled in Malta. In the king's household-book, under 12th and 13th August of that year, there are some entries of certain payments stated to have been made to Maister Broke's servant, bringing cake for the king, which, if they refer to Sir Richard, show that he was then about the court. After serving with the knights for a time, Sir Richard became commander of the commandery of Mount St. John, in Cleveland.[1] When the king was pushing on the dissolution of monasteries, Sir William Weston being the lord prior of the order, the king, in the hope of inducing him to surrender the revenues of the knights, offered him a pension of £1000 a year for his life; but the prior, proving to be an oak which could not be bent, rejected the offer, and the king thereupon, in 1540, obtained an act (32 Henry VIII.) by which the order was entirely suppressed and dissolved, and Sir William, whom neither threats nor self-interest had been able to move, the same day died of grief. He was buried in his priory church at Clerkenwell.[2] An account of the disease, sufferings, death, and burial of the lord prior, has come down to us in the history of his order. Sir Richard Brooke, who is expressly mentioned in the act of dissolution as

[1] Gough's Camden's Brit. iii. 84 ; Notes and Queries, 1853, p. 191.
[2] "In the north wall of the chancel of the priory of Clerkenwell is a fair marble tomb, with the portraiture of a dead man lying upon his shroud, the most artificially cut in stone that ever man beheld ; all the plates of brass are stolen away, only some few pieces remaining, containing these words :—

"one of the compeers of the said order," was to have 100 marks as a yearly pension, and his name occurs in most of the histories of the order; but if he was present at the death and obsequies of the lord prior, he did not share his resolution to oppose the king's will, for, bowing to the fate which he could not avert, he conformed to the act of parliament, accepted his pension, and, being released by it from his religious vows, after being civilly dead was restored to life again, and became the founder of the family at Norton.[1]

After his release from his vows, Sir Richard married Christian, the daughter of John Carew of Haccomb, in Devonshire. Cromwell, the king's minister, who is commended for the great pains he took to bring up his son well, gave a strict charge to his tutor "to instruct him with good letters, honest manners, pastyme of instruments, and such other pastyme as should be meet and convenient for him;" but Christian, Sir Richard's wife, had a brother, afterwards Sir Peter Carew, who either had no such tutor, or was not disposed to profit by his instructions, for the historian who praises Cromwell for the care he took of his son's education, gives us at the same time a sad picture of the frowardness, refractoriness, and ill conduct of Sir Peter Carew.[2]

> " Hospitalitate inclytus, genere preclarus.
> Hanc urnam officii causa . . .
> Ecce quem cernis tuo nomini semper devotum
> Suscipe in sinum virgo Maria tuum.
> Spes me non fallat quam in te semper habebam
> Virgo da facilem . . .

This monument was erected to the memory of Sir William Weston, knight, Lord Prior of St. John's, Jerusalem, at the time of the dissolution of the said priory, to whom Henry VIII, for his maintenance, had allowed £1000 of yearly pension during his life. Of which sum he received never a penny, for so it fortuned that upon the 7th May 1540, being ascension day, and the same day of the dissolution of his house, he was dissolved by death, which struck him to the heart, at the first time when he heard of the dissolution of his order."—Weever's *Funeral Monuments*, p. 213. See also Sutherland's *Knights of Malta*, p. 115.

[1] Sutherland's Knights of Malta, ii. 114-15; Notes and Queries, 1861, p. 270. Villeneuve Bargemont, Monumens Historiques des grand Maitres de l'ordre de St. Jean. Paris, 1829. Cotton, MSS. 365, Otho, ix. [2] Froude's Hist. Eng. i. 38.

In the year 1545, Sir Richard contracted to purchase from the crown the manor of Norton, including the abbey with its members and appurtenances, and by letters-patent, dated the 10th December in that year, only little more than twelve months before the king's decease, they were conveyed to him. In the letters the king calls Sir Richard "dilectus servicus noster," and besides a sum of money, expresses the consideration to be "servitium antehac multipliciter impensum," and grants him in fee-simple, Norton, Stockham, Acton Grange, and Aston Grange in Cheshire, and Cuerdley in Lancashire. Unlike many similar grants of the possessions of the dissolved abbeys, this was in no sense a grant to a needy courtier, but a *bonâ fide* sale for a full and valuable consideration in money. The treasurer of the court of augmentations, Sir John Williams, who signs the letters, has also sealed them with a seal which represents a warrior bearing a shield, falling on one knee, which is evidently an impression from an old intaglio. The treasurer who selected such a seal when the art of engraving was at a low ebb, showed himself a man of taste by admiring such beauty in art.

In 2 and 3 Philip and Mary, 1555, Sir Richard Brooke sued the tenants of Cuerdley, in order to avoid certain leases which, as he alleged, they had obtained, contrary to the customs, from the prior of Jorvaulx, the successor, *sed longo intervallo*, of Scott's prior of that place in Ivanhoe.[1] Sir Richard's suspicions were natural.

In the 5 and 6 Philip and Mary, 1557, when a survey of Halton Castle, the park, and lordship, was directed to be made, there was then in the park a herd of deer. Sir Richard living near, and the crown having confidence in him, he was appointed one of the commissioners to make it. The report states what repair the castle was in, and how many trees were needed to repair it.[2] In 1563 and 1564, while Queen Elizabeth's reign was still young and the times critical, she made Sir Richard, in whose loyalty, ability, and experience she had full confidence, high sheriff of

[1] Duchy Calendar, ii. 192.   [2] Ibid. 173-5.

Preface.

Cheshire, and the result proved that she had not misjudged him, for he so filled his important office as to earn his quietus. In the family pedigree he is styled vice-admiral of England, by which it is not meant that he either held a maritime command, or that he was what is now called a lord of the admiralty. The office of vice-admiral, which was known to the constitution in very early times, was confined to some of the coasts, like that which was held by Sir John Eliot, who was vice-admiral of Devonshire in the reign of Charles I.[1] It seems to have been an office bearing a resemblance to a deputy-lieutenant's commission on land; and the venerable Lambarde, who gives us a commission for the office, intimates that it had some perquisites attached to it.[2] In the 11th year of the queen's reign, 1569, the life of Sir Richard Brooke, which had been very varied, and had had many trials and troubles, came to a close, and he died, leaving his wife Christian, and five children—Thomas, Christian, Prudence, Jane, and Martha—surviving him. His widow afterwards married Ralph Done, of the good Cheshire house of Crowton, and she is mentioned as being then Done's wife in some proceedings of the Cuerdley tenants, which took place in 1570.[3] Sir Richard's daughter Jane was contracted when very young, to Edward Boteler of Bewsey, but the marriage never took place, and the bridegroom's refusal to complete the marriage was among the first steps he took in his way to ruin: his daughter Prudence married Hugh Starkey the traveller, who in 1565 was present at the siege of Malta, which, from his former connection with its defenders, must have given her father satisfaction.[4] Sir Richard was carried to Runcorn for burial, and in altering that church in 1847, an incised slab was found, which, from its bearing the figure of a Maltese cross and chain upon it, was believed to have covered his remains.

[1] Disraeli's Life and Reign of Charles I. 319-20.
[2] Eirenarcha, 17, 18, 19.
[3] Duchy Calendar, ii. 401.
[4] Notes and Queries, 1855.

Preface.

THOMAS BROOKE, Esq., Sir Richard's son and successor, added to the family estate by purchasing and laying to it the township of Thelwall. In the year 1578 he served the office of high sheriff of Cheshire, and in 1580 he filled the office a second time. Both were years of comparative peace, and consequently the duties of the sheriff were less onerous than at some other times.

In the latter year we read that one Thomas White, a London merchant, fitted out a sort of bucaneering expedition, which captured and made prize on the high seas of a vessel which had on board a valuable cargo of 1400 chests of quicksilver, and what in some countries would have been even of more value, two million indulgences, but these had here lost their market. In August 1597, the queen having been at great charges about the war in the Low Countries, and having incurred debts, "money had to be found" to meet them, and she therefore issued out privy seals, and commissioned Sir Hugh Cholmondeley, her deputy-lieutenant, to collect those miscalled loans. The whole sum to be raised in Cheshire was £1675, and towards it Mr. Brooke contributed £25.[1]

On the 3d August 1619, Mr. Brooke and his eldest son and heir-apparent, Richard Brooke, joined in conveying the hall and demesne of Thelwall, and the fishery in the Mersey, with various other hereditaments there, to Sir Richard Grosvenor and others, with a view to a family settlement. Mr. Brooke, who was three times married, had a family of eighteen children, one of whom, George, his second son by his first wife, was drowned in Warrington Water, which discredits the efficacy of a look upon the face of St. Christopher, whose effigy at Norton George Brooke could not help seeing every day :—

> Christophori faciem die quocunque tueris
> Illo nempe die malâ morte non morieris.

Alice, Mr. Brooke's eldest daughter by Ellen Gerard, his third wife,

---

[1] Calendar of Privy Seals, Chetham Miscellanies, vol. iv.

Preface.

married Thomas Birch, Esq. of Birch, and Peter, his second son by her, took sides with the Parliament in the great civil war, and rose to be a colonel in their army. He was elected member for Newton, was a frequent speaker in the House, and in 1652 he bought the estate of Mere, and was the founder of the family there. He was knighted after the Restoration, and in 1669 he was sheriff of Cheshire. His father, Mr. Brooke, died in 1622, and in 1627 his mother married, at Warrington, Edward Bridgeman, Esq., a brother of the bishop of that name. Mr. Brooke was succeeded by his eldest son,

RICHARD BROOKE, who, having been knighted in Ireland, was afterwards Sir Richard Brooke, knight. He was twice married, and left children of each marriage. One of his daughters, Elizabeth, who married Tourell Joseeline, was the authoress of a work called "The Mother's Legacy to her Unborn Child," which was first printed at Oxford in 1624, and has been often reprinted since.[1] Sir Richard died on 10th April 1632, having enjoyed the estate but ten years. His inquisition *post mortem*, taken as usual soon after he died, contains many particulars of the house at Norton as it then was, which will be found at length in the ensuing work. He was succeeded by his eldest son,

HENRY BROOKE, afterwards Sir Henry Brooke, the first baronet of his family. Sir Henry, who at his father's death was just of age, was still a young man on the breaking out of the great civil war, when, like many others of his age, he joined the Parliament party. In 1643 he became a colonel in their army, and was made a commissioner for levying the assessment ordered to be made for carrying on the war, which made him obnoxious to the King's party, who decided to besiege his house. When they had taken up their position, a contemporary of his own party tells us

[1] Notes and Queries, 1851.

—"A man upon his tower, with a flag in his hand, cryde them ayme while they discharged their cannon, saying, 'Wide, my lord, on the right hand; now wide two yards on the left; two yards over, my lord,' etc. He made them swell for anger, when they could not endamage the house, for they only wounded one man, lost 46 of their own, and their canonier: then, in devilish rage, they burnt a barn and corne worth, as is valued, £1000; set fire to another, but more execution was made on the man that attempted it than the barn, for he was blinded in firing the barn, and so found wandering in the fields, and confest he had £5 given him for his service. After this they plundered Mr. Brooke's tenants, and returned home with shame and hatred of all the country. To this worthy man's rescue we could not go, because the march [from Nantwich] was long and full of hazard, and we thought their aim was to tire us out upon that service, upon which they might put us every day, by reason of Halton Castle in their possession, and but half a mile from Norton."[1]

In the year 1644, Richard Grosvenor, Esquire, having been made sheriff by the King, the Parliament, by a stretch of their power, appointed Colonel Brooke to the same office, and they continued him in it for four years, so that the country saw the anomaly of two sheriffs.

In the first year of his office Mr. Brooke was appealed to by Mrs. Lettice Legh of Lyme, the guardian of her infant children, to relieve her of a surcharge made upon her for a horse soldier, when he wrote her the following letter :—

Most noble Ladie—The respects that in my own particular I have receaved from you commandes mee in anie thing wthin my power to serve you: but in this concerning the horse I am but the deputie leevetnts serv^{t}ant, and dare not doe anie thinge in that kind wthout theire p'mission. I well remember when ye list was p^{r}duced y^r busines had a debate, and the gentlemen could not resolve why the lord of Darbie for anie p'ticular respect should weaken the standing forces of ye countie, and therefore, as I remember, they thought fit that one horse at least should be shewed here. I p'fess, ladie, my owne brothers are not spared, as when you please you may know from my brother Hyde, whoe wth my coozen Crewe, I am confident, will

---

[1] Hist. Ches. pref. xli.

give you better satisfaction than I can possible by letter. I most earnestly entreat you take not unkindly w^t I write, nor thincke y_t I have forgotten that noble ingagement you have laid on all the gentry of the countie, to which I must justly add one lately to myselfe in that undisputed . . . you sent mee. These and many more make mee soe whollie yor servant, that w^tev^rʒis in my simple power I say againe you shall most freelie command. But this being the contrey's, not mine, 'tis not in my power. I most humblie therefore crave yor p'don, and hartily beg of you to esteeme me never the lesse,

Ladie, yor most affectionate servant,

H. BROOKE.

Daresburie, Satterday night, 1644.

Addressed—
      For the right w^{oss't} Mrs. Leigh, at Lyme,
            Theise P'sent.

From the year 1646 to the year 1651 Colonel Brooke was seneschal of the Widnes court-leet at Farnworth, which had then an extensive jurisdiction, and in 1652 Newcome expressly calls him Colonel Henry Brooke.[1] He was afterwards elected to parliament, and sat as knight of the shire for his native county. For the active service he did his party both in and out of parliament, he is abused in the scurrilous lines which Mr. Halliwell has preserved—

Brooke, mad as a hare,
At Halton doth stare.[2]

Colonel Brooke, who was made a baronet at the Restoration, and of whom some other particulars will be found in the ensuing pages, died in 1664, and was succeeded by his eldest son,

SIR RICHARD BROOKE, baronet, who while his father was seneschal of Halton Castle during the interregnum, served under him as its constable, which was then an office of some importance. In 1667 he was high sheriff of Cheshire. In the parish of Runcorn, which had long an unenviable fame for its tithe suits, but which are now happily laid at rest for ever, there began about this time to be an uneasy feeling on that subject, and Sir Richard through some friend seems to have asked counsel from Sir

---

[1] Newcome's Autobiography, Chet. Soc. i. 39.   [2] Ashm. MSS. 36, 37, Art. 93, p. 78.

Preface.

William Dugdale as to whether he could set up any claims to exemption from tithes on all or any part of his estate, and this letter, the original of which is preserved at Norton, was received from Sir William in reply:—

To Walter Chetwynd, Esq., Stafford.

Honoured Sir—By yours of the 15th instant (which came to my hands yesterday), I perceive that . . is no sure man of his word, so that, unlesse you continue your importunitie, I must never expect any of those things that belonge to our parish, though they will be of no advantage to him if he keepe them till domesday. The next opportunity I have with Sir Joseph Williamson, I will speake with him concerning that Lieger-booke; but I cannot expect that my moving him therein can be so effectuall as your appearing in it would be.

As to your queries concerning Norton Abbey, I suppose it is in order to an exemption from payment of tithes for some lands wch have heretofore belong'd thereto. W^{ch} if it be, your friende will have a very difficult worke to make these lands capable of such a priviledge: for though it was founded before the Lateran councill, it was none of those orders (viz. Cistertians or Templars) wch had that priviledge for the lands wch they were possess'd of before that time; it being of the order of canons of St. Augustine; some of wch monasteries had speciall bulls for that purpose, as Leicester Abby for one. Neither was it one of the greater houses for wch the act of dissolution in 30 Hen. VIII. tooke care for preserving their priviledges in as ample manner as the monks or-canons held them, for it being under £200 in value per annum was dissolv'd in 27 Hen. VIII. and not reviv'd again as Croxden in your county of Stafford, and two or three more in all England were. Its foundation was first at Runcorne in Cheshire in Anno 1133, and afterwards translated to Norton, as you will see in page 187 of the second volume of the Monasticon.

This is all I can saye to you herein, and for news, ye Prince of Orange and his lady went hence yesterday, but I doubt they are windbound as yet, it blowing full east; and that I heare not for certaine who shall be archb^p of Canterbury. Many ghesses there are, wch be according to men's fancies. I shall not come into the country till twelfe day be past; so heartily wishing you good health, I rest your most obliged servant, and reall honourer,

WM. DUGDALE.

Herald's Office, neere Paul's Wharfe, 21 Nov. 1677.

My most humble service to noble Sr Wolsten and your worthy mother. Sir John Cotton is not like to be here this winter.

Sir Richard, who died in 1709, was succeeded by his eldest son,

SIR THOMAS BROOKE, baronet, who was high sheriff of the county in 1720, and was afterwards appointed by the crown to the honorary office of constable of Chester Castle. He married Grace, the daughter of Roger Wilbraham, and had a family of six sons and three daughters. Pusey, one of the sons, who became surveyor-general of the counties of Hants and Dorset, and collector of customs at the port of Portsmouth, could not in that distant sphere of duty forget his old home at Norton, for by his will, dated in 1767, he founded at Halton a set of almshouses for "six poor decayed and honest servants," who were to be appointed by his brother John during his life, and afterwards by the head of the house of Norton for the time being. Thomas, another son, while living at Ashton Hayes in 1784, was elected M.P. for Newton. Sir Thomas witnessed and probably took part in the improvement of the Mersey, where it ran through his estate, and in removing the weirs and other obstructions in which were found to impede its free navigation. He died in 1737, and his eldest son having predeceased him, he was succeeded by his grandson,

Sir Richard Brooke, baronet, who was high sheriff of Cheshire in 1752. The present mansion at Norton, which has the usual features of other great houses of the Georgian period, was probably Sir Richard's work, and it is to be regretted that in building it more of the old house was not preserved. It was in his time also that the Sankey canal was cut through his Lancashire estate in Cuerdley, and that the Bridgewater canal was made through the grounds at Norton, his Cheshire estate, when Sir Richard successfully resisted some of its great promoter's first and rather arbitrary designs respecting it.

Sir Richard died on 6th July 1781, and was succeeded by his eldest son,

Sir Richard Brooke, baronet, who was high sheriff of the county in 1787, and died at an early age in 1795. In 1807 his son Thomas Brooke was elected member for the borough of Newton. Sir Richard was succeeded by his eldest son of his own name,

Sir Richard Brooke, baronet, the late representative of the family, who was born at Norton on the 18th August 1785, and was still a minor when his father died. At the general election in 1812, he stood candidate for the city of Chester, and was beaten on the poll by only a narrow majority of 27, in favour of Mr. (afterwards Sir John Grey) Egerton (baronet), after which he never again sought parliamentary honours. In 1817 he served as high sheriff of Cheshire, an office which seemed almost hereditary in his family. Loving a country life, and having rural tastes and pursuits, he lived much at home, and gave attention to his estate, which in his time so much increased in productiveness, that more wheat was grown at last upon a single farm in Norton, than was produced by the whole of it when he came to the property. Planting young trees and carefully looking after his woods and timber was his amusement, and had he been educated in the school of woods and mines, after the manner which is common in Germany, and which might be introduced with advantage among our gentlemen at home, it would have become his passion as it was Evelyn's. He knew also the value of having good roads in the country, and took pleasure in looking after, and widening and improving, those of his own estate and neighbourhood. In his discharge of the duties of an active county magistrate he was exemplary in his patient attention to the cases coming before him, and brought to their decision so much common sense, that he was seldom if ever wrong, while sometimes his sagacity enabled him to detect the falsehood of a serious charge. Upon one occasion, when a woman who had charged two men who were in custody with a gross assault, Sir Richard, suspecting from something in her manner that her story was false, pursued his investigation until out of her own mouth she was convicted of falsehood, when, instead of the accused, she herself was committed to prison—a result which was amply justified by what transpired afterwards. While he was a minor the proprietors of the Old Quay Navigation cut a canal from Runcorn to Warrington to avoid the neaps in the river, and so have always a passage open from Runcorn to Manchester, and this canal for a considerable distance was made through Sir Richard's Cheshire estate. At a later period the proprietors of the Saukey canal extended it from Sankey to Widnes, and this extension was made chiefly through Sir Richard's Cuerdley estate in Lancashire. These two canals, with the Bridgewater canal cut in his ancestor's time, made the system of artificial water communication more complete in the valley of the Mersey than almost any other in the world. For a long series of years boats upon these canals, after the fashion of a Dutch *treckschuit*, afforded a popular and cheap mode of travelling from Runcorn and the intermediate places to Manchester; and Southey, in his Don Manuel Espriella, describes very pleasantly the view he had of the country in travelling in this way, from such a boat at London bridge upon the Bridgewater canal. But Sir Richard saw introduced one of the greatest of modern improvements—the railway system, which has now covered the country as with an iron network; not, however, to curtail but to assist the inhabitants in their movements, and which, revolutionising all former modes, has so changed our travelling habits as to make near neighbours of persons and places the most far off and remote. Sir Richard, at the request of the promoters of the Chester and Warrington railway, cut the first sod of that line; and when the work was approaching completion, he was waited upon by a working mason with a portfolio, who requested from him a seal or a drawing of his coat of arms, that he might engrave it over the mouth of the north tunnel, which stood on his estate. After giving him an impression of his seal without the motto, the man requested to have this also, when Sir Richard wrote it down for him thus—" Faste withoute Fraude," which contains an allusion to the badger, the family crest. Expressing his surprise that it was not in Latin, which he thought would read better, the mason produced from the portfolio the drawings of some of the Brooke hatchments in Runcorn, and asked Sir Richard whether "resurgam," the word under one of these, would not do, to which he replied that such a word over a tunnel would be interpreted to mean "I may go in, but shall I come out?" But Sir Richard was also permitted to see introduced that other great wonder, the electric telegraph, whose feats have distanced Puck's boast to "put a girdle about the earth in forty minutes," by accomplishing it in so many seconds. When the tithe suits—that long-standing hereditary sore of the parish of Runcorn, which it was Sir Richard's good fortune to see ended—were near their last gasp, Sir Richard went to Oxford to see the dean and chapter, whose clerk had raised some unfair obstacles at the last moment. When they with their clerk were met, the latter began a vulgar tirade against his opponents, but when he saw Sir Richard with his pencil in his hand, he stopped to ask if he was taking notes,—"Why, yes, I am," he said, "but will you tell me how you spell that word chaps?" In his coarseness he had applied this term to his opponents, but Sir Richard's question was so polite and happy a rebuke, that the dean and chapter no longer hesitated, but directed the dispute to be settled.

After living to advanced years, and earning

"That which should accompany old age,
As honour, love, obedience, troops of friends,"

Sir Richard died at Norton on the 11th November 1865, and was buried in the family vault at Runcorn. He was succeeded by a son of his own name,

SIR RICHARD BROOKE, the seventh baronet, who upon his father's decease removed to, and has since resided at, the family seat at Norton, employing himself in the useful but unobtrusive duties of his station as a country gentleman, and indulging a taste for the pencil, which is hereditary in his family, and which he found ample opportunities for indulging during his travels in Palestine and Egypt. Like most of his ancestors, he has served the office of high sheriff of the county, and he commanded for a time, with the rank of colonel, a neighbouring volunteer rifle corps, for which he was well qualified by the commission he had previously held in the Guards. As a county magistrate Sir Richard gives time and attention to the duties of a justice of the peace, which in his, or in any other populous neighbour-

Preface. xxv

hood, are neither light nor trifling, though they are oftener repaid by abuse than praise—so much more common is ill-nature than justice, the temper of a Cynic than that of an Aristides!

Since he came to the estate, Sir Richard has cleared and re-opened, after it had been hidden since the building of the present mansion, the original doorway of the old priory, a beautiful piece of work, and almost as perfect as when the Norman masons left it, which is once more devoted to its original purpose, and made the entrance to the house. The restoration of an ornament so rarely to be found entitles him to the thanks of all who love the "music of the eye," that charm which consists in the grace of form and the harmony of proportion in architecture. In the course of making some alterations of the ground near the house, he also discovered a series of sculptured slabs, lying where they had been originally placed, above the remains of the former priors and abbots of Norton, or of others who were thought worthy of such a burial. Deeply buried beneath the mould and green sward which more than three centuries had heaped on them, and which had served to preserve their freshness, the slabs lay entire and *in situ*, clearly indicating what was before unknown, that there had once stood the church of St. Mary of Norton. Sir Richard, with reverent hands, has put a fence round the place, which will prevent the slabs from injury. Their discovery gave occasion to some anonymous writer to print and circulate the following copy of verses which he pretended to have found in the British Museum :—

" Nortune frerys, els theyr bonys
Rest aneath great carven stonys
That, whiles Englonde loves ye ryghte,
Hedde must bide fro mortale syghte—
Meane tyme oder hape befalle
Brokes now course aboon theym alle,
Brokes yat manne, so over fain,
Can ne fathome, no nor drayne.
—Still ane oder daye shal bee
Whan a lorde of yat contree—
(Dykon sonne of Dykon sonne

d

Preface.

> Of hys pares ye formast one,)
> Wol his fader's courte astore,
> Wel those heddn depes explore;—
> Than shal yat home-closet felde
> Harvest all unwott of yelde.
> Than shal those ones beryd stonys
> Rered ore holie frerys bonys
> Courte ye lyght of daye againe.—
> Than take hede ! Yf ther romano
> Anie gode menne in yat daye
> Did theym for old Englonde praie."

Though there is abundant internal evidence that the lines are not, as the writer pretends, ancient, there can be no harm in heartily responding to their concluding prayer.

In the fine vaulted old chamber into which the newly-opened entrance to the house leads, its hospitable owner, over the hearth which was made for warming it with a fire, has placed these lines:—

> "Though warmth the coming guest to cheer,
> Is kindled on the hearth-stone here ;
> Still warmer, when he mounts the stair,
> The welcome that awaits him there."

The fire to the coming guest burns warmer and brighter as he reads these lines of welcome.

If it be true, as Dr. Johnson somewhere says, that "much of our knowledge we must snatch, not take," even an inattentive observer may gain something from wall inscriptions like the foregoing, and that which adorns the banqueting room at Knebworth, in which we are at no loss to recognise the pen of the writer :—

> "Read the Rede of this Old Roof Tree.
> Here be trust fast. Opinion free.
> Knightly Right Hand. Christian knee.
> Worth in all. Wit in some.
> Laughter open. Slander dumb.
> Hearth where rooted Friendships go.
> Safe as altar even to foe.
> And the sparks that upward go

Preface.

> When the hearth flame dies below,
> If thy sap in them may be,
> Fear no winter, Old Roof Tree."

And here we bring to a close our review of the house of Norton. Except in a few instances where circumstances seemed to call for a fuller account, our notices of the heads of the house have been but brief: a biography of ten generations could not have been compressed in a small space. But though greater prominence has been given to some than to other members of the family, all the Brookes are said to have lived much at home, loving the country and country pursuits, discharging their public duties as magistrates, deputy-lieutenants, grand jurors, and sheriffs, exercising hospitality to their neighbours, and not forgetting the poor.

> " Servare modum finemque tueri
> Naturamque sequi"

might have been their motto, for prudence, which is the root of all virtue, has been their guiding star.

In 1562 an Arthur Brooke translated from the Italian the story which was the ground-work of Shakspere's "Romeo and Juliet;"[1] and in 1588 a Humphrey Brooke of Liverpool communicated to the queen's ministers the first intelligence of the sailing of the great Armada.[2] The author would have rejoiced if he had been able to connect either of these men, but especially the first, with the Norton genealogical tree. An old family, like one of its own hereditary oaks, while it gives shade and shelter, remains stationary itself, sends off many a healthy sapling to serve their country at the bar, in the senate, or in the field. Sir Philip Broke, who, with his much smaller ship the "Shannon," fought and captured the American vessel "Chesapeake," claimed alliance with Norton; and Colonel Brooke, the late baronet's brother, fought at Waterloo, and the present baronet's brother has won a general's commission by his service abroad and at home.

It is now the author's pleasing duty to acknowledge his obligations for the assistance he has received.

[1] Watt's Bibliotheca.   [2] Hist. Lanc. iv. 71.

Preface.

To Sir Richard Brooke, baronet, he is indebted for the means of referring to the king's letters-patent to his ancestors, and the original papers respecting Aston chapel, as well as for a photograph of the Norton doorway.

To Lady Brooke he owes his thanks for a drawing of the statue of St. Christopher, and to the Honourable Miss Adela Bootle-Wilbraham for a drawing of the Norton slabs.

To his friend Frank Renaud, Esq., he is indebted for a drawing of the Halton window.

To Rowland Eyles Egerton-Warburton, Esq., he owes his thanks for permission to refer so frequently to his Arley Charters.

To Mr. John Owen, of Manchester, the painstaking antiquary, who first drew attention to many of the Daresbury relics, he owes his best thanks for his drawings of some of them, and for a sight of his copious notes on the architecture of that church.

The view of the doorway at Norton has been produced by the heliotype process, and to the author's regret it fails to do justice to the original photograph from which it was taken.

For all the other illustrations the author is indebted to his wife's pencil, from whose drawings in anastatic ink they have been produced in such a shape as, he flatters himself, will atone for some of the faults of his volume.

PART I.

Far roves the eye across the dewy plains
Whither yon hoar time-tottering castle rears
Its crumbling ruins on the rocky hill.
Of Norman Lupus once the warlike meed,
Where are its towers, its battlements, its walls,
The proud defence of all the country round!
Ah! seen no more, save that a mouldering pile,
Wrapt in the ivy's strong embrace, survives
To tell the fate that waits all human things.

       HEWSEY. *A Poem*, p. 14.

HALTON

CHAPTER I.

INTRODUCTORY.

WHO that has ever sailed on the broad bosom of the majestic Rhine, where, deep and swift, it flows between the mountains which border it on either hand, has not wondered when he looked up and saw

> High from their fields of air look down
> The eyries of a vanished race;
> Homes of the mighty whose renown
> Hath passed and left no trace?

Such a scene is indeed well calculated to carry back the mind to other ages, when those crumbling towers, which now crest every height that commands an advantageous reach of the river, were the strongholds of ancient knights and barons, who were wont from thence to sally forth either to make inroads on their defenceless neighbours, or to levy black mail from the traffickers on the river, carrying back for ransom captives to their dungeons, where daylight became but gloom to their eyes, and music but heaviness to their ears. Those were times and men whom it is perhaps pleasanter, as it is certainly safer, to contemplate rather at a distance than near at hand. How is it, then, that while the foreign scene calls up a crowd of ideas and associations, we look with comparative indifference upon similar scenes at home? Perhaps in travelling we carry with us a magic glass that invests with unusual interest every object that is new and strange. But, whatever the cause may be, there must be some reason for the difference, or the castle at Halton, looking boldly forth upon a river of wider renown than the Rhine, would challenge like attention with either Rolandseck or the Drachenfels, the Mausthurm or Stolzenfels, and call before us pictures equally vivid, and with more power to interest us because they are local and belong to our own history and neighbourhood.

In our comparatively flat country the commanding height on which Halton stands was at all times too conspicuous to be overlooked. In the year 79 Agricola must have marched near it, but he has left no trace of his footsteps. Those pigs of lead found on Norton Marsh, and bearing Roman inscriptions, as mentioned by Camden, must have been derelicts of later times. In the Saxon times, however, Halton became a sort of central point to the surrounding neighbourhood, and the four towns of Norton, Aston, Sutton, and Weston, or as the people call it from the blasts which sweep on it from the Mersey "Windy Weston," received their names from the direction in which they stand relatively north, east, south, and west to the hill of Halton. We hear nothing, however, of any fortress erected here by the Saxons. The danger they apprehended seems to have been principally from the west, either from the Strathclwydian Britons, or the Danes, those invading foes who made the river their highway for plunder, and used it as their gate of entrance into the interior of the country.[1] It was the habit of these daring marauders to sail boldly up the river to some convenient place, and there drawing their boats ashore to raise a hasty entrenchment, from whence they might sally out to collect their plunder, and to which they might ultimately return with it when it was time for them to quit the neighbourhood and sail from our shores.[2] Several earthworks, which are traditionally said to have had such an origin are still to be seen on the banks of the Mersey and its tributary the Irwell. (1.) One of these, once better known to the sportsman in pursuit of wild-fowl than it is now, is an entrenchment raised on Cuerdley Marsh, almost within sight of the castle at Halton. (2.) A second may be seen higher up the Mersey, on its Cheshire shore, about five miles above Warrington, and at the junction of the Bollin with that river. This, which is called "Mickley Hills," consists of several great mounds, the largest of which, now overgrown with large trees, has an imposing look when viewed over the flat meadows which surround it. No foundations of any kind have been found in these hills; but though we are not bound to hold the same opinion of them as a former proprietor, who said they

[1] Archæological Journal, No. 66, p. 100.   [2] Foreign Quarterly Rev. xii. p. 290.

were as old as Noah's flood, we may yet take it as the general opinion of the country that they are of great antiquity. (3.) At Hyle Wood in Pendleton, on the river Irwell, there remains a third of these entrenchments. Here there is a large oblong tumulus, which tradition, with the general acquiescence of all antiquaries (except the historian of Manchester, who puts in a plea for its Roman origin), has always ascribed to the Danes, and held to be their work.[1]

To curb the advance of these invaders who made so lawless a use of our noble river, the heroic Elfleda built a strong and solid stone fortress on the Castle Rock at Runcorn, at the point where the river is narrowest and the situation most commanding, and where an invading navy might best be held in check. Elfleda, who was one of the daughters of the immortal Alfred, and was worthy of her sire, married Eldred, Duke and Governor of Mercia for the king. She survived her husband eight years, and as Governess of Mercia during a troublesome period, in which the kingdom was infested by the invaders we have spoken of, she governed her province with surpassing skill and ability. "Not without good reason did King Edward, her brother, entrust her with the government of Mercia during her widowed life, for by the wise and politic order she used in all her doings the king was greatly furthered and assisted, but especially in the repairing and building of towns and castles, wherein she showed her noble magnificence, in so much that during her government it is recorded that she did build and repair those towns whose names here ensue:— Tamworth beside Lichfield, Stafford, Warwick, Shrewsbury, Watersbury or Weddesbury; Edisburie, or rather Eadsburie, in the forest of Delamere beside Chester; Brimsburie bridge, upon Severne; Runcorne, at the mouth of the river of Mercia, with others. Moreover by her help the citie of Chester, which by the Danes had been greatly defaced, being newly repaired and fortified by her with walls and turrets, was greatly enlarged, so that the castle, which stood without the walls before that time, was now brought within the compass of the new wall."[2] This restoration of Chester is thus alluded to by the Monk of Chester:—

"This Elfleda Duchess, with mickle royalty,
Re-edified Chester and fortified it full right."

In that age the saints were held in great reverence and honour, and Elfleda,

[1] Whittaker's Manchester, l. 240.   [2] Hollinshed's Chronicles.

a virtuous and valorous princess, showed that she was not wanting in this respect by translating the body of St. Oswald, king and martyr, from the abbey of Bardney to Gloucester, and there erecting a monastery over it. To her, also, it is said, belonged the building of the first church at Runcorn. Runcorn, the place which Elfleda selected as the site of her castle intended to repress the inroads of the fleets on the Mersey, is not mentioned in the Domesday survey, which perhaps is a sign of the great devastation which had then befallen this part of the country. Huntington calls it Rumcoven, and other early chroniclers Runcoven or Runcofan, and by the last name it occurs in an Anglo-Saxon inscription given in the addenda to Weever's Funeral Monuments, and in the Saxon Chronicle. The name is probably derived from Roncaria or Runcaria, a word mentioned in Coke upon Littleton, as meaning a heath full of briars and brambles. Here, in the year 916, the castle was erected on a flat, triangular-shaped rock, which on the river side was defended by a raised mound of earth, and on the land side by a deep ditch more than six yards wide. On the rock where Elfleda's castle stood there now stands the south pier of the great railway viaduct which here spans the Mersey. A tracing of the site of the castle, taken just before the iron horse set his foot upon it and trode out its last fading vestiges, now alone preserves the remembrance of Elfleda's castle. Her erection, and the raising of the wonderful viaduct, mark two distinct eras —the one was civilisation just emerging from barbarism, the other civilisation attained, between which the contrast is extreme. Elfleda's fortress, however, had done its work before the work of war gave way to the work of peace.

On the 12th June 919, this great princess departed this life at Tamworth, and upon her tomb was placed a Latin epitaph to record her merits, which an old writer has thus translated :—

   O puissant Elfled, O thou maid,
    Of men the dread and fear ;
   O puissant Elfled, worthie maid,
    The name of man to beare.
   A noble nature hath thee made
    A maiden mild to bee ;
   Thy virtue also hath procurde
    A manlie name to thee.

   It doothe but onlie thee become
    Of sexe to change the name ;

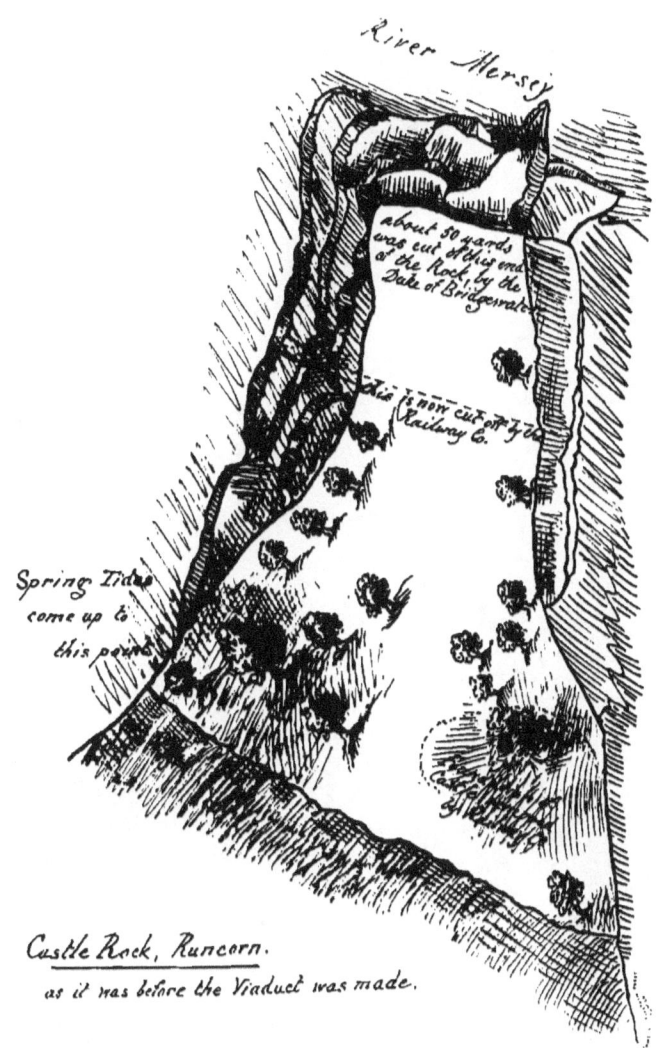

> A puissant queene, a king art thou,
> Preparing trophies of fame;
> Now marvel not so much at Cæ-
> sar's Triumphs trim to view,
> O manlike maiden more renown'd
> Than Cæsar was, adieu.

There are some Saxon coins, which have on the obverse "Eadred Rex," and on the reverse, "Othbrim on Ring," which Camden, who gives a print of them, thinks may probably have been coined at Runcorn, or, as he says, Ringhornan, which by mistake he tells us is in Lancashire.[1] And in Mr. Thoresby's catalogue of Saxon coins there is one (No. 102) which has on the reverse the inscription, "Leodmer on Rine," which he conjectures to have been also coined at Runcorn about the year 1017. If these coins were really from a Runcorn mint, the credit of establishing it must be ascribed to Elfleda.

Up to the time of the era of the conquest these seem to be the principal notices of the neighbourhood which time has left us. The Normans, however, had no soooner obtained a footing here, and seen that danger no longer threatened them from the sea, than their eyes caught a sight of the bold rock at Halton, and they saw the great advantage it would be of in securing their new possessions, and controlling the conquered people. Of the castle which they built, and the long series of its illustrious possessors who inhabited it, some account will be given in the following pages.

[1] Camden's Britannia, Gibson's Edit. 1695, p. 143.

CHAPTER II.

NIGEL, FIRST BARON.

IN the year 1070, as we are told, William the Conqueror bestowed the county of Chester on Hugh Lupus, one of his Norman earls, "to hold as freely by the sword as he himself held England by the crown." What the sword had won the sword must hold, and the Norman earl, the better to secure his possessions, at once divided his palatinate into eight or more baronies, one of which was Halton.

I. Nigel, the first baron of Halton, was a brother Norman. It has been sometimes thought that he bore the forename of Robert.[1] According to Pecham he was the son of Ivo, Count of Constantia, in Normandy, and Emme, his wife,[2] and the ballad of the earls of Chester, enumerating the barons, says "Nigel of Halton was the first." The editor of Mamecestre suggests, but I think without sufficient grounds, that Nigel was one of the five barons mentioned in the Domesday survey, who held the manor or hundred of Salford.[3] If Nigel really was the son of that Ivo de Constantia who encountered and slew, as they left the ships, the English whom King Ethelred sent to France, he did not bring with him a name or associations likely to endear him to his new dependants. Nigel was not slow in selecting the place for the head of his barony, and he wisely chose Halton, its highest part, and there placed the stronghold that was to overawe his new acquisitions. The silvan scene which then reached from this hill to the banks of the wide Mersey, the beauty of its glades, and the verdure of its velvet turf, spread their charms in vain before eyes which taste had not yet opened to appreciate them. Not so, however, the round-topped woods of Norton. These did not fail to attract Nigel's regard, for they sheltered the wild animals which it was his pleasure to pursue in the chase, and fed and fattened those herds of deer or swine which helped to supply the rude but bountiful hospitality of his table. Halton derives its names from Allt

---

[1] Hist. Cheshire, i. 147.   [2] Hist. Cheshire, i. 506.   [3] Mamecestre, Chet. Soc. p. 29.

or Alt, a hill or cliff, to which its situation corresponds.[1] We cannot agree with a late writer, who offers a very different explanation. He says the word is a hybrid, made up of the British word Halen, salt, and the Saxon ton, and he quotes the Domesday survey to prove that there was then a wych (or salt house) there.[2] But this is altogether a mistake. The wych of Halton was at Northwich. Nigel probably drew the ground-plan of his castle, built and fortified the gateway and the walls of its outer ballium, and raised the donjon tower at the north-west corner where the rock is steepest and most defensible. The views of the castle, before it was dismantled, give a good idea of the plan, but there is probably no part of the present remains which can be said to belong to the founder's original structure, unless it be a solitary carved corbel brought from thence, and now deposited in the Warrington Museum.[3] Though an earlier foundation than Beeston, and resembling that castle in its general plan, Halton wants the grandeur which Beeston derives from its broad and deep moat, a feature which Halton must always have wanted. King, in his Vale Royal, affects to set out the privileges which Hugh Lupus granted to Nigel, and amongst these was the right to embattle (*kernellare*) his castle. But this licence to embattle was of later origin than Nigel's time, and no such right could then have been granted.[4] Nigel conferred the church of Runcorn on Wolfat, or Wolfrith, a priest, the brother of Hudard, his seneschal, both Normans like himself.[5] Sir Peter Leycester thinks that the office of constable of the earl's host was not conferred on the barons of Halton until his successor's time, but in the service of Hugh Lupus Nigel won for him the castle of Rhuddlan. The memory of his other victories, if he achieved any, has perished with him, wanting a bard or a chronicler to record them. King, who places the taking of Rhuddlan in 1098, must be mistaken in the date, for the name of Nigel as in possession of any Cheshire lands does not occur in the Domesday survey made in 1087, and Nigel must have been then dead.[6] Rhuddlan was probably taken in 1078, and Nigel died soon after. The arms which have been since assigned to this baron are *gules* four fusils in pale *or*.[7]

[1] Philological Journal, 1855, p. 219.
[2] Ethnology of Cheshire names by Professor Earle in Arch. Journal of 1866, p. 99.
[3] See the Plate, *post*.
[4] Hist. Cheshire, i. 98.
[5] Greswell's Runcorn, p. 9.
[6] Hist. Cheshire, i. 147.
[7] See further, as to this Baron, Lacy's Nobility, and Peckham's Complete Gent[s]. Hist. Cheshire, i. 122.

CHAPTER III.

WILLIAM FITZ NIGEL, SECOND BARON.

NIGEL transmitted Halton to his son, William fitz Nigel, who occurs in the Domesday survey as then holding the broad lands of the barony. In 1093 he is a witness to a charter of Hugh Lupus and his countess,[1] and to two other charters of earls Richard and Randle; and he and his brother Richard, in 1106, witness a charter to St. Werburgh's.[2] He was made constable and marshal of the earl's host, which involved no less than the leading of the host in its advance and guarding the rear on a retreat, a post as honourable as it was dangerous. This post, probably by mistake in confusing *constabularius* with *senescallus*, has been ascribed to the baron of Montalt instead of the Baron of Halton: Roger de Montalt tenet lxvj bovatas terræ de comite Cestriæ per id servitium quod debet esse primus in exercitu eundo in Walliam et extremus in redeundo.[3] The baron of Halton was also the hereditary head of the earl's council; and, speaking in the first person, the earl calls him *hereditarie supremum consiliarium post me super omnes optimates et barones totius terræ meæ*.[4]

Between the year 1101, when Richard II., earl of Chester, succeeded to the earldom, and 1120, when he died, we read this story, which possibly was the occasion of William fitz Nigel's being made constable:—"Earl Richard having gone on pilgrimage to Holywell, the Welshmen took advantage of his situation, and raised a force to intercept him; but he contrived to send word to his constable, William fitz Nigel, who hastily assembled a great host and marched with them towards the little isle of Hilbree, expecting to find shipping to transport them across, but no ships were there. The constable, however, prayed to St. Werburgh, when *the dry sands*, from that circumstance since called *the Constable's sands*, appeared

---

[1] Chester Arch. Journal, part iii. 293-5.
[2] Hist. Ches. I. 17; and Sir P. Leycester, 117-119; and Amicia Tracts, Chetham Soc. 391.
[3] Lib. Nig. de Scacc. p. 325; and Testa de Nevil, 325.   [4] Hist. Ches. pref. xxx.

in sight, and he marched his host over them, relieved his master, and brought him safe back to Chester. On his return he gave thanks to the saint, and made an offering to her of the village of Newton."[1] As Baron of Halton, William fitz Nigel, for each knight's fee he held, in time of war with the Welsh, was bound to find one horse and furniture or two without furniture.[2] In the year 1133 William fitz Nigel founded a house of canons regular at Runcorn, which was afterwards removed, and became the well-known Priory of Norton. By a strange confusion of geography, the author of the Vale Royal tells us Norton is in Wirrall over against Liverpool.[3] About the same time he and his son granted one third of Thelwall to the monastery of St. Peter and St. Paul at Shrewsbury.[4] He appears also to have given Daresbury Chapel to the canons of Norton.[5] In 1135 William fitz Nigel witnessed the grant of the church of Buildwas to the abbey of that name.[6] Of William fitz Nigel and his son, William fitz William, we have in an old charter a picture which is almost dramatic. The charter begins by calling on all Christian people, as well French as English, to give ear to it, and then in circumstantial terms details how these two great men having met on a certain day at the house of Hugh fitz Odard, the castle seneschal (and son of that Odard who held Weston at the time of the Domesday survey), and having found him sick, they, probably as they stood by his bedside, upon his entreaty and in compassion for him, granted all his lands to his son Hugh; and the sick seneschal in return, and feeling he no longer needed them, gave William fitz Nigel his coat of mail and his war-horse, and his son gave William's son a palfrey and a noble soar hawk.[7] The seneschal had a sword of office, which it is said is still in the possession of the Kilmoreys, but that was not given up, probably because the dying man clung to it too closely to part with it even then. William fitz Nigel's wife was a sister of Walter and a daughter of Gilbert de Gant, one of those Flanders men who are thought to have served William the Conqueror in the conquest of England as volunteers, and only for personal rewards. William fitz Nigel had a daughter Maud, who married Aubert de Grelley,[8] and he died in 1134, and was buried at Chester. He was succeeded by his son William fitz William.

[1] Life of St. Werburgh. See also Bradshaw's ballad in Colonel Egerton Leigh's Cheshire Ballads, p. 1, et seq.   [2] Camden.   [3] Hist. Ches. i. 147.
[4] Chartulary of that abbey.   [5] Hist. Ches. i. 539.
[6] Archæological Journal for 1858, p. 322.   [7] Hist. Ches. i. 507 in notis.   [8] Ibid. i. 539.

CHAPTER IV.

WILLIAM FITZ WILLIAM, EUSTACE FITZ JOHN, RICHARD FITZ EUSTACE—THIRD, FOURTH, AND FIFTH BARONS.

IN or about the year 1135, WILLIAM FITZ WILLIAM succeeded his father, and became the third baron of Halton. In the year 1140, almost before the house of canons regular of the order of St. Augustine, founded by his father, had become settled at Runcorn, William fitz William removed them from that place to Norton, where in a new home, first as a priory, and afterwards as an abbey, they flourished in great splendour until that storm-cloud burst under Henry VIII., and swept the religious houses away. The charter of removal, which may be seen at length in the History of Cheshire,[1] is witnessed by William the chaplain, probably the same who witnessed the charter already mentioned as made at the bedside of Hugh fitz Odard, and who was probably William de Dutton. The payment of tithes and the division of England into parishes had been established before this time, but what are called arbitrary consecrations of tithes were not then wholly out of use, and every man, though bound to pay his tithes somewhere, might in certain cases elect to pay them to whatever church or religious house he would. It became common, therefore, for a great landowner who had founded a religious house, to confer on it the tithes of his possessions. This practice was no doubt followed by William fitz William, when he gave the tithes of his lands in Thelwall to his religious house at Norton, in return for which they were to offer up prayers and masses for himself and his family, and this will account for Thelwall, though distant from Runcorn, and cut off from it by two other parishes, being still in that parish. But William fitz William's religious leanings were shown by another grant, in which he joined his father in conveying to the abbey of St. Peter and St. Paul at Shrewsbury, a third part of the village of Thelwall, " in wood, and in plain, and in water," and this he did

[1] Hist. Ches. i. 508.

for the good of the souls of William and his father, and in order that they might obtain mercy, and that St. Peter, by the prayers of his servants, might open to them the Kingdom of Heaven.[1]

That he had a pious regard for his father's memory appears from his giving to the Abbey of St. Werburgh as sustenance one half of Raby in Wirrall, which had been anciently given thereunto by his father.[2]

In the reign of King Stephen, and probably to avoid the troubles of the time, William fitz William transported himself to Normandy, where he died childless, probably before the year 1150, and in him ended the male line of Nigel, the first baron of Halton, for Robert fitz Nigel, who in 1157 became the fourth Abbot of Chester, if he was Nigel's son, became civilly dead when he received the tonsure.[3]

EUSTACE FITZ JOHN, who had married for his second wife Agnes de Gant, the last baron's sister, succeeded him as fourth baron of Halton, and had the barony with the hereditary constableship of Cheshire confirmed to him by Earl Randle Gernons. Eustace succeeded to the castle of Knaresboro', and the other inheritance of his uncle, Serlo de Burgh, and he aggrandised himself by both his marriages. His first wife, Beatrix, the daughter and heir of Ivo de Vescy, brought him the baronies of Malton and Alnwick, and his second, the great barony of Halton. Living in the troublous times of a disputed succession, he adhered to the side of his master, the Earl of Chester, for which King Stephen fiercely attacked his castle of Malton, and Eustace as vigorously defended it, and though Hoveden, who was of the other party, stigmatises him as a traitor for this, he ought rather to be commended for it, since he owed allegiance to his palatine lord.[4] He seems to have given to Hugh de Cathewic, probably the Hugh fitz Hugh whom William fitz Nigel and his son visited, pasture for 100 sheep, on condition that he finished the church at Norton, according to the foundation of William fitz Nigel and his son.[5]

Like most of the great men in that age, he tried to atone for his faults by founding, with the consent of his first wife, the abbeys of Malton and Alnwick; and the house of Walton, with the consent of his second. He met his death in discharging his high office of constable, in a war with the Welsh in 1157. The chronicler who records his death says he fell at the

[1] Chartulary of the Abbey of Shrewsbury.   [2] Hist. Ches. i. 508.
[3] Ibid.   [4] Ibid.   [5] Ibid. i. 504 *in notis*.

same time as Robert de Curcy, a great nobleman, and very many others, and that he was aged, great, and wise, and renowned amongst the princes of the land for his wisdom and riches.[1] Between the years 1153 and 1157, he was witness to a charter made by Hugh Cyveliok and his mother.[2] The arms which have been since assigned to this baron are, quarterly *or* and *gules* a bordure *vair* impaling Nigel's arms as above.

RICHARD FITZ EUSTACE, the son of the last baron by Agnes, his second wife, succeeded his father as fifth baron of Halton. In 1165, while Richard was baron of Halton, Henry II., with a view to overawe the Welsh, came to Chester, and remained there some time.[3] Possibly their success in the battle in which the late constable fell had emboldened the Welsh, and made the king's presence necessary. Richard married Albreda, the daughter of Robert de Lizours, and half-sister of Robert de Lacy, baron of Pomfret, the consequences of which were very important, for she ultimately became heir to the Lacys, and greatly increased the wealth and importance of the barons of Halton. About 1170, while Richard was baron of Halton, a charter was made in his court which shows the simplicity of the times, when bargains seem to have been not far removed from barter. One Gilbert Brito, son of Hugh fitz Pagan, granted in way of sale to Adam fitz Hugh de Dutton eight bovates of land in Budwurth, belonging to his fee, and which before the whole hundred court of Halton he had bought from Andrew fitz Geoffrey Percy, son of Sigard, daughter of Wulnet de Budwurthe, for three marks and three shillings in money, and two and a half ells of burnet cloth, and for which the said Adam now gave the said Gilbert one two-year-old colt and two marks, as relief, before the hundred court.[4] According to Leycester, besides his other lands, Richard held a knight's fee at Smathe, in Yorkshire. There is an engraving of the seal of Richard fitz Eustace in the Vetusta Monumenta, which is copied in the History of Cheshire.[5] In his work on ancient armour, Meyrick out of this seal has drawn a representation of Richard in a hauberk, covered with little plates sewn on in the manner of tiles, which may give us some idea of what that coat of mail was which Hugh fitz Odard gave to William fitz Nigel on his deathbed.[6] Meyrick, who calls this baron Richard fitz

[1] Hist. Ches. i. 508. [2] Chet. Soc. 194. [3] Litt. Hen. ii. 410.
[4] Arley Charters, Box 1. 89. [5] Hist. Ches. i. 509.
[6] Meyrick's Ancient Armour, i. 35.

Hugh, gives the date of his seal as 1141, and makes him " standard-bearer of England "—the first two are clearly mistakes, and for the last there appears to be no authority. Richard died about 1172, leaving a son by his wife, Aubrey, by whom he was succeeded in his title and honours.[1] The arms which have been assigned to this baron are, quarterly *or* and *gules*, impaling *or* a chief *azure*.

[1] Hist. Ches. i. 509.

CHAPTER V.

JOHN FITZ RICHARD.

JOHN FITZ RICHARD, who succeeded his father as sixth baron of Halton, had a brother Robert, who, from his being the head of the English house of St. John of Jerusalem, was called the Hospitaller, and he occurs as a witness in one of the Arley charters.[1] This John, in the time of Henry II., gave Clifton to Geoffrey de Dutton, *scilicet de uxore desponsatâ*, for his homage and service, and performing the service of half a knight's fee at the castle of Halton.[2] In this baron's time, and for some time after, the halls of Halton, like other great castles, were thronged with a crowd of vassals and retainers who were housed and fed at their lord's cost.[3] But there was at least one retainer of a different kind in John fitz Richard's halls, for he had the rare merit in that age of being a patron of science, and of maintaining, probably at Halton, an excellent astronomer, or as he was then called an astrologer, an ecclesiastic named William, who wrote an able work on the planetary conjunctions of the year 1186.[4] In this baron's time, charters for the transfer of land became somewhat more frequent. By one of these, in which he styles himself Constable of Chester, John fitz Richard grants to his favoured vassal, Adam de Dutton, his "demesne apple yard in Halton, with the messuage, wherein Levinge lived, and a meadow near the Caldewelle, in Clifton, rendering yearly a soar hawk at the feast of *St. Peter ad vincula*." By another charter, in which he again styles himself the Constable, he grants to the same Adam "his demesne toft in Halton, with its orchard, and a meadow in Clifton, which was surrounded by a dyke." One of the witnesses to this last charter is Radulf, the baron's cook, a personage who was of some importance in an ancient castle.[5] These two charters have reference to the same property, and in an age of supposed simplicity it seems strange

---

[1] Box i. 58.   [2] Hist. Ches. i. 525.   [3] Litt. Hen. II. 2 vol. ii. 333.
[4] Hist. Ches. i. 510.   [5] Arley Charters, box i. Nos. 44, 81.

that they should thus multiply charters for one and the same object; but our ancestors, living in times when might often made right, were rarely content to rest upon a single charter, but generally took the precaution to have it repeated more than once, and sometimes in more languages than one. Moreover, if there were several parties to a charter, there were the same number of parts of it prepared, and each of them had his own part delivered to him.

By another charter he gave Hield in Aston by Budworth to Methroso Punterling, rendering a Welsh lance yearly on St. Bartholomew's day.[1] If Punterling had to win his lance every year from some Welsh enemy, his tenure of Hield must have been troublesome.

"In the year 1178," says Whittaker, "when the veneration of mankind for monastic institutions was at its height, and when a partial reform of the Benedictine order under St. Bernard had directed for a time the bounty of kings and nobles into that channel, John, Constable of Chester, founded a monastery of Cistercians at Stanlaw not far from Halton."[2] In his charter of foundation, the founder grants the monks a house near St. Michael's in Chester, reserving to himself a right to hold his court of pleas there at his pleasure, but he was not to require hospitality at the monks' expense.[3] From the foundation of the abbey, the abbot of Stanlaw was one of the earl's spiritual peers, and had a seat in the palatinate parliament until the abbey was finally removed to Whalley. More than a century afterwards it was the burial-place of the lords of Halton, and as it could always be seen from their castle walls, it was no inappropriate reminder to them, in the midst of their greatness, to remember their end. To John fitz Richard, as we learn from two charters, both specimens of the simplicity of the times, is owing the first foundation of the ferry at Runcorn. By the first charter, Richard de More granted to his son W'goon, two bovates in Roncover, late the lands of Beatrix of Higher Roncover, and a toft and a croft in Widnesse, which John, the constable of Chester, had given him, with the lands acquired by him from other persons, rendering yearly to God, and St. John, and the Holy House of the Hospital at Jerusalem, two shillings at the nativity of Saint Mary, and finding one-half the necessaries for the passage of the ship of Widnesse for ever, for all who should

---

[1] Hist. Ches. i. 510.
[2] The monastic chroniclers differ as to the date of this foundation, some placing it in 1163 and some in 1172. (Hist. Whalley, edit. 1872, p. 83.)   [3] Hist. Ches. i. 509.

pass over there in the love of God.¹ The second charter, dated in 1190 (it is not common to find dated charters at so early a period), explains the first. By it Garnier de Naplouse, grand prior of the English brotherhood of the Knights Hospitallers, granted lands in Platt and elsewhere to Richard de la More and his heirs, in consideration of his paying 4s. yearly at Michaelmas, and keeping in repair on the river Mersey, at Runcorn, the vessel which John, constable of Chester, for the love of God, had formerly provided to carry across the stream those who desired it, upon condition that one third part of the chattels of Richard and his heirs in succession at the death of each were reserved to the brotherhood for the good of his soul.² This baron was friendly to both the templars and hospitallers, and gave to the former one carucate and to the latter two carucates in frank almoign.³ He confirmed William fitz Nigel and his son's grants to the abbey of Shrewsbury, and witnessed Cyveliok's grant to Stanlaw.⁴

In 1181, John fitz Richard and Richard Peche, Bishop of Coventry, were sent by the king to govern his new conquests in Ireland, and to keep Dublin safely, in the place of Hugh de Lacy, whom the king recalled in displeasure, on account of his marrying, without license, a daughter of the king of Connaught. A few years afterwards he went with half Europe on the crusade, and there, while engaged in that historic siege, the siege of Tyre, in the year 1190, he died.⁵ John fitz Richard married Alice, the sister of William Mandeville, and had by her a son and heir, Roger, who succeeded him, besides two sons, Eustace and Richard, each of whom assumed the name of "De Cestria," a third son, called Peter, and a daughter, Alice, who married Rob. de Hulton.⁶ John's mother, Albreda, sister of the whole blood, and not half-sister as was long supposed, to Albert de Lacy, the last of the Lacys of the Domesday survey,⁷ through her brother succeeded to a great inheritance and a greater name, the name of Lacy, which afterwards became famous, not at Halton only, but throughout all England.

¹ Hist. Ches. i. 498.
² Hist. of the ancient chapel of Birch (Chetham Soc. p. 14, and appendix 189), where the charter is given at length.   ³ Testa de Nevil, p. 403.
⁴ Hist. Ches. i. 27.   ⁵ Ibid. i. 510.   ⁶ Hist. Lanc. iii. 40.
⁷ Ibid. iv. 765, appendix.

CHAPTER VI.

ROGER, SEVENTH BARON.

ROGER, who succeeded as seventh baron of Halton, was a stern warrior, which, in an age that loved *sobriquets*, procured him the unenviable surname of "Hell." In 1196, however, when he took the name of Lacy, which he was the first of his family to assume, he bore a noble surname, and a name which any one might be proud to own. It was this baron who, being at Chester at the fair when news arrived that his master, Earl Randle Blundeville, was shut up and hard pressed by the Welsh in Rhuddlan Castle, mustered all the musicians, singers, beggars, and idle strollers, who were then assembled in great numbers at the fair, and hastily marched with them to the earl's rescue. Perceiving the approach of this great multitude, and mistaking them for an armed force, the Welshmen stood for awhile amazed, and then, like the French in a later age at the sight of Talbot, exclaiming that "the devil was in arms," they were seized with a sudden panic and fled, leaving the way to the fortress open for the entrance of Roger, who quickly entered it with his rabble rout, and relieved the earl in triumph. In gratitude for his vassal's service, and to perpetuate the memory of his deliverance, the earl conferred on him in perpetuity the rule and government of all the musicians, singers, beggars, and idle strollers within the earldom, so that without his license no such person might exercise his calling within the limits of the earl's dominions. The exercise of a similar right to govern minstrels seems to have been not unknown to a later possessor of the barony of Halton in another portion of his dominions, the honour of Tutbury, as we may see from this curious mandate :—

John, by the grace of God, king of Castile and Leon and Duke of Lancaster, to all them who shall see or hear these our letters—greeting. Know ye that we have ordained, constituted, and assigned to our well-beloved the king of the minstrels, in our honour of Tutbury, who is, or for the time shall be, to apprehend and arrest all the minstrels in our said honour and franchise that refuse to do the service and minstrelsy as appertain to them to do from ancient times at

Tutbury aforesaid yearly, on the days of the assumption of Our Lady, giving and granting to the said king of the minstrels for the time being full power and commandment to make them reasonably to justify, and to constrain them to do their services and minstrelsies in manner as belongeth to them, and as it hath been there and of ancient times accustomed. In witness of which thing we have caused these our letters to be made patent.

Given under our privy seal, at our castle of Tutbury, the 22d day of August, in the 4th year of the reign of the most sweet king Richard II., 1381.[1]

    Roger, though both by name and nature stern and severe, was not destitute of feeling for the unfortunate. His brother Richard, who has been already mentioned, had the misfortune to be afflicted with leprosy, and compassionating his misfortune, Roger conferred on him the township of Moor, and an annuity of 6s. a year, issuing to him out of the twelve bovates of land in Aston which he had granted to Adam de Dutton. But his brother's misfortune disposed him to do something for others who were similarly afflicted. At Edisforth (the nobleman's ford), the site according to Whitaker, of the great battle recorded in the Saxon Chronicle, and fought in 798, in a romantic spot on the Yorkshire bank of the Ribble, about a mile from the castle of Clitheroe, which Roger had inherited from his ancestors, there stood a hospital for lepers, or as it was the fashion to call it, from the spotted appearance of its inmates, a messle house.[2] Remembering his brother's affliction, Roger gave to this leper house four acres of land at Baldwin Hill. Diseases, like empires, have hitherto rolled westward, and the East, the cradle of our race, and the birthplace of our truest liberty, seems also to be the fount and spring of our most fatal maladies. In that region leprosy has always prevailed, and a very ancient scandal, refuted by Josephus, would have it that the Jews were driven out of Egypt because they were lepers; to which a lively modern writer adds, that the Egyptians were singular in the choice of a king, for they did not require him to be virtuous, but they would on no account tolerate a candidate with red hair, there being in their minds some connection between that complexion and leprosy.

    It is not unlikely that, in some of the many invasions of disease from the East, the leprosy made a swoop upon Europe. The form in which it first appeared was probably the black leprosy—the *elephas elephantiasis*, or leprosy of the Arabians—so named from its rendering the skin like that of the elephant—scabrous, dark coloured, and furrowed over with tubercles. It was not, I think, the leprosy of Scripture, which was perhaps the white

[1] History of Tutbury, 5.   [2] Hist. Whalley, 34.

leprosy, a form of disease still met with in the East, and which, when it attacks a dark skin, looks like whitewash upon a discoloured wall. In the time of Roger Lacy, leprosy was rampant not only in England, but all over Europe. It must indeed have been very common, when so small a place as Clitheroe required an entire hospital for such unfortunates. Like the Jews of old, our ancestors required that the houses for lepers should be outside their towns, and generally at a little distance from them. St. Nicholas, at Edisforth, was so situated, so was the hospital of St. Giles, at Boughton, near Chester, so also was the French Malmaison, and so also was that most famous of them all, the hospital of St. James's in London, which, from being once a leper house, has risen to the dignity of being the state palace of our English sovereigns. It was required of all lepers that they should dwell apart, and the infected who transgressed this rule might be removed by a special writ provided for the purpose.[1] When the leper begged he was required to sound a rattle to warn all persons of his presence, and he was to receive such alms as were offered him in a clap dish, just as Tristrem did in the thirteenth century, of whom we read that

" Cup and clapper he bare,
As he a measle ware."

When crowds violate her rules, nature avenges herself by the generation of contagious diseases, just as hereditary diseases are the result of a systematic disregard of her rules among successive individuals of the same family. When Robert de Ferrars, Earl of Derby, was taken prisoner, and lost his estates after the battle of Evesham, one of the chroniclers indulges in this reflection upon it : "And thus, of all his great inheritance, nothing now remained or was left to him but the gout in his hands and feet, which his father and grandfather had had before him." Robert de Ferrars was not a solitary instance of the heir coming in for no other inheritance from his ancestor but a poor constitution or a hereditary disease.

When the leprosy first appeared here, it was fostered by the dress, habits, and mode of living, of our ancestors. Woollen not sufficiently cleansed or washed was worn next to the skin, and a diet of fish and salted provisions was too extensively used by the people. After a time, however, the disease was modified by endemic influences, and it gradually disappeared with the introduction of a more frequent wearing of linen, and the

[1] Paris and Fonblanque's Med. Juris. i. 86.

more general use of fruit, vegetables, and good bread, with improved habits of cleanliness. Before the 10th Ed. II. (1317), the house of Edisforth had ceased to be any longer used for its original purpose; but the Lacy fret and their rampant lion still remain on its front, to attest Roger Lacy's bounty to its ancient inmates. So "shines a good deed in a naughty world."

Let us now resume the history of the house of Halton. In 1191 Roger Lacy took the cross and served in that land

> "Over whose acres walked those blessed feet,
> Which *eighteen* hundred years ago were nailed
> For our advantage on the bitter cross."

But before he set out he granted one half of Comberbach in free alms to the hospital of St. John of Jerusalem, and Richard, his leprous brother, was one of the many witnesses to the grant.[1]

The next year he was present with Richard Cœur de Lion at that historic event, the storming of Acre. After the death of the great leader, under whom he had served with distinction, Roger was one of the great barons whom John, Cœur de Lion's successor, most feared, and was therefore most desirous to secure in his interest. In 1199 he was summoned to swear fealty to the king, and when this was performed and his homage done, the king restored to him his castle of Pomfret, but detained his son as a hostage.

In the following year, when the King of Scotland was coming to do his homage to King John, Roger Lacy was one of the great nobles sent to give him safe conduct; and after the king's coronation, he was the first of the great barons who put down their names as having witnessed the King of Scotland's homage at Lincoln.

In 1201 William Marshall, Earl of Pembroke, and Roger Lacy, constable of Chester, each with a hundred soldiers (*centum soldariis*), knights who fought for pay (whence our English soldiers), were sent into Normandy to put down the king's enemies. In those old times men seem to have fought without scruple for any usurper who paid them.[2]

In the 4th year of John's reign (1202), Randle, Earl of Chester, having fallen under the king's suspicion, and being required to find sureties for his fidelity, the two great constables, William Humet, constable of Nor-

[1] Hist. Ches. i. 454. [2] Ibid. 510.

mandy, and Roger Lacy, constable of Chester, came forward and became sureties for him.[1]

The historian of Cheshire, who has printed a charter made in the shrievalty of Richard Wibbenbury, and witnessed by "Roger Hell *senescall*," (not constable) of Cheshire, suggests that the *sobriquet* here used is an interpolation, but it is surely more than this, and the whole deed must be spurious unless Wibbenbury was sheriff at some earlier date than 1233, the first and only time in which his name appears in the list of sheriffs.[2]

In Roger's Lacy's time, a charter of Alizia, daughter of Randle de Aston, to Adam de Dutton, mentions a yearly fair as being then held at Halton on St. Bartholomew's day, and reserves two white gloves, *de uno nūmo*, meaning, I suppose, a pair, to be paid yearly *ad nundinas Haltoniæ*.[3]

On the 22d March 1203, Roger Lacy, as constable, and Henry de Rolleston, who probably held some office under him, were commanded to let William Marshal, Earl of Pembroke, have six *carettæ* (loaded wains) of wine, quit of all tolls.[4] This had no doubt reference to the expedition to Normandy, which occupied at least two years. In 1204 Roger Lacy was shut up in the Castle *De Rupe Andeliacâ*, that is "Château Gailliard," or "Saucy Castle." This castle, which is a very strong place, opposite Les Andelys, on the Seine, was the last hope and stronghold of the English in Normandy. So important was it esteemed that the King himself wrote a letter to Roger Lacy, exhorting him to maintain it.[5] Roger had boldly held it for seven months, when the Earl of Pembroke, his colleague, a man of great vigour and capacity, being ordered to relieve him, marched a force of 3000 horse and 400 foot towards the place, but owing to the Flotilla, on which he trusted to destroy the floating bridge over the Seine, not arriving in time, he was repulsed, and obliged to abandon the attempt.[6] Pressed to the last extremity, and finding that relief was no longer to be expected, Roger made a desperate sortie from the castle, but in attempting to cut his way through the besiegers was made prisoner. The King of France was so struck with his valour that he would not allow him to be kept a close prisoner, and King John levied an aid and paid his ransom.[7] In 6 John (1204), Roger, who was again at home, and employed in the king's service, received 60 marks towards fortifying the castle of Carlisle. The

[1] Hist. Ches. i. 33, *in notis*. [2] Ibid. iii. 308. [3] Arley Charters, i. 22.
[4] Archæologia Cambrensis, July 1859, p. 194. [5] Hist. Ches. i. 511.
[6] Arch. Camb., July 1859, p. 195. [7] Hist. Ches. i. 510; and Patent Roll 5 John.

order to pay this money to the Constable of Chester miscalls him Robert. Royal scribes, it seems, were not exempt from slips of the pen, even in writing records.

Richard the leper, Roger's brother, at his death was not taken for interment to Stanlaw, but was carried to Norton, and found his last resting place in the priory there.

Roger Lacy gave Nether and Little Peover to Osbert de Wethale, reserving 6s. 8d. rent and foreign service for the 20th part of a knight's fee. In Sir Peter Leycester's time the rent of 6s. 8d. still continued to be paid for this land at Halton.

Roger added to the family estates the barony of Penwortham, which he purchased from Robert Bushel. He also increased the possessions of Stanlaw Abbey by giving it the church of Rochdale, the lordship of Merland, with its pleasant Mere well stocked with fish, a great help to the monks' table, and the town of Little Woolton, with other lands in Lancashire. In 1205, 6, and 7, the office of High Sheriff of Lancashire, an office at that time never filled but by a great personage, was conferred by the king upon Roger Lacy. In virtue of this office he held a tourn or court twice a year, for the trial of causes and the despatch of business, when all persons, as well peers as others within his bailiwick, except the bishop, who had been excused by the Conqueror, were required to attend and assist him. As the presiding officer he had to dispense justice in the causes which came before him. This was not so remarkable as his occasionally presiding to administer justice, as we are told he did in his own court at Clitheroe. The obverse and reverse of the seal of Roger Lacy may be seen engraved in the "History of Cheshire and the History of Whalley."[1]

Roger Lacy married Maude de Clare, and having ended his busy life on 1st October 1211, was carried in great honour to his last resting-place in the family-burial place at Stanlaw.[2] Besides his son and successor, John, he had a daughter, who married Geoffrey, son of Robert, the dean of Whalley. Like his father, Roger confirmed his ancestor's gifts to the abbey of Shrewsbury. It has been stated[3] that King John gave five pounds to the chapel at Halton: if so, the gift must have been made in this baron's time, when the king probably visited Halton from Liverpool or Chester, in the years 1206 and 1208.

[1] Cheshire i. 511; and Whalley, p. 178.   [2] Hist. Ches. i. 511.
[3] Notitia Cest. Chet. Soc. ii. 358.

CHAPTER VII.

JOHN LACY AND EDMUND LACY, EIGHTH AND NINTH BARONS.

JOHN LACY, who succeeded his father, Roger, as eighth baron of Halton, about the year 1212 conferred the right of licensing minstrels, which Earl Randle had given to his father, upon his seneschal, Hugh de Dutton, who and whose successors continued to enjoy it down to the reign of George IV., it having been reserved to them in every vagrant act to that time.

John Lacy joined the barons and friends of freedom when they rose against King John, and took those proceedings which led to the granting of the Great Charter at Runymede, and which have ever since reflected so much honour on all who were concerned in them. The weight of his character afterwards caused him to be chosen as one of the barons who were to see the conditions of the Charter faithfully observed by the king. Probably it was on this account that an attempt was afterwards made to deprive him of his Lancashire forests.[1] It was certainly for no better reason that in the year 1216 he was excommunicated by the Pope. But for these his services in the cause of freedom, history now awards him a different and a far juster meed. In 1218 he took the cross, and was present with his master, the Earl of Chester, at the siege of Damietta; and no doubt at his return he witnessed the earl engaged in the building of Beeston castle. In 1224 he joined the earl and many others in remonstrating with the king against the conduct of the Chief Justice, Hubert de Burgh, who was charged with not duly executing the laws, and with exasperating the king against the nobles.[2]

In 1230, King Henry III. conferred on John Lacy the valuable manor of Collingham and Bardsey, then held under the Crown by the abbot of Kirkstall, at a rent of £90 a year, a very great sum in those days, which shows that he was high in the king's favour.[3] But he proved that he could give as well as receive, for about this time he gave Eccles to Stanlaw.[4]

[1] 5th Report on Pub. Records.   [2] Hist. Ches. i. 35.   [3] Ibid. 513.
[4] Madox' Fam. Anglic. 5.

John Lacy married, first, Alice, daughter of William de Aquila, who died without issue, and was buried at Norton, before the year 1231. In or about the following year he married Margaret, daughter and coheir of Robert de Quency, son and heir of Saher de Quency, Earl of Winchester. Robert had married Hawys, fourth sister and coheiress of Randle Blundeville, Earl of Chester and Lincoln, and on the distribution of his lands, she had given to her the latter earldom, *scilicet quantum ad eum pertinuit ut inde comitissa existat*. From Hawys the earldom of Lincoln descended to Margaret, and from her to her husband, John Lacy, who was thus in possession when Henry III., on 23d November 1232, regranted it him by patent, to hold to him and the heirs of his body by Margaret his wife, the effect of which was probably to continue the earldom to the husband and wife for their lives, and the life of the survivor of them, and then to their heirs in tail. The king's confirmation of his title to the earldom, with a bribe, politely called a subsidy, of 1000 marks to him and the Earl of Chester, detached both of them from the party of Richard, the earl marshal, and brought them over to the side of the king. In John Lacy's time, a fishery in the Mersey must have been of some account, since Philip de Orreby thought it worth his while to obtain from him a grant of it to him and his heirs, and to have a boat on the river, and with one net to fish throughout the limits of Halton (Hathelton), rendering yearly therefor sixpence or a pair of spurs.[1] Like the rest of his ancestors, John Lacy increased the possessions of the house of Stanlaw, by granting it the two medieties of the rectory of Blackburn, in Lancashire.[2]

In 1236, when the king's marriage with Queen Elinor was about to be solemnised with great pomp, and all the great men of the kingdom were to use the offices and places which of ancient right their ancestors had ever used at the coronations of the kings of England, the Earl of Chester carried in state before the king the *curtein*, or sword of St. Edward, to signify that he was an earl palatine, and had the right and power to restrain the king if he should offer to do amiss; and he had John Lacy, his constable, attending upon him, to beat back the people with a rod, or staff, whenever they chanced to press too disorderly upon him.[3] Amongst many other privileges obtained for the honour of Clitheroe, John Lacy had a grant of the right to have a *furca*, or gallows, there and at Tottington.[4] The rise of

[1] Hist. Ches. i. 573.
[2] Hist. Ches. i. 9.
[3] Hist. Whalley, 179.
[4] Hist. Whalley, 179 n.

the Lacys was the decline of Halton, for when they had acquired the earldom of Lincoln "the greater glory dimmed the less," and the castle of Lincoln being more palatial than Halton, the latter from that time became but their secondary home, and only an occasional residence. John Lacy died on 22d July 1240, and was buried beside his ancestors at Stanlaw. His seal is engraved in the History of Cheshire.[1] On his heater-shaped shield he seems to bear the coat with the label of five points assigned to him in the History of Whalley.[2] Gilbert de Barton was at one time John Lacy's seneschal at Halton.[3] At another time Alan the clerk, probably Alan le Norcis, was such seneschal, after having first been bailiff between 1237 and 1240. William de Wambwelle was his bailiff at "Alton."[4] Vaughan, who, in his British Antiquities, makes John Lacy marry Gwenliant, daughter of Llewellyn, Prince of Wales, was under a mistake.[5] In Lyson's History of Cheshire[6] there is a story of John Lacy being summoned to parliament in 1269, which is probably a mistake for Henry de Lacy.

EDMUND LACY, son of the last baron by Margaret, his second wife, succeeded his father as ninth baron of Halton, but his mother being alive and surviving him, he never attained to the title of Earl of Lincoln. He was educated at Court, under the immediate eye of King Henry III., and with his sanction, by the contrivance of Peter of Savoy, but to the great dissatisfaction of the nobles and people of England, and without his own consent, he was married in the year 1247 to Alice de Saluces, a foreign lady, the daughter of a nobleman of Provence, who was related to the Queen.[7] The marriage took place at Woodstock, and the King was present at the ceremonial. In 1256 we have an account of the marriage of his son, which almost reads like a Gazette announcement:—Anno Gratiæ 1256 die Veneris proximâ ante natale domini circa horam diei primam facta est hæc conventio inter dominum Edmundum de Lacy ex unâ parte et dominum Willielmum Longepée ex alterâ et quia prælocutum fuerat in Vasconiâ super maritagio Henrici filii et hæredis dicti Edmundi et Margaritæ filiæ et hæredis dicti Willielmi dictâ die ex consensu partium completum est.[8]

[1] Hist. Ches. i. 513. [2] Hist. Whal. p. 61. [3] Harland's Hist. Eccles. p. 8.
[4] Arley Charters, Box i. 70, 6, 4 ; and Misc. Pal. p. 11.
[5] Amicia Tracts, Chet. Soc. p. 214. [6] Hist. Ches. p. 350. [7] Hist. Whalley, 170.
[8] Amicia Tracts, Chet. Soc. 239.

For some reason which does not appear, this baron alienated to Sir Geoffrey fitz Geoffrey de Dutton *totam terram suam de Thelwall, cum wera et piscaria et stalagiis suis*—that is, according to the historian of Cheshire, two third parts of his patrimony in Thelwall, and also all the land he had in Thelwall, which he had of the gift of the abbot and convent of Evesham.[1] These lands the abbot and convent had originally acquired by the gift of Randle, Earl of Chester.

In 1254 he went, with many other nobles, on the King's affairs to Bordeaux, and on his return home through France he probably was present and witnessed the meeting of the Kings of France and England at Chartres.[2] In 1257 he is expressly called constabularius Cestriæ.[3]

On the 5th June 1258 he died, and was buried with his ancestors at Stanlaw.[4] The seal of this baron, which is large and fine, is engraved in the History of Whalley.[5] It represents him on the obverse as arrayed in complete armour, mounted on a charger in full career, and brandishing his sword. The reverse has a shield bearing the three garbs of Cheshire, the country of the *Cornavii*, which, with the Lacy knot, was afterwards a favourite family bearing. Some heralds have thought these sheaves of corn in the arms meant nothing but a pun on the Latin name of the county, and it is certain if they were used thus early, that they were not adopted because Randle Blundeville, a later earl, was born at Blanchminster or Whitchurch.

[1] Hist. Ches. i. 546. [2] Holinshed. [3] Amicia Tracts, Chet. Soc. 239.
[4] Hist. Whal. 179. [5] Ibid. 178.

CHAPTER VIII.

HENRY DE LACY, TENTH BARON.

HENRY DE LACY, who succeeded his father as tenth Baron of Halton, and afterwards became Earl of Lincoln, attained a degree of eminence far above all his ancestors, and his name is found largely interwoven with our national annals. "In his days," says Sir Peter Leycester, referring to a contemporary charter, "a fair was and had been from ancient times kept at Halton on St. Mary's day (Sept. 8)."[1] Walter de Warren was the bailiff of Halton when Henry succeeded to it.[2] Henry de Lacy had scarcely entered upon his inheritance when the king, on 6th February 1259, issued his command to the sheriffs of every county in which any part of the honour of Lancaster lay, not to hinder either William le Butiller (probably the Lord of Warrington), the keeper of that honour, or any of his bailiffs, from doing what to such keeping belonged, the king having committed to him it and the whole county of Lancaster.[3] This mandate, which at that time only concerned the Lacys directly as lords of Clitheroe, at a later period, after Halton had become part of the honour of Lancaster, directly concerned also the lords of that honour. The time of Henry de Lacy's rule at Halton was a busy one. We are told by Dr. Whitaker that the mode of putting thieves taken in the fact to death by beheading was a practice peculiar to the Earls of Chester, and that it thence came to be called "the Cheshire custom." Upon succeeding to the honour of Clitheroe, the Halton Lacys are supposed to have introduced this Cheshire custom there; and if so, the Halifax and Scottish "maidens," and their sister, the French "guillotine," with its ugly name and its hateful associations, were probably an offspring of the barony of Halton.[4] In 1272, Henry de Lacy, who, not long before King Henry's death had received knighthood from his royal hand, rose high in favour with his son and successor, Edward I., whom in

[1] Hist. Ches. i. 506.
[2] Arley Deeds, Box i. 33.
[3] Dodsworth.
[4] Hist. Whal. 261-2.

energy, bravery, and decision of character he very much resembled. We hardly wonder, therefore, to find him soon afterwards the king's chief counsellor and friend. In 1272 he assisted Earl Edmund, the king's brother, at the siege and taking of Chartley Castle, then forcibly withheld from him by the King's rebellious vassal, Robert de Ferrars, once lord of the honour of West Derby, and, as such, Lord Paramount of Warrington.

But Henry de Lacy, who had introduced *the maiden* into his Lancashire possessions, introduced also something far more valuable—an institution calculated to improve and humanise society, as that was to punish offenders. His ancestors, as we have seen, had founded a religious house at Stanlaw. Though called, like every Cistercian house, a "Locus Benedictus," the abbey at Stanlaw in some respects hardly deserved its name. Standing on the shores of the river Mersey, its situation was low and unpleasant. At spring tides it was nearly inaccessible, while the sea, which made continual inroads upon the adjoining lands, sometimes even threatened the abbey itself. After enduring these inconveniences more than a century, the monks, who had now acquired large possessions in Lancashire, were beginning to sigh for a new home. None knew better than they how to choose a site for a house, and, casting about for such a place, their eyes lighted upon the parish of Whalley, one of the livings belonging to their patron. Here "the glebe was warm, fertile, and spacious; the tithery extensive, the incumbent aged, and the patron bountiful." The monks, who were importunate beggars, supplicated their patron for Whalley. They did not supplicate in vain, for on the 1st January 1283, Henry de Lacy granted them the coveted advowson and a license for the translation of their house from Stanlaw to that place.[1] and, which seems singular, on the very same day, Einion, bishop of Bangor, issued an indulgence of thirty days to all who should give aid to the monks of Stanlaw in their removal to a new home.[2] The charity of a Welsh bishop towards an English abbey at such a juncture, when his country was being overrun from England, could not have been spontaneous; but probably Henry de Lacy was with the invaders, and his influence was used on behalf of Stanlaw.

In 12 Edw. I. (1 Jan. 1284), Henry de Lacy granted the church of Whalley to the monks of Stanlaw.[3] In the great civil war (*temp.* Car. I.)

[1] Hist. Whalley, 62.   [2] Ibid. 115.   [3] Madox Form. Angl. 261.

Sir Henry de Lacy was governor of Denbigh for the king, and when he could hold out the fortress no longer, he threw the key into the moat, rather than surrender it to his sovereign's enemies, and there, long after, it was found. In 1284, probably in reward for his services in the Welsh wars, the king bestowed on Henry de Lacy the lordship of Denbigh, when, in addition to his other titles, he assumed that of Lord of Roos and Rowynock. Over the gateway of Denbigh Castle stands an effigy of Henry in his robes, and hence we may perhaps assume that to him belongs some part of the honour of erecting this grand old fortress. Here, or at Pomfret, another of his castles—for the tradition varies—his eldest son and heir-apparent met his death by a fall from the castle battlements.[1] The old feeling for lepers was not yet dead, for, by his charter of 30th September 1285, Henry de Lacy confirmed the grant made by Henry and Ellen Torboc to the prior and canons of Burscough, upon condition that one leper from Widnes, if any such there were, should at all times be received and entertained in their house, and also that a mass for Henry de Lacy, Earl of Lincoln, and his countess, should be celebrated every year at Easter, and that after their death, they should be entered in the martyrology of Burscough, and have their names entered in the canon.[2] Three days before he died, Earl Hugh, the founder of St. Werburgh's, considering it a safe passport to heavenly bliss, caused himself to be shorn a monk of his own abbey.[3] But in that age there were many who put their trust in vicarious services, besides those who

> Dying, put on the weeds of Dominic;
> Or, in Franciscan, thought to pass disguised.

And in this respect Henry de Lacy, though an enlightened person, was not before his time, for he believed in the efficacy of the purchase of such steps towards heaven.[4]

In 1286, his mother being dead, Henry de Lacy then styled himself Earl of Lincoln, Constable of Chester, and Lord of Roos and Rowynock. By an inquisition taken at Chester on Tuesday next after the Ascension, 16 Edw. I. (11th May 1288), to ascertain what services were due to the king from his Cheshire tenants in his wars in Wales, it was found that Henry de Lacy held eight knights' fees in Halton by that service.[5]

[1] Hist. Whalley, 180.   [2] Hist. Lan. iii. 718 *in notis*, and 720, 721.
[3] Hist. Ches. i. 162.   [4] Kennett's Par. Ant. i. 434.   [5] Original *penes me*.

When King Edward I., in the seventeenth year of his reign (1289), returned home after an absence of three years in his French dominions, he issued a commission, in which the Earl of Lincoln was named the chief commissioner, to reform abuses in the courts of law, and especially in the court of Common Pleas. In the following year (1290) the commissioners made their report, and several of the judges having been found guilty of erasing and altering records to the perversion of justice, heavy (and as it was thought) disproportionate fines were imposed upon them. The charge against Sir Ralph de Heugham, the Chief Justice, and the author of more than one text-book on the law, was, that he had reduced the fine set upon a very poor man from 13s. 4d. to 6s. 8d.—not, one would think, a very aggravated offence, seeing that at that time the Chief Justice's whole salary was only 60 marks a year.[1] If there was really corruption amongst the judges, and we are bound in some measure to believe it, to the Baron of Halton belongs the credit of being the means to redress it. In connection with the fine imposed on the Chief Justice, we are told that the amount was laid out in building a turret at Westminster, in which was placed a clock, by which is probably meant a bell [*cloche*], which might be heard all over Westminster Hall.[2] The disproportion between the alleged offences and the fines generally imposed has induced a suspicion that in issuing the commission which led to them, our English Justinian had in view the possibility by such means of replenishing an exhausted exchequer, as well as reforming the law.

Henry de Lacy's seneschal of Halton at this time was Nicholas Leycester, an ancestor of our great Cheshire antiquary, and a man then much employed in public business.[3] It was probably Leycester's position as Lacy's seneschal that led to his marriage with the widow of Robert de Denbigh.

At this time we have this charter affecting Henry de Lacy:—A Touts ceaux Felippe, que fuit femme Monr. Tho. de Dutton, Salute. Sachez moy aver graunte—a toute ma vie à mon cher seigneur Sire Henri de Lasci, counte de Nicole & conestable de Cestre, toute le droit & le cleyme que je avoy en une pechery que est appelle Chiploade, en le countée de Cestre. Done à Lundres 24 jour de Maij 18 Ed. I. (1290).[4] Chiploade was a fishery on the Mersey at Thelwall, and Phelipe was the wife of Thomas de

---

[1] Blackstone's Com. iii. 409. [2] Ibid. [3] Hist. Ches. i. 461, 514.
[4] Amicia Tracts, by Chet. Soc. 239.

Dutton of that place, to whom Geoffrey de Dutton, who held Thelwall under Edmund de Lacy, had granted it.[1]

From a deed of Henry de Lacy, dated at Stanlaw 19th January 1292, it appears that certain works, probably additions or repairs to the castle, were then going on at Halton, for Henry le Norreys, in the event of his failing to complete a grant which he had made to the abbot and convent of Stanlaw, then bound himself to pay xxs. towards the completion of the works in question.[2]

Henry de Lacy's charter, as we have seen, for the translation of the monastery at Stanlaw to Whalley, bore date on New Year's day 1283, but the abbot and convent had to endure a long delay before they could enter upon their new home.

At the time of the charter, Peter de Cestria was in possession of the living, and although already an old man, he lived on for ten years afterwards, and the monks, thus made to feel the pains of hope deferred, had their impatience further quickened by several events which in the interim occurred at Stanlaw. In 1287 the great tower of their church gave way, and fell down, and two years afterwards a fire broke out, and consumed the greater part of the abbey. At the death of Peter de Cestria, therefore, the monks would gladly have removed to Whalley, but there were further obstacles to be overcome, and for which they must still wait.

In 1293 Henry de Lacy was sent on an embassy to France, to demand satisfaction for certain outrages committed by the French upon our English merchants, and if possible to obtain redress without resorting to war.

In 1294, despairing of male issue, he surrendered all his lands to the King, who re-granted them to him for life, and after his decease to Thomas, Earl of Lancaster, and Alice his wife, and the heirs of their bodies, failing which they were to remain over to Earl Edmund, the King's brother.[3] By this act the honour of Clitheroe became united to that of Lancaster.

The appropriation of the living of Whalley to Stanlaw Abbey by the Pope's bull, and its ratification by Henry de Lacy, which had been so long waited for, were not completed before 1295; and on the 4th April following, Geoffrey de Norbury, eighth abbot of Stanlaw, and his convent, took possession of the deanery or parsonage of Whalley, which was to be their abode during the erection of the new monastery.[4] Henry de Lacy granted

[1] See a copy of the charter *me penes*.
[2] Hist. Whal. p. 181.
[3] Miscel. Pal. 44.
[4] Ibid. 623.

his burgesses of Congleton a charter making the place a free borough, and gives them a gild merchant and other privileges.[1]

The Lacys, and other great patrons of Stanlaw, had for several generations found their last resting-place in its precincts; and when the monastery was translated to Whalley, their remains, as is intimated in Bishop Einion's indulgence, were to be translated also. In due time they were doubtless removed to the new "Locus Benedictus" at Whalley, and there re-intombed in magnificent tombs, but no research has yet discovered the place of their re-burial.[2]

On the morrow of St. Barnabas (12th June 1296), Henry de Lacy with great ceremony laid the first stone of the great Abbey of Whalley, and in that act was rung the final death-knell of the ancient Abbey of Stanlaw.[3] In the same year, the king having lost his brother Edmund, who had been commander-in-chief in Gascony, and Viceroy of Aquitain, appointed Henry de Lacy to succeed him in both those high offices.

Two years afterwards, he and the Lord St. John, going to the relief of Bellegarde, then invested by the French, were encountered by the Count of Artois, at the head of a large force, and a battle ensued, in which each party claimed the victory. In this battle, darkness coming on, and Henry being separated from his men, passed the night in a wood, and returning the next morning to Bayonne, was received with great joy by his friends. The next year he raised the siege of St. Catherine, driving off the people of Toulouse, by whom it was invested. The next year, the Kings of England and France having concluded a truce, Henry de Lacy returned home.[4] But he seems to have been allowed but little rest, for in 1298, being with the king in Scotland, he led the van in the great battle of Falkirk, fought on the 22d July in that year, when the Scotch are said to have left on the field the incredible number of 40,000 men.[5] It seems strange still to find in Falkirk churchyard several tombstones which preserve the names of the heroes who on that fatal day fell in defence of their country, and still stranger to find among them one of a Scotchman who died fighting on the English side. These monuments, however, may be but renewals of some older ones which were there. In 1300, Edward, Prince of Wales and Earl of Chester, having come to Chester, Henry Earl of Lincoln attended amongst other

---

[1] An exemplification of the charter is enrolled at Chester in the Patent Rolls, 10 Hen. VIII.
[2] Hist. Whal. 113.   [3] Ibid. 67.   [4] Holinshed's Chronicles, 1297.
[5] Hume's Hist. Eng. ii. 304.

nobles to do his homage.¹ And in the same year the Lord Walter de Vernon is mentioned as the Earl's bailiff at Halton.²

In the Parliament which was held at Carlisle in 1307, Henry de Lacy bore a part, being placed above all the peers except the Prince of Wales; and afterwards, when Edward II. advanced into Scotland, he left Henry de Lacy protector of the realm in his absence.

Henry was twice married; first in 1256, when he was only six years of age, to Margaret, daughter of William Longespée, by whom he had issue a daughter, Alice, who alone survived him; and, secondly, to Joan, daughter of William Martin, Lord Kaimes, by whom he had no issue.

Henry de Lacy, who lived much in London, died there at his great house, called, from the title of his earldom, "Lincoln's Inn," on the 5th February 1310, at the age of 60, worn out by labours rather than years. The house which had been the warrior's abode afterwards passed into the hands of the lawyers, and has been ever since one of their most celebrated resorts. *Cedant arma togæ.* Henry de Lacy was not carried to Whalley for interment, but was buried in St. Paul's, to which he had been a benefactor, under a magnificent tomb, on which was laid his figure as a cross-legged knight in link mail.³ An old plea to a *quo warranto* claims for him the right to hold a weekly market and two fairs at Halton, franchises which were more likely to have been the acquisition of Henry himself than of any other baron of Halton. The Lacys, not spelt as some have fancifully spelt it, "De la Sees," must have been popular in their time, for when that bold rebel, Jack Cade, wished to vaunt of his connection with a noble house, he could think of none nobler than they. "My wife," he said, "is descended from the Lacys."

As Henry de Lacy left no male issue, his great name and its glory may be said to have died with him. Two of his seals and two of his daughter Alice's have been engraved, and may be seen in the History of Whalley.⁴ In one of Alice's seals, Longespec is impaled with the shield of Lacy. After his death, a great inquisition was taken of his estates in 1311, and I give the portion relating to great Merclisden as a specimen of the whole, and as showing the rental of a township at that time, and what land realised per acre :—

¹ Hist. Ches. i. 194-5.   ² Arley Deeds.   ³ Hist. Whal. 180.
⁴ Ibid. pp. 169, 174, 178.

Value in Merelesden Magna.

	£	s.	d.
350 acres in demesne to divers tenants at will	5	11	8
Certain cotaril for four tofts	0	2	0
Twelve customary tenants for twelve oxgangs in bondage	1	17	6
Works (boon services) remitted	0	6	4
Fishery	0	0	10½
	7	18	4½

I also give part of the Inquisition which was taken after his death at Lincoln, by which it was found that he had the constableship of the castle of Lincoln in right of his wife Margaret Longespee, by the service of having the custody of the prisoners therein, and of being its constable, to which pertained the wardship of it, and other profits, worth 40s. per annum; that he had 100s. per annum in rents from certain free tenants in the bail of the castle belonging to the constableship; from certain other tenants in Kesteven paying to the wardship of the castle he had £4 : 5s., and from certain other like tenants in Lindsey £2 : 16 : 10, and that Alice, his daughter, by Margaret his wife, was his next heir, and was then 26 years old.

In old times Halton was frequently called Halton*shire*, and the bailiffs had the power to execute criminals, but they were bound to present their heads at Chester.[1]

[1] Hist. Ches. i. 281.

CHAPTER IX.

THOMAS OF LANCASTER, ELEVENTH BARON.

THOMAS, Earl of Lancaster, who was cousin-german to the King, was summoned by him to take part in his wars in Scotland in 1298, and in 1300, when he was 25 years old, he was again serving at the siege of Caerlaverock. He had married, as we have seen, Alice, the daughter of Henry de Lacy, succeeding in her right as the eleventh baron of Halton. In compliance with a bad custom of that age, she was married to the Earl at the early age of nine years, and if this marriage were made, as it is said to have been, without her consent, the circumstance may palliate, though it cannot wholly excuse, the disorders and irregularities into which in her after-life she was betrayed. There were originally four children of her father and mother: Alice herself, her sister Margaret, and two brothers, Edmund and John. The sister died a natural death, but tradition has it that her brother Edmund was drowned in the draw-well of Denbigh Castle, and that John, the other brother, running hurriedly on the leads at Pomfret, stumbled and fell from one of the turrets of the castle, and was killed by the fall. Alice, who of all the children alone survived her father, immediately on his death became his heir, and inherited his vast estates, the rental of which was estimated at 10,000 marks a-year, at that time a prodigious sum. On her marriage with Thomas of Lancaster, the great name of Lacy quailed before the still greater name of her lord, for Thomas of Lancaster was nearly allied to the king, and the first prince of the blood, and so the name of Lacy went out, and the barony of Halton became linked to the illustrious house of Plantagenet. Alice, who survived her first husband, afterwards became the wife, first of Eubulo L.'Estrange, and secondly of Hugh de Frenes, and afterwards died in the year 1348, without leaving issue by any of her husbands. Thomas, who was Earl of Lancaster, and also, by inheritance from his father, high sheriff of that county, was a man of great power and influence, and when to his own rich inheritance was added that of his wife, his wealth and possessions were equal to his high station. One consequence of his marriage with the heiress of Lacy was to transfer to the honour, afterwards the duchy of Lancaster, with Alice's other possessions, the manor of Congleton, which until now had belonged to the honour of Halton.[1] In the year 1311, when he had only just become possessed of the Lacy inheritance, he had a dispute with the chapter of St. Asaph respecting some aids which the chapter refused to pay, as having been granted without their consent.[2] In 1317 Preyeres was his seneschal, and Henry del Bruche his receiver, at Halton.[3] In a short time he was advanced by the King to the high honour of being made the chief of his Privy Council. This office had been well filled by Henry de Lacy, the late Baron of Halton, but Thomas of Lancaster, by his want of strength of character, was little fitted to be his successor. During his rule over Halton, the castle was broken into and robbed, in 13 Edward II. (1319), by William de Huxley and other felons. William's share of the plunder was small, being only a basnet. The *basnet*, the *salade*, and the *helm*, all of them head pieces of armour, seem at times to have descended to lower uses, and to have established a relation between themselves and the kitchen. The *basin* is derived from the basnet, and thus Mambrino's helmet, which had been degraded to a basin, was only returning to its original purpose when it became a helmet again; *salade* is well-known as a preparation of uncooked or half-cooked vegetables; and it stung Othello to the quick to think of the base use that might at last await his own head-gear, when he exclaimed

"Let huswives make a skillet of my helm!"

William de Huxley and his co-felons being indicted for their offence at Chester, he pleaded that he was a clergyman or clerk, and could not be tried by the temporal courts, but was entitled to be tried by the bishop; whereupon proclamation was made to ascertain whether he really were a clerk or not, and no claim being made for him by the bishop in answer to the proclamation, he was tried, and the jury found him guilty, and notwithstanding his plea, they further found that this pretended clerk was one of a gang of common robbers. Breaking into a castle to rob it must have been rare, even in William de Huxley's time; breaking out of a castle was

---

[1] Lyson's Ches. 490. [2] Arch. Cambrensis, 3d series, lvi. 441.
[3] Orig. charter, *me penes*.

common then, and has been common enough ever since. His trying to evade the consequences of his crime by pleading that he was a clerk, and able to read, which should have been the means of teaching him better, sounds now very strange to us. But out of the respect formerly paid to learning, at the time when learning was scarce, and reading a rare accomplishment, the clergy first, and afterwards all who could read, were allowed benefit of clergy, and escaped with a less punishment than other offenders. Whenever a person not actually in orders claimed this benefit, the court was wont to test his power of reading by requiring him to read a verse or two of one of the Psalms. The 51st Psalm was usually and not inappropriately selected. William of Deloraine, in "The Lay of the Last Minstrel," when he boasted

> Letter or line know I never a one
> Wer't my neck verse at Hairibee,

was more entitled to indulgence for his crime than a clerkly offender, who, forgetting his better knowledge, transgressed the law. And so the Legislature at length thought, for in the 8 Geo. IV. (1827) they abolished this benefit of clergy finally and for ever.

About this period the neighbourhood seems to have been much infested by bands of robbers, a circumstance which led the learned historian of Cheshire to appropriate to our Halton the sarcastic notice found in "Piers Plowman's Vision," where we read—

> There the pass of Haulton
> Poverté may pass without fear of robbynge.

Later inquiries, however, set on foot by our respected townsman Dr. Kendrick, seem to prove that to the pass at Alton, on the borders of Surrey and Hampshire, and not to our Halton, belongs the poet's censure, which implies that although its "gentlemen of the shade" let the poor go free, they made the rich pay for both.

In February 1322, Thomas of Lancaster having risen in arms against his sovereign, with the avowed purpose of compelling him to put away his favourites, the Spensers, took up a position on the banks of the Trent, in Staffordshire, at the head of a large force, prepared to dispute the king's passage over the river. The earl had command of the bridge at Burton; but the king, while making a feint of attacking it, threw a part of his forces across the river at a ford about five miles higher up, and coming upon the earl's flank, compelled him to fall back hastily, and in some disorder, upon his headquarters at Tutbury. He had scarcely arrived there before the king was thundering at the castle gates. To sally out in front, and march through Staffordshire, was impossible; to cross the river Dove, in his rear, where there was neither a bridge nor a ford, and thence retreat through Derbyshire, was both difficult and dangerous. But to attempt it seemed the earl's only alternative. Committing, therefore, the baggage and the military chest to Henry de Leycester, his cofferer (the son probably of Henry de Lacy's former seneschal), he set out under the shade of night to make his way across the Dove; and, notwithstanding that the stream was then in flood, he himself effected the passage in safety; but his cofferer was less fortunate, for his guards being seized with a sudden panic, allowed the money chest, containing more than 100,000 pieces of silver, to fall from their hold in the dark, and drop into the river, where it sank and was lost. Moments were too precious to be wasted in the attempt to recover it, and so, embedding itself by its weight where it fell, the chest remained beneath the river until the month of June 1831, a period of more than 500 years, when in deepening and widening the Dove, the chest and its contents were discovered, and some of the coins found their way to the Warrington Museum, where they may now be seen.[1] Having taken possession of the earl's vacated castle on the 10th March 1322, the king did not loiter there, but pushing on at once, he arrived at Borough-bridge just after his rebellious subject had been defeated at that place, where he had been stopped by Sir Andrew de Harcla. The earl surrendered to Sir Andrew on the 16th March 1322, and the next day the king received the surrender of the earl's great ally, Sir Robert de Holland, and his kinsmen, Sir John and Sir Richard de Holland, who had followed their master's fortunes until his star finally set. From Borough-bridge the earl was conducted to Pontefract, and shut up in a tower which he had himself built there opposite the Black Friars. But the sword was impatient for vengeance, and having been tried and found guilty of treason, the earl, being led to execution with great indignity, was beheaded on a hill outside the town on the 22d March 1322.[2] Some of his adherents, and among them Sir William Touchet, Sir William fitz William, Sir Waryne Lisle, Sir Henry Bradburne, Sir William Cherry, and John Page, Esquire, were hanged about the same time; but Sir Robert Holland and his two kinsmen

[1] Penny Magazine, Nov. 1834, p. 430.   [2] Leland's Collectanea, p. 465.

experienced the king's clemency, and though their estates were forfeited, their lives were spared. Their escaping thus countenances the idea that at the last moment they deserted their master, and joined the king. A historian informs us that Thomas of Lancaster was a weak man and a bad subject—bustling without vigour, and intriguing without abilities. He lived, however, in a style of princely magnificence, and the particulars of his housekeeping for a single year may be seen in the household book kept by his cofferer, which is printed in the "History of Lancashire."[1] In this account there is no mention of Halton; but two items in it relating to the Countess Alice, its owner, show that she was then living at Pickering. One of these gives us the expenses of her house in the pantry, buttery, and kitchen; and the other the sum paid for her wine, wax, and spices, and the clothes and furs of her wardrobe—both together amounting to no less than £440 : 0 : 9, a large sum in those days.

On the death of Thomas of Lancaster his estates were seized as forfeited for treason, and probably because the abbot of Shrewsbury had shown sympathy with his cause, in 17th Edward II. (1323), an inquisition found that Wilgreave (a place in Thelwall), containing a carucate of land with a rent of 20s. in the Manor of Weston, and a fishery in the Mersey belonging to the abbey, had been escheated to the king since the 13th August then last, by reason of the abbot having withheld for sixty years a chantry founded in the chapel of Wilgreave for the souls of the king's progenitors, who had given those lands, rent, and fishery to sustain the same.[2] The possessions of the chantry had been conferred, as we have seen, on the abbey of Shrewsbury by William fitz Nigel and William fitz William, Barons of Halton, and could only be said to be the gift of the king's progenitors, inasmuch as some of the king's ancestors, and particularly Henry III., had confirmed the gift.

Shortly after the death of his rebellious vassal, the king came on a progress into this neighbourhood. He had been here on at least two previous occasions: on the 1st July, 3d Edward I. (1310), when he was at Chester, and the day following at Nantwich, and on the 31st July, 13th Edward II. (1319), when he was again at Chester.[3] But in his present visit he had a deeper purpose. The Earl of Lancaster, though his death had been ignominious, had befriended the monks, the clergy, and the church, and by them, and all whom they could influence—and their power at

[1] Hist. Lanc. i. 132-3. [2] Dodsworth. [3] Hartshorne's Itinerary of Edward II.

that time was great—he was idolised. It was given out that he was a martyr, and then that he was a saint; a chapel was erected to him on the spot where he had suffered, a litany was composed in his honour, and miracles were alleged to be wrought at his tomb. This posthumous popularity, which for a time went on increasing, was very offensive to the king, who thought it should be checked, and, if possible, suppressed. The pretended miracles were denied by royal proclamation, just as was done afterwards in France, when a similar proclamation by a French monarch was greeted with a pasquinade—

"De part le roi defense a Dieu,
De faire miracles en ce lieu."

On the 23d October 1323, the king was at Liverpool, and from that place he wrote a letter commanding his commissioners to proscribe the miracles said to be wrought at the tomb of two adherents of the earl. But the popular belief in the earl's sanctity was so perverse, that even so late as 1361, in the will of Humphrey de Bohun, Earl of Essex, there is this passage: "a un home d'aler a Poumfret et offrir illocques a la toumbe de Thomas jadys de Lancastre xl^s."[1] From Liverpool the king sailed up the river to Ince on the 30th October. From Ince he came to Halton, where he remained from the 1st to the 3d of November, visiting Norton on one of those days, and Vale Royal on another. On the 4th, 5th, and 6th, he was at Ince; from whence he probably visited the neighbouring house of Stanlaw.[2] In his visits to these religious houses, all doubtless infected by the Lancaster heresy, there was good policy. The king no doubt made his offering at the shrine of St. Mary of Norton, and at the altars of the other houses. Unhappily, however, no chronicler has recorded his visits, or the account of them, if there were any, has perished; otherwise we might have had as lively and graphic a picture of them as Joscelin de Brakelond has left us in his gossiping account of King John's visit to the shrine of St. Edmund at Bury.[3] But the king was not wholly engrossed by the pursuit of the dead earl's adherents, for in his progress he indulged his taste for music and minstrelsy. Who sang for him at Halton we are not informed, but at Wherlton, Alianor Rede and Alice de Wherlton received 4s. for singing before the king the song of "Simon de Montfort" and other songs. Simon de Montfort was the hero of many

[1] Nichol's Roy. Wills, 54. [2] Hartshorne's Itinerary of Edward II.
[3] Chronicles of Joscelin de Brakelond.

popular songs. But the songstresses showed little judgment in singing his praises before the king. Like Thomas of Lancaster, he had risen against his sovereign, and like him had fallen. Like him, too, the people had canonised him after his death, calling him St. Simon the righteous. Miracles, too, were said to be wrought by his body and at his tomb. He fell in the battle of Evesham, in Warwickshire, and was buried in the abbey there, a place then very inaccessible from Lancashire. Yet, William the rector, and Richard the hermit, of Warrington, the former of whom seems to have been present in the battle, actually travelled to Evesham to bear votive candles to the saint's tomb, and no less than eight Warrington persons are said to have been cured, either by his appearing to them, or by the application of his fillet.[1]

But in following the king's progress, after the late earl's adherents, a great antiquary (lately deceased) thinks he has discovered another personage of more extensive popularity, with whose name we have all been familiar from childhood, but whose real history is so obscure that it has sometimes been thought he was not a real man of flesh and blood, but only an impersonation of certain popular qualities—the ballad hero, Robin Hood. The comely king of the ballad he believes to be no other than King Edward II., and it is certain that during this royal progress a person of the name of Robin Hood, an outlaw, probably, in the cause of Thomas of Lancaster, did enter the King's service, and remain in it as his valet at the wages of threepence a day, from about December 1323 until the November of the following year, when, finding a Court life wearisome, and his yearning for the green wood having been quickened by seeing some young men practising with the bow, he sought and obtained his discharge precisely as the ballad describes the outlaw to have done :—

"Alas!" then said good Robin Hood,
"Alas! and well away!
If I dwell longer with the king,
Sorrow will me slay."

So forth then wente Robin Hood,
Tyll he came to our kynge;
"My Lord, the kynge of Engelande,
Graunte me my askynge.

---

[1] Rishanger's Chronicles, published by the Camden Soc. 74, *et passim*.

" I made a chapel in Bernysdale,
  That semely is to se ;
  It is of Mary Magdalene,
  And thereto wolde I be.

" I might never in this seven night,
  No tyme to slepe ne wynke ;
  Nether all these seven days,
  Nether ete ne drynke.

" Me longeth sore to Bernysdale,
  I may not be therefro ;
  Barefote and wolwarde I have hyght,
  Thyder for to go."[1]

The ballad of Robin Hood, as given in the Percy Relics, contains nothing that seems to contradict this, and one passage in it rather looks to our neighbourhood, and to the outlaw as a redresser of wrong, for there the ruined knight, speaking of his son, tells the outlaw

" He slew a knight of Lancashire,
  And a squire bold ;
  For to save him in his right,
  My goodes he 'th set and solde."

Fordun, the Scottish chronicler, who lived near the end of the reign of King Edward III., gives us under the year 1260 this account of the outlaw :—" At this time, amongst the outlaws and banished men, rose that famous robber Roben Hode, with Little John and their accomplices, on whom the multitude are very merry in their plays, and of whom the clown and ballard singers delight to sing."[2]

It seems strange that a Scottish chronicler should be the first to mention our celebrated outlaw, and almost as strange that he should fix his date nearly a century after the reign of Richard I., in which he is generally supposed to have lived. These discrepancies, added to the freshness of the story at the time when Fordun lived and wrote, may make us hesitate before we reject the antiquary's conjecture that the outlaw lived in the time of Edward II., and was for a while in his service.

After Thomas of Lancaster's death, the king seized on his possessions, and retained them until his own death. On the 24th December, 20 Edward II. (1326), Sir Hugh de Dutton, who had married Joan, a

[1] Hunter's Historical Tracts.   [2] Fordun ii. 104.

daughter of Sir Robert de Holland, was appointed by the king, and as if he owed the Hollands a favour, Seneschal of Halton, but he held the office only a year, for he died in the first year of the following reign, and it may be a question whether his death was not hastened by Henry of Lancaster's hatred against the Hollands and their kindred.[1] In the next reign we shall hear more of Thomas of Lancaster's possessions, and of his successors in the barony of Halton. His seal is alluded to in the Archæological Journal, No. 96, 316; and he bore for his arms *gules* three lions passant gardant *or*, with a label of France; his mother's shield of arms was, *azure* semé of fleurs de lis *or*.

[1] Sir P. Leycester's Hist. Ches. i. 477.

CHAPTER X.

HENRY OF LANCASTER, TWELFTH BARON.

HENRY OF LANCASTER, Lord of Monmouth, surnamed Grismond from the place of his birth, had served, like his brother, in the king's wars in Scotland in 1298, and at the siege of Caerlaverock in 1300, and in the reign of Edward II. he had attended by command to meet the king and queen at Dover on their return from France. Upon the death of his brother, Thomas of Lancaster, he would have immediately succeeded to the earldom of Lancaster, and have become what Sir Peter Leycester calls him, the twelfth Baron of Halton, had not his brother's attainder stood in the way, and prevented his stepping at once into his inheritance. But even had this not been so, he could not have taken the Lacy possessions, for these, or at least so much of them as the king had not seized on the plea that the Lady Alice, the earl's widow, had married Eubulo L'Estrange without first obtaining his license, remained with her for her life under the settlement made by Henry, Earl of Lincoln. All her lands in Lancashire, Cheshire, and Yorkshire, with the lordship of Denbigh and the castle of Bullingbrook, the lion's share of her inheritance, had been seized by the king, and a diminished income of 3000 marks a-year for her life was all that remained to her.

In the 20th Edward II., when the king's power was tottering, Henry of Monmouth, probably after the king's deposition, and in the regency of his son, was granted the custody of the castle and honour of Tutbury and Pickering, and on the 24th December in the same year, probably by the same authority, Sir Hugh Dutton was made seneschal or steward of Halton.[1] Henry of Monmouth did not forget or forgive his brother's death or the treatment he had received from the king. He willingly joined the queen's party against her husband's favourites, the Spensers, and he was one of those sent by the queen and the Prince of Wales to

[1] Hist. Ches. I. 477.

find out the king in his hiding-place. They found and took him, with Spenser and other favourites, in Wales, when the king was committed to his custody to keep, and he conducted him to his castle at Kenilworth. Some disgrace was supposed to attach to Henry's name from the way in which he was said to have kept his royal prisoner.[1] But later research has cleared his character from this stain, and a historian tells us that as his sovereign's keeper he was touched with generous feelings towards him, and treated him with so much gentleness, that he was even suspected of intending to favour the king still further, on which account the prisoner was taken out of his hands.[2]

In the first year of the following reign, however, Thomas of Lancaster's irregular attainder was reversed. A chapel was erected over his remains, and on the 8th June 1327 Robert de Weryngton, clerk, the overseer of the work, was authorised to collect money to complete it.[3] The young king received knighthood at the hands of Henry of Monmouth, who also helped to find him a wife, for he was of the council who sent ambassadors to ask the hand of Philippa of Hainault. Henry now became possessed of all the lands and lordships which had been seized on his brother's death, with the earldoms of Lancaster and Leicester, and all the other lands of which Edmund, his father, and Thomas, his brother, were formerly possessed. He was now called Earl of Lancaster and Leicester, and Seneschal of England.[4] Shortly afterwards writs to the various receivers were issued, which announced to them that the new earl had done homage for his late brother's lands, and that thenceforth they were to account to him for all the rents. Twenty-seven at least of such writs were issued, but none of them occurs as addressed to the steward seneschal, or other officer at Halton. At this time Halton was probably a part of those possessions of the Lady Alice which the late king had seized, and which was still in the hands of the Crown. Sir Robert de Holland, though he had followed his master the Earl of Lancaster to Borough Bridge, was suspected not to have kept true faith with him in his last extremity, and was on that account in such disfavour with the new earl that he had been set upon and slain. Sir Hugh Dutton, the lately appointed seneschal of Halton, had married a daughter of Sir Robert, and as he died about the same time as Sir Robert, there is reason to suspect that he was involved in his father-in-

[1] Hist. Ches. i. 517.   [2] Hume's Hist. Eng. ii. 358.   [3] Rymer's Fœdera, ii. 707.
[4] Hist. Ches. i. 517.

law's discredit, and shared his fate. But we are not left to doubt as to the reason why the seneschal of Halton was omitted when writs were addressed to the receivers of the other Lancaster estates. The new king and his mother, Isabel, for services rendered them by Sir William Clinton in France, had promised to find him lands of the value of £200 a-year, and the king in his first year, in satisfaction of his promise, and because Sir William, confiding in it, *se posuerat ad vexillum*—meaning, perhaps, that he had joined the king and the queen-mother against the late king and his favourites, granted him the castle, manor, and hundred of Halton, in the counties of Lancaster and Chester. Sir William was a great warrior, and in the same year, by the king's command, he met John, Earl of Hainault, at Dover, and marched with him and his host to join the king and aid him in his wars in Scotland.[1] Under this grant of Halton to Sir Wm. Clinton, the barony probably remained dissociated from the earldom of Lancaster during the lifetime of the Lady Alice, the late earl's widow, and if so, Henry Grismond was not, as Sir Peter Leycester styles him, the twelfth Baron of Halton, but the barony either remained in abeyance or was vested in Sir William Clinton during Lady Alice's life, who outlived Henry Grismond.[2]

After the death of Sir Hugh Dutton, the seneschal of Halton, in 1st Edward III. (1327), Sir William Clinton seems to have appointed Sir Hugh Venables to succeed him, and in 19th Edward III., Venables having died, Sir William Clinton, now become Earl of Huntingdon, by a deed dated at Maxstock, appointed Thomas Dutton, *quamdiu se bene gesserit*, to be his seneschal governor and receiver of Halton and of all his manors and lands in Cheshire and Lancashire, at a farm rent of 440 marks a-year.[3]

The following inquisition on Halton, which gives us an estimate of its value, was taken at this time:—

"Halton, in the county of Chester, is worth 148 0 20¼."

An extent of the castle of Halton, with the appurtenances, made there on Wednesday next after the feast of Saint James the Apostle, 2d Edw. III. (27th July 1328), before Robert de Aspull and Roger de Gildesburgh, assigned, by the king's writ, to make the said extent by the oath of Hamo de Ashley and eleven others (who are named), who say on their oath—

[1] Collins' Peerage, ii. 184; and Hist. Lan. iv. 307.   [2] Hist. Ches. i. 517.   [3] Ibid.

"That there is a certain castle there built, with a stone wall embattled, which, in time of peace, costs more than it yields, unless the lord there shall be in possession of it. And the pasture of the same castle cannot be extended, because it is common, up to the walls, to all the tenants of the town of Halton. And they say that there are 65 acres and a half of land there, formerly held in demesne, which are let to farm to divers tenants for 43s. 8d. at 8d. for the acre, and no more, because the same tenants, of the fruits of the same land, shall give a tenth and the tenth of a tenth, by custom anciently used; also they say that there are ten acres of meadow there, which are worth by the year 12s.—the price of the acre, 14d.—less in the whole by 4d. There is a several pasture called Astmore, worth by the year 9s.; and one windmill and two watermills, worth by the year, deducting reprizes, 26s. 8d."[1]

Henry Grismond seems to have had from the king a grant of certain *jura regalia* in tail, which his son afterwards surrendered. He married Maud, the daughter of Sir Patric de Chaworth, Lord of Kidwelly and Agmore, in Carmarthenshire and Glamorganshire, and as she was her father's sole heir, Henry, by this prudent marriage, advanced his interest and increased his already large estate. By his marriage he had issue a son, of his own name, and six daughters. He began, but did not live to finish, a hospital at Leicester for 100 poor persons. He died on the 22d September, 19th Edward III. (1345), aged about 70, and was buried at Leicester, *in ecclesiâ canonicorum*, the collegiate church which he had founded. The king and queen, the queen-mother, and nearly all the archbishops, bishops, earls, and barons of the whole kingdom, honoured his burial with their presence; but his son, being then in Gascony on the king's affairs, was prevented from joining in this last tribute to his father's remains.[2] The earl bore for his arms, *gules* three lions passant gardant *or*, England, with a baton *azure*.

Kuerden has preserved an imperfect note of the inquisition taken after the earl's death, from which it appears that the manor of Warrington and various other possessions in Lancashire were held under him by Sir William Boteler.

[1] Inquisitions, 2 Edw. III.   [2] Hist. Ches. i. 517.

CHAPTER XI.

HENRY, DUKE OF LANCASTER, THIRTEENTH BARON.

HENRY OF LANCASTER, who had been created Earl of Derby in his father's lifetime, upon his death succeeded to his titles also, and became Earl of Lancaster, Derby, and Leicester, as well as Seneschal of England. Upon the death of Lady Alice, his uncle's widow, if not before, he also became thirteenth Baron of Halton and Constable of Chester. Besides his other names, he had also what was not unusual in that age, an uncomplimentary *sobriquet*, that of "Tort Coll.," or wry neck, in allusion to a personal deformity. According to Froissart, who by a prolepsis calls him Earl of Derby before he had attained that title, he was one of that gallant party who, in 1322, accompanied the king to France, to do his homage for Guienne.[1]

On 28th December, 7th Edward III. (1333), by his father's grant, dated at Kenilworth, he acquired the town and castle of Kidwelly, with the territory of Carnwarthland.[2]

In the expedition to Scotland, where he accompanied the king in 9th Edward III. (1335), he gave such proofs of his valour and military skill as won for him a grant of the forfeited lands of Peter de Kymeringham, at Berwick-upon-Tweed.[3]

On the 7th April in the next year (1336) we find him acting as Captain-General of the English army in Scotland, and in the next month he was made a banneret, and his Scottish services were soon afterwards rewarded with a coronet, the title of Earl of Derby, and a grant of 1000 marks a-year to support it, to be paid out of the customs of London, Boston, and Hull, until the king should find him lands or rents of that value. The patent expressly states that the payment was to be in addition to the £20 a-year usually given in lieu of the *tertium denarium de placitis comitatus*, which the earls anciently had.[4] He was still young when he

[1] Froissart, i. 32.   [2] Hist. Lanc. i. 136.   [3] Ibid.   [4] Ibid.

received these gifts and honours, but his devotion to a military life, and his capacity for it, acquired him even then among his followers and companions the name of "The soldiers' father."[1]

King Edward III., before he called himself King of France, a title which, a historian informs us, created an animosity between France and England, which lasted for centuries, sought, and by courting the friendship of Jacob Von Arteveldt, the brewer of Ghent, secured, an alliance with the Flemings.[2] A party of the nobles of that country, having possessed themselves of the island of Cadsand, between the havens of Sluys and Flushing, began to harass and distress the English commerce. Upon this news reaching the King's ears, he was heard to say, "We will soon settle that business;" and thereupon, having given the Earl of Derby, Sir Walter Manny, and others, orders to hold themselves in readiness, they shortly afterwards, with a force of 600 men-at-arms and 2000 archers, set sail from the Thames. As they neared Cadsand, they caused their trumpets to sound a defiance, but no parley was sought, and so, ordering the archers to draw their bows stiff and strong, they set up a great shout. The first discharge did such mischief and maimed and hurt so many, that they compelled the force which guarded the haven to give way, upon which the English knights and barons landing, renewed the fight on shore with swords, lances, and battle-axes. On both sides the battle was stoutly maintained. But the gallant Earl of Derby, true to his character as a valiant knight, advancing too far on the first assault, and being struck down, would have been slain had not Sir Walter Manny, rushing heroically to his aid, covered him when down, and then raised him up with the cry of "Lancaster for the Earl of Derby." At length, however, the Flemings were put to rout, many prisoners were taken, and amongst them their commander, whose ransom enriched Sir Walter Manny. More than 3000 were left dead upon the field.[3]

A warrior in those times was often alternately an admiral as well as a general, and fought at sea as well as on land. In the great sea fight fought before Sluys on 23d June 1340, the earl was serving with the king on board the fleet.[4]

In 1340, the king, being in Flanders prosecuting in person the war with France, was compelled by circumstances to conclude a truce, when

[1] Capgrave de Illustribus Henricis, p. 161.   [2] Hume's Hist. Eng. ii. 397.
[3] Froissart, lib. iv. 1, c. 30; and Smollett's Hist. Eng. iii. 357.   [4] Froissart, i. 73.

his Flemish allies, becoming clamorous for the promised subsidies, and money not arriving from England to pay them, he took the resolution to return to England, and leaving his trusty soldier, the Earl of Derby, in the not very enviable position of a pledge, or pawn, for the payment of his debts, he sailed home from Zealand.[1] There seems at this time to have been scarcely any public affair of importance in which the Earl of Derby's aid was not sought. One of the articles of the late truce having stipulated that, if possible, it should be converted into a permanent peace, an embassy which assigned the second place to the Earl of Derby was sent about this time to the Pope, to endeavour, by his mediation, to bring about this object; but the ambassadors were expressly charged in their commission, dated 17 Ed. III., 1343, to treat with the Pope neither as *Pope*, nor even as judge, but simply as a private person, who, being the common friend of both parties, might suggest or find out some mode of settling the differences between them, in which we may see how early began the jealousy of our monarchs against admitting the Pope to have authority in England in the olden time. The Holy Father, however, does not seem to have been much in favour, for when Lord Morley about this time held public jousts in Smithfield, a knight apparelled like the Pope, and twelve others apparelled like cardinals, entered the lists, and we must suppose were worsted, as the chronicler does not inform us of their success, which he would hardly have failed to do had it occurred.[2]

In the month of August 1342 (Froissart places it in this year, and though the old chronicler's dates are not always correct, he seems in this instance to be right), by the king's command, a great feast, pageant, and tournament, were held in London, to which there came very many lords, ladies, and knights, as well from Flanders, Hainault, and Brabant, as from England. All the ladies present, except the Countess of Salisbury, who was dressed with studied plainness, vied with each other in the splendour of their attire, and the antique pageant presented a scene of very great magnificence. Among the other nobles present were the Earl of Derby, and his father (Henry of Lancaster), to whom, instead of his son, the chronicler, by mistake, applies the epithet of "Tort Coll." The pageant, which opened with splendour, ended in a tragedy which clouded it with gloom. John, Lord Beaumont, a "handsome hardy knight, bearing on his shield *azure* semé of fleurs de lis *or*, a lion rampant *or*, and a baton *gules*,"

[1] Smollett's Hist. Eng. iii. 374.   [2] Holinshed's Chron. 385-6.

and gallantly riding in the lists, was unfortunately killed. He was doubly allied to the house of Lancaster, for he had married the Earl of Derby's sister and the earl had married his, and his death was an especial grief to his father-in-law and brother-in-law. Froissart tells us that Lord Beaumont was the son of the viscount of that name, in which he has made a strange mistake, since the title of viscount was unknown in England until 12th February 1440, nearly a century afterwards, when John Beaumont was raised to that title, and was the first viscount ever created in England. In conferring such a title upon a John Beaumont nearly a century before the event, Froissart was rather uttering a prophecy than either committing an anachronism or using a prolepsis.

On the 24th March 1344, the Earls of Derby and Arundel were constituted governors of Aquitaine, from which office the Earl of Derby was discharged on 1st February 1347.[1]

The following year the earl was made the king's captain and lieutenant in Gascony on the 10th May, and on the 20th of that month he had a protection upon his going abroad to his government.[2]

In the same year, the king having put an end to the truce with France, sent a force of 600 men-at-arms, and the same number of archers, into Guienne for the defence of that province. At its head he placed the Earl of Derby, the most accomplished prince in his court, and who possessed in a high degree the virtues of justice and humanity, as well as those of valour and conduct. His commission gives us an insight into the pay of the earl and his soldiers. He was to have 8s. a day, every banneret 4s., every knight 2s., every esquire 1s., and every archer 6d. But, not content with merely protecting and cherishing his province, the earl, on his arrival in it, made a successful invasion on the enemy.[3] He attacked and took the strong town of Bergerac, and when the inhabitants craved his mercy, he proclaimed through the host that mercy must and should be shown to all who claimed it. In June he went back to England, and then returned, bringing fresh succours to Guienne.[4] After which 50 towns and cities submitted before his arms to the King of England, and he defeated the Count de Lisle, who came against him with an army, took prisoners a great number of his followers, amongst whom were 23 persons of quality, and drove the rest of his forces in complete rout from the field.

[1] Fœdera, iii. 9, 104. [2] Ibid. 37, 39. [3] Hollinshed's Chron. 367.
[4] Smollett's Hist. Eng. iii. 396.

He was in the habit of giving up to his soldiers the greater part of the booty taken, and on one occasion having, we are told, promised the booty of a particular place to whoever should find it, a private soldier, who had the good fortune to find a great chest of money, thinking the treasure too great for him to keep, brought it to the earl, but the latter said his promise did not depend on the greatness or smallness of the sum, and told him that he must keep what he had found as his own.[1] At Bergerac, however, the booty proved so large, that out of the share left to him, the earl was able to spend no less than 52,000 marks in the repair and rebuilding of his palace in the Savoy, then an open and rural neighbourhood, looking out upon the clear and unpolluted Thames, and not then as now a place jostled on all sides by houses and buildings, and crowded by noisy streets. In this palace John, King of France, while he was a prisoner in England, resided for a time as the guest of its owner. We may understand the horrors of this campaign from a story told by Froissart, who says that a messenger from a besieged town, being taken with letters upon him asking their friends outside for succour, was barbarously put into an engine and shot back into the town, with his letters tied round his neck.[2] In the year 1345, while the earl was still prosecuting the war in Guienne, his father died, but the importance of the king's affairs prevented him from returning to pay the last tribute of respect to his father's remains.

The following year (1346) was rendered memorable by the great victory of Crecy, from which his important engagements in Guienne kept the Earl of Derby away, doubtless to his great chagrin, since it lost him a share in the glories of that memorable day. In his own province, however, he was a most popular hero everywhere, and in every battle the only cry was "Derby for ever."

On 3d February 1346, the king being about to go abroad, commanded the earl to bring him 200 Welshmen from Monmouth and the neighbourhood, and the like number from Kidwelly and the neighbourhood, and the command seems to have been urgent, for in the following April it was repeated.[3]

On the 27th March 1346, the king ordered the archers, who were going to Gascony, under the charge of the earl, to appear at Tothill to be reviewed.[4]

[1] Hume's Hist. Eng. ii. 423.   [2] Froissart's Chron. p. 135.   [3] Ibid. 68.   [4] Ibid. 77.

On the 14th May 1347, the earl received the king's orders to hasten to him in France, to resist the French, and he gave orders to the admiral to provide shipping to transport him and his forces across the sea.[1]

In the following month the earl made a favourable report of the loyalty of the Gascons, and the king ordered 2000 florins to be paid to the burgesses of Regula, in that province.[2]

After the siege of Poictiers (1347), where he won still further renown, he was appointed, with William de Clinton, Earl of Huntingdon, and others, to hear and determine all causes and disputes relating to arms.[3] No record of the judgments of the Court in these picturesque disputes has come down to us, but the age was heraldic, and the Court's not infrequent decisions, if they had been preserved, would have been full of curious traits of the time and its usages. Such a record we have in the Scrope and Grosvenor controversy in the next reign. The earl's retinue, which at this time was very large, consisted of 800 men-at-arms and 2000 archers, with 30 banners, and his hospitality must have been proportionate, for he spent in his own house, every day, the large sum of £100. On his return to England, it was found that, besides his pay from the king, he had spent in these wars in France £17,000 of his own money. To make him some amends for this great outlay, the king, while he was encamped before Calais, in 21 Ed. III. (1348), granted to him and his heirs-male the castle and town of Bergerac, and also the lands and goods of all the prisoners taken by him at St. John de Angelyn, until they had paid their ransoms,[4] and soon afterwards he obtained another grant to himself and his heirs-male of the castle of Horeston, in the county of Derby, with an annual rent of £40, issuing out of the town of Derby.

In 1349 the earl surrendered to the king the grant in tail of *jura regalia* which had been made to his father, because they appeared to the king and his council to be *ad maximum damnum et nimiam exhæredationem regis*. But by a subsequent charter the same rights were regranted to him to hold for his life only; and it is expressly said that the county of Lancaster was to have the same palatine rights as the county of Chester.

In the 23d Edward III. (1349), the Lady Alice being then dead, to whom the earldom of Lincoln, an old possession of her family, had belonged for her life, it was conferred upon the Earl of Derby, who, in

---

[1] Froissart's Chron. 121.   [2] Ibid.   [3] Ibid. i. 171.   [4] Ibid.

addition to his other titles, had now that of Earl of Lincoln.[1] In the same year the king constituted him his lieutenant and captain-general in the parts of Poictou. In the same year also the king instituted the celebrated Order of the Garter. Steps had been taken towards forming it as early as the year 1344, and this perhaps misled Froissart, and Holinshed after him, to state that it was established in that year, although it really seems not to have been fully instituted until St. George's Day, 1349.[2] The body was to consist of 25 knights, besides the sovereign; and after the Prince of Wales, the second of the original knights nominated was the Earl of Derby, now become Earl of Lancaster, Leicester, and Lincoln, as well as of Derby. Holinshed, alluding to the well-known incident which is said to have given rise to the Order, says that though it had a mean beginning, Ovid's maxim, *Nobilitas sub amore jacet*, is an authority for it.[3]

On the 6th March, 25 Edward III. (1351) the earl was advanced to still higher honour, the king, to reward his merit, creating him a duke, and his county a county palatine. Except the Black Prince, no subject had before been made a duke in England, and in the person of the Earl of Derby, Lancaster for the first time became a dukedom, and Henry, Duke of Lancaster, became, with the above exception, the first subject duke. The king, about the same time, made him admiral of his whole fleet from the Thames westward.

There being now a lull in the king's wars, the duke, who hated ease and idleness, took service under the Teutonic Knights, who had been attacked by the Saracens in Prussia, after which he went forward to Cyprus and Rhodes, and other parts of the East, returning by Grenada, in Spain, where he put to rout the enemies of the Cross, and acquired by his noble deeds such fame that the young nobles of France and Germany flocked in crowds to his standard, to learn under it the art of war.[4]

In the year 1353, when the Lords Richard de Wylughby and William de Scharshall came into Cheshire to hold an eyre, the measure was so unpopular that they had to be protected; and the duke was one of their protectors.[5] This is the entry made of it :—

"Sederunt justiciarii ap⁴ Cestriam super le Eyre magno tempore et in defensionem eorum, ne compatriotæ eos nocerent assistebant prope in patriâ,

[1] Hist. Ches. i. 517. [2] Hume's Hist. Eng. ii. 447. [3] Holinshed, 366.
[4] Capgrave de Ill. Henricis. Smollett's Hist. Eng. iii. 436. [5] Hist. Ches. i. 195.

princeps Walliæ Henricus dux Lancastriæ, etc. Justiciarii dom⁴· Ricardus de Wylughby, dom⁴· Willielmus Scharshall."¹

In the 28 Edward III. (1354), the duke was sent to Avignon to obtain, if possible, the Pope's confirmation of the peace which had been concluded between France and England.² Returning home from his embassy he was arrested, and placed in confinement until he had paid a large ransom. On his release, he declared that Otho, Duke of Brunswick, who had contrived his imprisonment, had been guilty of conduct unworthy of a man of honour, on hearing which Otho sent him a challenge, and defied him to single combat. The challenge was accepted, and the duke passed the sea in great state to meet his challenger. An attempt was made in vain to heal the quarrel, and a day was fixed for deciding it by arms. But when the combatants entered the lists, Otho's courage seemed to fail him; he turned pale, mounted his horse reluctantly, dropped his shield three times, and appeared so disconcerted, that his friends would not in such a state suffer him to commence the combat. At first they proposed that both parties should withdraw from the lists, but the Duke of Lancaster would agree to no terms unless his adversary would either fight or acknowledge himself vanquished. The Duke of Brunswick at length submitted himself to the judgment of the King of France, who ordered him to renounce his challenge; and, to effect a reconciliation between them, entertained both parties and their suites at a magnificent banquet. The Duke of Lancaster afterwards returned home in triumph, and brought with him as present from the King of France a precious relic, which he afterwards gave to his collegiate church in Leicester, a spine from the Saviour's crown of thorns.³

The next year (1355) the king appointed him his lieutenant in Brittany. A little later in the year he was with the king in the marches of Calais, prepared to give battle to the French King, but the latter avoided an encounter, and the King of England returned home.⁴

In 1356 the duke led a reinforcement into Normandy to defend that possession of the Crown. From thence, after raising the sieges of Port Audemer and Breteuil, and reducing Vernueil, he retired into Brittany, where the state of affairs much needed his presence.⁵

On the 19th September 1356, the great battle of Poictiers was fought,

¹ Hist. Ches. i. 195. ² Smollett's History of England, iii. 436. ³ Ibid. iii. 436-7.
⁴ Ibid. 441-3. ⁵ Ibid. 447.

but the duke being engaged on the king's affairs elsewhere, again lost the glory of sharing in that great victory. But how near he was to being actually present in the battle we may see from the Black Prince's letter to the city of London after the victory, in which he says, " Going from Tours, we had the intention of meeting with our most dear cousin, the Duke of Lancaster, of whom we had had most certain news that he would make haste to draw near us."

The following year (1357) he invested Rennes, and pushed on the siege so closely, that the town agreed to pay him 100,000 crowns as an indemnity for his expenses, and to receive a governor of his choosing.[1]

Two years afterwards (in 1359), the king, intending to invade France with a large army, sent the duke before him to prevent disorders among the knights and their followers, who were encamped and awaiting him at Calais: and when the king afterwards made his unsuccessful attack on Rheims, he was with him: and he was again with him when he was overtaken by the great hailstorm near Chartres, in which 1000 men and 6000 horses were struck dead in an instant—a calamity so like a judgment, and which so concurred with the good advice the duke had given the king, that he was now disposed to consent to a peace.[2] The high and exalted rank to which the Barons of Halton had now attained, has left us of late but few notices of their ancient barony, but the Duke of Lancaster, as Constable and Marshal of Chester and Baron of Halton was sued, in a *quo warranto*, at the suit of the king, about 33 Ed. III. (1359); and in his plea to this writ we again meet with a notice of Halton. Amongst other things the duke claimed the right to have his castle at Halton *battlemented* (kernellatum)—to have a prison there, and to take castle-ward—to hold there twice a-year a view of frank-pledge of all resiants within the burghs of Halton and Congleton—to have his burgesses free of all tolls throughout the county of Chester (except toll of salt in the Wyches). He also claimed to hold a weekly market on Saturday and two fairs a-year, one on the four days next before Lady Day, and the other on the day and morrow of St. Catherine, and to take stallage of all chapmen within these following vills of his said manor—viz. (1) Halton, (2) Runcorn, (3) Weston, (4) Clifton, (5) Sutton, (6) Aston-by-Sutton, (7) Middleton, (8) Aston-Grange, (9) Stockham, (10) Norton, (11) Preston, (12) Daresbury, (13)

[1] Smollett's Hist. Eng. iii. 456.
[2] Hume's Hist. Eng. ii. 467; Smollett's Hist. Eng. iii. 462-4.

Newton, (14) Keckwick, (15) Moore, (16) Acton Grange, (17) Higher Walton, (18) Lower Walton, (19) Hull, (20) Appleton, (21) Thelwall, (22) Stretton, (23) Hatton (24) Nether Whitley, (25) Higher Whitley, (26) Comberbach, (27) Great Budworth, (28) Aston-by-Budworth (29) Marbury, (30) Cogshall, (31) Bartington, (32) Little Leigh, and (33) Dutton. He claimed also to have the channel of the Mersey free and kept open for a barge of eight oars, between Freshpool and his fishery at Thelwall.[1] In right of his said manor he also claimed to be Marshal and Constable of Chester. On the part of his serjeants, he claimed the right to *behead* (*decollare*) all thieves taken with the mainour who confessed their offence. As Baron of Halton he also claimed to hold a court of all pleas arising within his barony, exclusive of the earl's Court at Chester, pleas appertaining to the *earl's sword* only excepted. It is singular that in the exemplification of this plea, on 15th August, 29 Eliz., the duke is called Henry de Lacy.

He also claimed not to be compelled to do service to the earl beyond the Clwyd (in Wales), nor anywhere beyond the bounds of the county, except of his own free will, and at the earl's costs.[2]

This claim, which expressly connects the duke with his ancient barony of Halton, affords some insight into the extent of his rights (rights which were then of great value), and the account of Hugh de Preston, his bailiff, the same year, to William Blaby, the auditor, gives a few particulars which are curious. He accounts for—(1.) Three halfpence for a Manchester knife with a horn haft, out of Millington. (2.) One shilling from Adam Clayton, for his tenement in Thelwall, in lieu of a pair of stag leather gloves, furred with fox-skin. (3.) Two shillings from Nether Walton, for the liberty of taking salmon in the Mersey at Lady-day. (4.) Sixpence for a pair of white spurs, from Wm. Mobberley, for his lands in Plumley.[3] The right to call for suit and service from the centre of Warrington bridge, which was formerly in use at Halton Court, probably arose out of the duke's right to have the river Mersey kept free and open from Freshpool to his fishery at Thelwall.

[1] In 1 Hen. IV. John de Eton was commanded to clear all obstructions in the Dee, and to bring the nets to Chester Castle.—Hist. Ches. ii. 450-1.
In the reign of Ed. IV. a royal order issued that all fish-weirs on the Mersey should be reduced in width, so as to enable an eight-oared boat to pass up the river, and enable the salmon to reach the higher parts of the stream.—Baines's Hist. Liverpool, 8.

[2] Hist. Ches. i. 519, *in notis*.   [3] Ibid. i. 519-520.

The duke married Isabel, daughter of Henry, Lord Beaumont, by whom he had issue two daughters, but no male issue. Like others in that age, he showed himself not indifferent to the claims of the Church, by making it various gifts. He gave two liveries, called the Black liveries, to the recluses of St. Helen, at Pontefract, and founded in the churchyard at Whalley a hermitage for two other recluses. He gave large possessions, and amongst them the bailiwick of Blackburnshire, to the monks at Whalley,[1] and he finished what his father had begun, the hospital at Leicester for 100 poor infirm persons. He also founded a great college at Newark, and set in it a dean, twelve canons, 13 vicars-choral, three clerks, six choristers, and a verger. Age and a life of labour were now telling upon the duke's strength, and he prepared for his end. By his will, dated at his castle at Leicester, 15th March, 35 Edward III. (1361), calling himself Duke of Lancaster, Earl of Derby, Lincoln, and Leicester, Steward of England, and Lord of Brigerac and Beaufort, he bequeaths his body to be buried in the collegiate church of Leicester. Nine days afterwards he died of the plague, which was then raging in England, and which was more especially virulent amongst the prelates and nobility of the realm. The duke, who began life with the ugly *sobriquet* of "Wry-neck," earned for himself a far better name before he died, when he was called "The good Duke of Lancaster." An old chronicler says of him that from his earliest years he was strong in virtue, steadily holding fast the fear of the Lord, and keeping his commands, in which he had been brought up. He was grave and courteous in conversation, never indulging in flattery or giving way to deceit; and he was temperate at all times and in all things. Labour was so habitual to him from his youth, that rather than be idle he sought employment in the wars against the infidels when his services were not required at home. Esteeming abstinence a prime virtue, and knowing that self-indulgence is the *mother* of vice and the *stepmother* of virtue, it was his habit, that he might better resist temptation, to repeat the saying of Augustine, that "It is a less evil to want than to abound."[2]

When the duke had retired from the wars and returned home, he devoted his leisure to writing a book, called "Mercy, Gramercy." In the first part of this book, called "Mercy," he recalls to mind, by way of confession, whatever he had done amiss, and asks God forgiveness. In the second part, called "Gramercy," or thanksgiving, he offers God thanks for

[1] Hist. Whal. 182.   [2] Capgrave de Ill. Henricis.

all the benefits he had so bountifully bestowed upon him.[1] One of the duke's good works was the founding of a priory at Preston.[2]

Amongst the Barons of Halton we have had one, Roger, who had a profane *sobriquet*; another, Thomas, who was called a saint; but Henry, Duke of Lancaster, the first of these barons who was an author, obtained a name which was the opposite of Roger's, and one still better than Thomas's, for he was deservedly called "the good Duke of Lancaster." In the inquisition after his death William Boteler was found to have held under him Warrington and other lands, and Halton Ronkore, and More, with the bailiwick of Halton, and the town and serjeanty of Widnes, were found to be a part of the duke's vast and numerous possessions. The duke's will is printed in Nichol's Royal Wills, p. 83. In Boutell's Heraldry (Historical and Popular, p. 235) is an effigy of the duke, and his Inq. P. M. is given at length in the Hist. of Lanc. (I. 336).

[1] Capgrave de Ill. Henricis, 161.   [2] Hist. Richmondshire, ii. 428.

CHAPTER XII.

JOHN OF GAUNT, FOURTEENTH BARON.

ON the death of the good Duke Henry, the barony of Halton devolved upon JOHN OF GAUNT, the husband of his daughter Blanche, who thereupon, in her right, became the fourteenth Baron of Halton. Gaunt, as a family name, was not now heard of for the first time in the annals of Halton. William fitz Nigel, the second baron, had married the daughter of Gilbert de Gaunt, a knight of Flanders, but the new Gaunt was in no way connected with the old, but sprang from the nobler stem of Plantagenet. Other possessors of Halton had claimed alliance with royalty, but none of them could so truly boast of their blood royal as John of Gaunt, who was the king's third (living) son, and took his surname of Gaunt from that celebrated city of his name in Flanders, in which he was born. There is a difference among the chroniclers as to the exact day of his birth, but it would seem to have been the 23d June 1340, for the king, with a great fleet and armament, set sail from Orewell on the 22d June,[1] and on the next day encountered and defeated the French fleet off Sluys, and hastening on the following day to Ghent, he found the queen had been delivered the day before of a prince, whom, from his being born on the Baptist's eve, he called John.[2] No wonder that a prince born almost within the sound and shouts and roar of a great victory should have grown up with warlike tastes, and should have spent almost all his life in the tented field. Owen Glendower would have said his birth was a sure presage of the circumstances of his life. In 1343 John de Montfort, Earl of Richmond (in Yorkshire), having been made prisoner by the King of France, the king's enemy, Edward III., availed himself of the circumstance to seize the earldom into his own hands, and, on the 20th of September, in the same year, he bestowed it upon his son John of Gaunt *per cincturam gladii*, at the same time

[1] Froissart, ii. 1129. [2] Hume's Hist. Eng. ii. 403.

granting him in tail all the castles, manors, prerogatives, and royalties enjoyed by the late earl. The poet Virgil has gratefully remembered and embalmed in verse the name of Caieta, the nurse of Æneas, and a more prosaic authority has preserved to us the name of the Flemish lady who nursed and tended the tender years of John of Gaunt. On the 22d of February 1346, the king granted to Isolda Newcman £10 a-year as that young Prince's nurse.[1] This was higher pay than Maud Plumpton received as rocker to the Black Prince, which was only ten marks instead of pounds, but the commission of neither of these ladies went so far as that of Alicia, the governess of Henry VI. when an infant, which gave her express authority to chastise her charge when necessary.[2] But even before this time, and so early as June 1345, when the royal infant was hardly out of his cradle, the king had set on foot a proposal to marry him to an infanta of Portugal.[3] Nothing having come of this matrimonial proposal, the king, in 1351, instructed his ambassador to treat with the Count of Flanders for a marriage between the young Earl of Richmond and his daughter.[4] From the nursery to the active business of life in those days was but a step. And princes of all men were treated as most precocious. King Edward III. was born 13th November 1312, and in 1315 a pardon, tested at Chester, issued in his name as Prince of Wales, to Adam Gough of Worthenbury, in consideration of services rendered to the prince's father in his Scottish wars.[5] There was little or no college or university training then to be gone through by a young prince. Young as he was, the Earl of Richmond, in the year 1354, was joined with the other princes and nobles who were framing instructions for the ambassadors about to be sent to the Pope to settle the treaty of peace with France.[6] When he was barely 15 years of age (1355), having probably been made a knight, John of Gaunt attended his father to the wars, and not inappropriately made his first campaign in Flanders, the country of his birth.[7] Four years later (1359), with the Pope's dispensation, he married his cousin Blanche, one of the two daughters and co-heiresses, and ultimately the sole heiress, of Henry, Duke of Lancaster.[8] The marriage took place at Reading, and was solemnised with great state, probably in the great abbey of that place. On the 6th February 1360, a charter was

[1] Fœdera, iii. 7.   [2] Acts of Priv. Coun. iii. 143, 191 ; and Kennett's Par. Ants. ii. 16.
[3] Ibid. 43.   [4] Ibid. 224.   [5] Dodsworth's MSS.
[6] Ibid. 284.   [7] Hist. of Lanc. i. 143.   [8] Ibid.

CHAPTER XII.

JOHN OF GAUNT, FOURTEENTH BARON.

ON the death of the good Duke Henry, the barony of Halton devolved upon JOHN OF GAUNT, the husband of his daughter Blanche, who thereupon, in her right, became the fourteenth Baron of Halton. Gaunt, as a family name, was not now heard of for the first time in the annals of Halton. William fitz Nigel, the second baron, had married the daughter of Gilbert de Gaunt, a knight of Flanders, but the new Gaunt was in no way connected with the old, but sprang from the nobler stem of Plantagenet. Other possessors of Halton had claimed alliance with royalty, but none of them could so truly boast of their blood royal as John of Gaunt, who was the king's third (living) son, and took his surname of Gaunt from that celebrated city of his name in Flanders, in which he was born. There is a difference among the chroniclers as to the exact day of his birth, but it would seem to have been the 23d June 1340, for the king, with a great fleet and armament, set sail from Orewell on the 22d June,[1] and on the next day encountered and defeated the French fleet off Sluys, and hastening on the following day to Ghent, he found the queen had been delivered the day before of a prince, whom, from his being born on the Baptist's eve, he called John.[2] No wonder that a prince born almost within the sound and shouts and roar of a great victory should have grown up with warlike tastes, and should have spent almost all his life in the tented field. Owen Glendower would have said his birth was a sure presage of the circumstances of his life. In 1343 John de Montfort, Earl of Richmond (in Yorkshire), having been made prisoner by the King of France, the king's enemy, Edward III., availed himself of the circumstance to seize the earldom into his own hands, and, on the 20th of September, in the same year, he bestowed it upon his son John of Gaunt *per cincturam gladii*, at the same time

[1] Froissart, ii. 1129.   [2] Hume's Hist. Eng. ii. 403.

granting him in tail all the castles, manors, prerogatives, and royalties enjoyed by the late earl. The poet Virgil has gratefully remembered and embalmed in verse the name of Caieta, the nurse of Æneas, and a more prosaic authority has preserved to us the name of the Flemish lady who nursed and tended the tender years of John of Gaunt. On the 22d of February 1346, the king granted to Isolda Neweman £10 a-year as that young Prince's nurse.[1] This was higher pay than Maud Plumpton received as rocker to the Black Prince, which was only ten marks instead of pounds, but the commission of neither of these ladies went so far as that of Alicia, the governess of Henry VI. when an infant, which gave her express authority to chastise her charge when necessary.[2] But even before this time, and so early as June 1345, when the royal infant was hardly out of his cradle, the king had set on foot a proposal to marry him to an infanta of Portugal.[3] Nothing having come of this matrimonial proposal, the king, in 1351, instructed his ambassador to treat with the Count of Flanders for a marriage between the young Earl of Richmond and his daughter.[4] From the nursery to the active business of life in those days was but a step. And princes of all men were treated as most precocious. King Edward III. was born 13th November 1312, and in 1315 a pardon, tested at Chester, issued in his name as Prince of Wales, to Adam Gough of Worthenbury, in consideration of services rendered to the prince's father in his Scottish wars.[5] There was little or no college or university training then to be gone through by a young prince. Young as he was, the Earl of Richmond, in the year 1354, was joined with the other princes and nobles who were framing instructions for the ambassadors about to be sent to the Pope to settle the treaty of peace with France.[6] When he was barely 15 years of age (1355), having probably been made a knight, John of Gaunt attended his father to the wars, and not inappropriately made his first campaign in Flanders, the country of his birth.[7] Four years later (1359), with the Pope's dispensation, he married his cousin Blanche, one of the two daughters and co-heiresses, and ultimately the sole heiress, of Henry, Duke of Lancaster.[8] The marriage took place at Reading, and was solemnised with great state, probably in the great abbey of that place. On the 6th February 1360, a charter was

[1] Fœdera, iii. 7.   [2] Acts of Priv. Coun. iii. 143, 191 ; and Kennett's Par. Ants. ii. 16.
[3] Ibid. 43.   [4] Ibid. 224.   [5] Dodsworth's MSS.
[6] Ibid. 284.   [7] Hist. of Lanc. i. 143.   [8] Ibid.

made by William de Thelwalle, sergeant-at-arms of "our Lord the King," whereby he granted to his brother Vivian the lands and tenements in Halton, which he had by inheritance from his mother Felicia, and also a piece of land in Thelwall, which he had by inheritance from William his father. A handsome seal of the Danyers' Arms, surrounded by the words, "S. Will de Braundistone," is appended to the deed, which, as there is no party or witness to the deed of that name, must have been a borrowed seal. The deed is witnessed by Geoffrey de Warburton, John de Anyers, and Thos. de Dutton, Knights; and Hugh de Clayton, of Thelwall; Adam de Martinscroft, of the same; Robert de Thelwall, and John, the clerk.[1]

Upon the death of the good Duke of Lancaster, on the 24th March 1361, John of Gaunt, Earl of Richmond, succeeded to the barony of Halton, and the Cheshire Records have this entry:—*de liberatione facienda exitus dominii de Halton Jōhi comiti Richemond. post mortem Henrici ducis Lancastriæ.*[2] There was formerly a peculiar custom in Halton, called "thistletake," which the lawyers explain to mean that if any one in driving his cattle over the commons of the manor suffered them to crop so much as a thistle, he should pay for each beast so allowed to graze one halfpenny to the Lord of the Fee.[3]

About this time Halton occurs amongst the duchy possessions, and we have the following account of its officers, and their fees ;—

THE HONOUR OF HALTON.

	£	s	d
The bailiff receives yearly	1	5	0
The same bailiff	3	0	0
The constable	6	13	4
The receiver	3	6	8
The attorney of its courts	2	0	0
The parker, or keeper of the park	3	6	8 [4]

The bailiff at this time was Hugh de Preston, the parker Richard de Pilkington, and Thomas de Dutton was the constable or governor, and also seneschal and receiver, and received the largest fees. All these officers had received their appointments from the Duke of Lancaster.

No previous baron of Halton could compare in greatness with him

---

[1] Charter, *penes* R. H. Wood, Esq.
[2] Ches. Records, 35 and 36 Ed. III.
[3] Blount's Law Dict., *sub voce*.
[4] Whitaker's Richmond, ii. 324.

who now called the castle of Halton his own; and of all its rulers none has left a name still so well remembered in the neighbourhood as John of Gaunt. He succeeded to the castle and all its honours at the very time that a strong ruler was needed, for on the 10th April, 35 Ed. III. (1361), the Earl of Chester, finding the neighbourhood much disturbed, issued a proclamation commanding that all persons found riding up and down the country armed with bows and arrows, or other arms, should be at once arrested and conveyed to Chester Castle.[1]

In 1361, being high in favour with his royal father, as was not unnatural, he obtained a special charter for divers franchises and privileges to himself and his heirs by his wife, Blanche—namely, the return of writs, pleas of *withernam*, felons' goods in all the lordships and lands whereof he was then possessed, with freedom for himself and his heirs, and all the residents upon the lands, and fees which belonged to her father from all manner of tolls, of what kind soever, throughout the whole of the kingdom. What should we now say to a country farmer who claimed exemption from tolls in our markets on such a ground as this? Yet this exemption was very much coveted in that age. Having now issue by his wife, and having done his homage, all the lands whereof her father died possessed were assigned to him in the same year. He had also, by the king's license, a grant to himself and his wife and their heirs of the castle of Bolingbroke (a name afterwards famous in our history as the name of the birthplace of John of Gaunt's greater son), with other manors in the counties of Stafford, Northumberland, and Derby. It could hardly be said at this time at Halton that a man might do what he would with his own, for Wm. de Hallum was compelled to sue out the Earl of Chester's pardon for taking a grant of ten marks a year from Halton without the king's consent.[2] The next year, upon the death, without issue, of Maud, the widow of William, Duke of Bavaria, John of Gaunt, in right of Blanche, his wife, Maud's sister, took the whole of the possessions belonging to her half of the estate of Henry, Duke of Lancaster, whereupon, on 13th November, 36 Edward III. (1362), he was in Parliament, in right of his wife Blanche, declared Duke of Lancaster, and Earl of Leicester, Lincoln, and Derby, and girding him with a sword, and setting a fur cap (probably that which is now the cap of maintenance in the Lancaster crest), with a circlet of gold and pearls, on his head, the king made him High Steward of England.[3]

[1] Cheshire Recog. Rolls. [2] Duchy Records. [3] Hist. Lanc. i. 144.

In April 1364, John, King of France, then a prisoner in England, died in the duke's palace of the Savoy.

With his new honours fresh upon him, the duke, who must have had many Cheshire retainers with him, amongst whom was Thomas Maisterson of Nantwich,[1] in 1366 joined his renowned brother, the Black Prince, at Bordeaux, to assist him in restoring Don Pedro to the throne of Castile, from which he had been driven for his cruelty. In the castle of Lormont, near Bordeaux, the ruins of which are still standing, Richard II., called from that circumstance Richard of Bordeaux, first saw the light about this time. The valour, skill, and ability of the Black Prince enabled him for a time to reinstate Don Pedro on his throne, but his triumph was short-lived. He was again driven from it not long after by the great Du Gueselin, who, on this occasion, as he went to the relief of Don Pedro's brother, exacted 100,000 livres from the Pope to pay his troops, for which, if the commander had not strenuously rejected his proposal, the Pope would have substituted his blessing and saved his livres. On the expedition of the Black Prince and his brother to carry back Don Pedro to Castile, the latter had doubtless been attended by some of his Lancashire tenants and retainers. One of these followers brought home with him from Oviedo a curious *compostella*, or certificate of pilgrimage, the virtue of which in those times was supposed to be so great, that Pope Eugenius "granted 1004 years and 40 days of pardon to all who should visit Oviedo and its relics, believing that the intercession of the saints, their owners, would save them," and which relics were removed to Oviedo by Pelayus, out of the way of the Moors, as a poet who describes them tells us—

> "The relics and the written works of saints,
> Toledo's treasure prized beyond all wealth,
> Their living and their dead remains;
> These to the mountain fastnesses they bore."[2]

The certificate intimates that by Divine command an ark, made by the Apostles, and full of heavenly mysteries and wonders, was transferred from Jerusalem into Africa, from Africa to Carthage, from Carthage to Seville, from Seville to Toledo, and from Toledo to the church of San Salvador, in Oviedo, in the Asturias, and then it goes on to particularise many of the relics and wonders contained in the ark, and concludes by making the pilgrim a partaker in all their benefits, and a member of the confraternity

---

[1] Hist. Ches. iii. 230. [2] Murray's Handbook of Spain.

of Oviedo, and as such entitled to the benefit of all their prayers in life and death.¹

In the battle of Navarete, fought on the 3d of April 1367, the Black Prince gained a great victory, and the duke, who had crossed the Pyrenees with his royal brother, was present, and did good service, leading the van in the battle. In crossing France, the duke reduced the fortress of Mont Paon, and made the garrison prisoners. He also took the strong fortress of Montcontour, where, to punish their obstinate resistance, he put the garrison to the sword. After these successes he returned with his new consort to England.²

In 1369, the duke, having been retained to serve the king for half-a-year, with 300 men at arms, 500 archers, three bannerets, 80 knights, and 216 esquires, was sent over the seas to give battle to the French, who had broken the truce; but a great sickness thinned his troops, and he returned home without hazarding a battle or accomplishing anything worthy of note. John of Gaunt landed at Harfleur, with a view to burn the shipping in the harbour, but the Count St. Pol defeated his design. He had not the skill of the Black Prince, and he cannot be said to have deserved the epithet of being a fortunate commander. But "sorrows seldom come single spies." At his return home he found to his great grief that his wife, Blanche, who was much respected and beloved, had been carried off in his absence in the great pestilence, and he arrived too late even to attend her obsequies, which had been celebrated with great pomp in St. Paul's cathedral.

In 1370 he marched an army of 25,000 men from Calais to Gascony, but he was so harassed by flying parties that not half his men reached their destination. But the campaign was not wholly without fruits of another kind. Instead of a victory he gained a wife, for he married Constance, the elder of the two daughters of Don Pedro, whom his brother, Henry Trastamare, had put to death for his cruelty after he had been reinstated by the Black Prince on the throne. After his marriage, the duke assumed the title of King of Castile and Leon.

Besides assuming the title of king, the duke also impaled with his own the arms of Castile and Leon, but afterwards, when he attempted by arms to enforce his claim to the kingdom, the attempt proved unsuccessful,

¹ From the original, in the possession of John Ireland Blackburne, Esq.
² Smollett's Hist. Eng. iv. 19.

and he found he had only boasted an empty title. In his expedition, however, he was supported by some of his Lancashire friends and retainers, and amongst those who were found in his retinue were John Donne, a former rector of Warrington, and Sir John Boteler, knight, the Lord of Warrington.[1] An act of clemency towards the Bishop of Limoges distinguished the duke at this time. The bishop had instigated the citizens of that city to a rebellion, in consequence of which it was besieged and taken by the Black Prince, who would at once have put the bishop to death if the duke had not interceded for him, and induced the prince to spare his life.[2]

John of Gaunt made Halton his occasional hunting seat, and of all the barons his name is best remembered there. He was notorious as a great builder and improver of his castles and domains ; witness the grand gateway of Lancaster Castle and the beautiful oriel now in Lincoln Castle. During the summer he resided often at that castle, but the oriel was only lately removed there from a house which he had in another part of the city, opposite the curious building called "John of Gaunt's stables," which he certainly did not build. Some of the large windows and cruciform arrow-slits, and some other of the best works at Halton, are his work, and so probably are two curious openings in the outer wall, near the two great windows of the north-west corner of the castle, the use of which is not exactly known. These openings are made at first a slant, and then they descend vertically, as if intended either for throwing out filth or pouring melted materials upon a besieging party. There is, however, one singularly beautiful trefoil-headed window in the outer wall, on the north side, now festooned with ivy, which is a work of Richard III.'s time; and there is a large window looking west, with perpendicular mullions, which is the work of a still later age. Within the castle enclosure there are the foot of an eight-sided cross, and a few mouldings lately discovered. The arched cellars still remain, and in one of them there is a well. The popular voice ascribes to John of Gaunt the name of the neighbouring Fiddlers' Ferry, in Cuerdley, which it is said was given to it after he had once passed over it with a party of stringed musicians, probably to examine the ancient earthworks on the adjoining marsh. These, which are now fast disappearing, consist of banks of earth about 2 yards high, with a ditch on the outer

---

[1] Fœdera, iii. 888 ; and Dugdale's Baronage, 653, citing the close roll.
[2] Smollett's History of England, iv. 16.

side, enclosing about 15 acres of land, and having their gateway or entrance guarded by a double wall. At many of his chief possessions the duke's name as John of Gaunt still lingers. At Lincoln, besides the oriel already mentioned, his house and stables are pointed out, and at Lancaster one of the towers in the castle bears his name, and one of the streets, where his horse once cast a shoe, is called John of Gaunt's corner, and a horse-shoe, renewed from time to time, is let into the pavement to commemorate the event.

Being about to cross the sea in the retinue of the king, in 46 Edward III. (1372), the duke, by his letters, commanded Sir John Boteler, knight, sheriff of Lancashire, Mawkyn de Rixton, Esquire, William Bradshaw, Esquire, Robert de Pilkington, and Nicholas de Atherton, to meet him, each of the first three with twenty archers, and each of the last two with ten. On the 18th of July, in the same year, he issued warrants to his receiver to pay each of them a month's wages in advance, at the rate of 6d. a-day; and on the 22d November following, the service being perhaps ended, a like warrant was issued to pay Sir John Boteler £56 : 8 : 8 for his wages.[1] Mawkyn de Rixton, or as he is elsewhere called, Mathew de Rixton, was employed by the king as a sort of admiral to collect ships at Liverpool.[2] Both he and his colleague, Robert de Pilkington, appear to have served the duke as well in peace as in war. On the 10th July, 46 Edward III. (1373), the former was appointed the duke's seneschal at Halton, and at the same time commanded to deliver to the prior and convent of Norton the tithes of their herbage and underwood in their parishes within the lordship of Halton, in the same manner as their predecessors had held them. Four days later the prior and convent had a warrant to receive from the keeper of Halton Park, according to custom, two bucks for the convent table.[3] This, which seems like the renewal of an old grant, probably signalised the election of a new prior (Prior Richard) to office. On the 9th January, 48 Edward III. (1375), the duke appointed Robert de Pilkington to succeed Mawkyn de Rixton as his seneschal at Halton.[4]

In July 1374, the duke, who had again been in France on the king's business, embarked on his return home,[5] and the next year was appointed one of the commissioners to settle the terms of the truce between

[1] Duchy Reg. 154ᵇ 160ᵇ. [2] Fœdera, iii. 891. [3] Duchy Records.
[4] Ibid. [5] Smollett's History of England, iv. 28.

England and France.¹ In that age it seems to have been almost always war or truce, and but very seldom peace. This year the duke levied an aid to marry his eldest daughter, of which the Lancashire portion is given in Whitaker's History of Richmondshire.²

About this time he received from the king a grant of several royal franchises, and in particular on the 28th February, 51 Edward III. (1377), the king conferred on him the right to have a chancery in his dukedom, with all other royalties belonging to a county palatine;³ and the same year he received a still more exclusively royal privilege—a license to coin gold, silver, and other monies, at Bayonne, Guysson Castle, or any other place within the seneschalcy of Landere, for two years, to commence from the 12th June then next.⁴ One or more of these coins would be a very acceptable addition to the Warrington Museum.

This year, by disregarding the petitions of the Londoners respecting their trade and other matters, the duke incurred great popular odium, which gave occasion to some serious riots, in the course of which his palace of the Savoy was sacked, and his life was even threatened, which induced him to withdraw from London for a time.⁵

But the year was fruitful in troubles. The duke having become acquainted with Wycliffe, "the morning star of the Reformation," who was born near Richmond, the place from which the duke took his first title, became the Reformer's patron, and when he was summoned before Courtney, Bishop of London, the duke accompanied him, and unfortunately still further increased his unpopularity by want of courtesy to the bishop, who stood very high in the public favour.

About Michaelmas of the same year, in order to win back some part of the popularity he had lost, the duke hired nine large ships of Bayonne, and with them attacked and took a fleet of fourteen French merchant vessels, all richly laden with wine.⁶ The enterprise, however, was little better than a privateering adventure, and any favour it won him was unworthily gained.

On the accession of Richard II., when a council was held to settle the ceremonial of the coronation, the Duke of Lancaster, as Earl of Leicester, claimed to be seneschal of England; as Earl of Lincoln, to be the king's carver; and as Duke of Lancaster, to carry the great sword of State,

¹ Smollett's History of England, iv. 31.   ² Hist. of Richmondshire, ii. 209.
³ Hist. Lanc. i. 145.   ⁴ Ibid.   ⁵ Ibid.   ⁶ Smollett's History of England, iv. 77.

curtana, before the king at his coronation. These claims being allowed, he then sat to hear and determine the applications of all such noblemen and others as claimed any right to do particular acts of service on the occasion.[1]

The same year, at Michaelmas, when it was proposed that the duke should attend a conference with the Commons on the king's affairs, he threw himself before the king, beseeching him to excuse him, as the Commons, he said, had traduced his character, by imputing to him designs which amounted to high treason. At the same time he protested his innocence, and declared himself ready to meet in single combat any one who should accuse him.[2] This readiness to appeal to single combat shortly grew into a kind of epidemic in the new reign.

In the year 1378 the duke led an army into Brittany, but failing to effect anything of importance, he very shortly returned home.[3] The French, who made merry over the duke's *fainéantise*, used on this occasion their taunting proverb, "Oh, John is as wise as his master."[4]

He had had granted to him by the late king authority to establish a treasury, with barons and other proper officers, within his duchy, which from that time came to be called his regality, and its proceedings to be recorded as occurring in the first, second, or other year of such regality.[5] Extracts from some of the close rolls of the duchy, and references to others, which show this, may be seen in the History of Lancashire.[6]

Henry of Bolingbroke, the duke's son, a name destined to be heard of hereafter, being now of sufficient age, his father levied the usual aid for making him a knight, and amongst his Lancashire tenants who paid this aid we find the name of Sir John Boteler, knight, lord of Warrington.[7] Nearly at the same time, the duke, under his assumed title of King of Castile and Leon, being about to proceed beyond the seas, Sir William Boteler, lord of Warrington, being one of his retinue, received the letters of protection usual in such case to protect him, his lands, and goods until the following Michaelmas.[8] In July the same year we learn the duke's destination, for he then sailed with a fleet and forces to St. Malo, in France, which city he besieged, but, not being able to reduce it, he returned home, and with him probably returned Sir John Boteler, within the limits of his

---

[1] Hist. Lanc. i. 147. [2] Smollett's Hist. England, iv. 74.
[3] Hume's History of England, iii. 5. [4] Froissart, ii. 169. [5] Hist. Lanc. i. 147.
[6] Ibid. i. 372. [7] Dodsworth's MSS. [8] Fœdera, v. 186.

letters of protection.[1] This expedition had cost much treasure and raised great expectations, and its miscarriage added fresh flame to the duke's unpopularity, which was still further aggravated by a circumstance of a more private nature which occurred at this time, and in which the duke was concerned. The Spanish Count Denia, who had been taken prisoner at Naverete, had been allowed to return home on leaving his son as a hostage for his ransom. But the count happening to die before the ransom was paid, the duke, who was desirous to use the son's influence in forwarding his own interest in Castile, procured an order to release him without payment of any ransom. The father's two captors, however, who had a right to the ransom, being informed of the duke's intention, raised their voices and remonstrated against it, and at the same time represented to the young count the personal injury and loss they should sustain by his release in this manner, which so wrought upon him, that, although he immediately disappeared and was lost sight of, he inwardly resolved that not even for liberty would he sacrifice his honour. Not to be foiled in his design, the duke caused several persons, suspected of being accessory to the young noble's disappearance or escape, to be apprehended, upon which the two captors, fearing to fall under suspicion, and thinking to escape the duke's anger, took sanctuary in Westminster Abbey.[2] Disregarding the sacredness of the place, the duke ventured to pursue them even there, and, in his attempt to drag them thence, one of them was killed. The survivor was at once taken to the Tower, where, at the instance of the duke, the king made him an offer of 500 marks in hand, and a pension of 400 marks a-year for life, if he would produce the young count, who had been his prisoner for ransom. The offer was not long in being accepted, for his keeper immediately produced the young prisoner, another Bayard *sans reproche*, who, as it was then discovered, had all this while been under his captor's care, and serving him in the capacity of page.[3] Truth is stranger than fiction, as this incident, which might furnish materials of a good romance, abundantly shows. The only real sufferer by the affair was the duke himself, who had not only broken sanctuary, but had caused the death of an innocent person, and all this in the prosecution of his own unjust and selfish interest.

In the summer of 1381, intending to bring the Scots to submission, the

[1] Smollett's Hist. Eng. iv. 79.   [2] Stanley's West. Abbey, 365.
[3] Smollett's Hist. Eng. iv. 81.

duke marched a large army to the north, but the result only led to the conclusion of another truce.¹ The expedition, however, though not fortunate for his fame, contributed to the duke's safety, by taking and detaining him from home during the continuance of Wat Tyler's rebellion, which occurred this year. One of the oaths taken by the rebel's followers bound them to bear true allegiance to King Richard II., and never to submit to a king whose name was John, which being evidently pointed at John of Gaunt, shows how great was the extent of his unpopularity, and leaves us no ground to wonder that the rebels in their fury proceeded to burn down his palace of the Savoy, and raze it to the ground. One of the demands the rebels made was that they should be allowed to buy and sell free of tolls in every market and fair throughout England,² and this may show us the value set upon the similar exemption claimed by Duke Henry on behalf of his Halton tenants, when he made his claim under the Halton *quo warranto*.

On the 27th February, 6 Richard II. (1383), the duke appointed William Appleton his serjeant or bailiff of Halton, at a salary of 40s. a-year, and shortly afterwards he retained William Appleton (friar) as his physician.³ If the physician, the friar, and the serjeant or bailiff, were one and the same person, the duke was strangely monopolised in mind, body, and estate; but after all the monopolist was probably not overpaid, and if the friar took the castle chapel and the castle inmates under his care whilst he was at Halton, he had no sinecure. The Appletons at this time seem to have been a rising family. One of them, Robert Appleton, Canon of York, was Chycheley's proxy, and in that character attended the deliberations of the Council of Constance in 1414.⁴

On the 7th April 1383, Thomas de Pilkington was appointed to be the duke's park-keeper at Halton, during pleasure.⁵ Of what kind were the deer then in the park at Halton?

In 1385, Ferdinand, master of the military order of St. James of Portugal, being about to cross the seas, most probably in order to press forward the duke's claim to his favourite *chateau en Espagne*, the crown of Castile, Sir John Boteler, knight, lord of Warrington, who on this occasion had agreed to accompany him, received the usual letters of protection to protect him and his estate during his absence from England.⁶

¹ Smollett's Hist. Eng. iv. 91. ² Ibid. 93. ³ Duchy Reg.
⁴ Hook's Archbishops, v. 66. ⁵ Duchy Records. ⁶ Fœdera, v. 434.

The next year the duke, with his wife and daughters—Philippa, daughter of Blanche, his first wife, and Catherine, daughter of Constance, his present wife—left England with the design of prosecuting his claim to Castile. The fleet which carried them and their large force, the flower of English chivalry, by which they were attended, set sail in the month of July. The expedition lasted some time, and at last ended in what was at the same time both a success and a failure. The duke lost his coveted kingdom, but he gained for both his daughters distinguished consorts, marrying Philippa, one of the two, to the King of Portugal, and Catherine, the other of them, to the Prince of the Asturias, who, on his father's death, became King of Spain; and thus, although he lost a throne, the duke placed his descendants on two thrones, the kingdoms of Portugal and Spain.[1] After securing these advantageous alliances for his daughters, and a large sum of money for himself, the duke resigned his claim to the crown of Castile, and returned home to England in the year 1389, and shortly afterwards, being appointed the king's lieutenant, he returned to his command in Guienne, but the Gascons remonstrating against the appointment, he returned home.

In January 1390, the king, in order to show his favour to him, created him Duke of Aquitaine.

At the conferences for a treaty of peace between France and England, in 1392, when the duke was one of the commissioners, he gained great favour in England by strenuously and successfully resisting the proposal of some of his colleagues either to give up to France the town and fortress of Calais, or to allow them to be demolished. William Mainwaring of Peover, going with the duke to Guienne, made his will before setting out, on the 3d September 1393.

The following year the king appointed him his lieutenant in Picardy. While he was abroad on this service the people of Lancashire and Cheshire then living under his and the Duke of Gloucester's government (the latter being then Chief Justice of Chester) rose in insurrection against their officers, and in 1394 Sir Thomas Talbot, the people's leader, threatened to waste and destroy the Duke of Lancaster's domains.[2]

In 1394 the duke was called Duke of Guienne and Lancaster.[3]

---

[1] Hume's Hist. Eng. iii. 13. [2] Smollett's Hist. Eng. iv. 171-2.
[3] Sir P. Leycester, lib. c. 283.

Halton.

In the same year the duke had the misfortune to lose his second wife, Constance of Castile.

In 1396, having gone to take possession of his new dukedom of Aquitaine, he was shortly afterwards recalled home on the king's business, and on his return, to the wonder of all men and the great mortification of his brothers, he married as his third wife Catherine Swinford, and obtained an Act to legitimatise her children born before the marriage. Catherine survived her husband, and was buried in Lincoln Cathedral, under a tomb, which, stripped of its brasses, still remains to be seen there.

In 1397 John Keckwick, one of the duke's neighbours at Halton, was retained by the king, on the 12th November, to serve him as one of his archers, at the wages of 6d. a-day.[1]

The Duke of Gloucester the same year was apprehended and suddenly hurried off to Calais by the king's orders. The Duke of Lancaster must bear the blame of having concurred in this act of violence, but he had certainly no share in his brother's subsequent death by violence in prison.

On the 8th August, 22 Richard II. (1398), not many months before his own deposition, the king granted the duke, whom he calls his "very dear uncle," the office of constable of the whole principality of Chester, to hold to him and the heirs-male of his body.[2] It will be remembered that almost from its first rise this office had been connected with the barony of Halton, and this re-grant of it, therefore, was probably sought by the duke only as confirmation to him and his heirs-male of the ancient and valued right of his family.

We now reach an important period in the life of the Duke of Lancaster —his introduction upon the pages of our great bard.

In the opening scene of the drama of "Richard II." the monarch thus addresses him :—

> "Old John of Gaunt, time-honoured Lancaster,
> Hast thou, according to thy oath and bond,
> Brought hither Henry Hereford, thy bold son,
> Here to make good his boisterous late appeal
> Against the Duke of Norfolk, Thomas Mowbray ?"

In this passage we have for the first time one of the few personages of this neighbourhood introduced by Shakspeare. John of Gaunt, although the father of Bolingbroke, now become Duke of Hereford, was one of the

---

[1] Ches. Records.　　　　　[2] Hist. Ches. i. 522.

commissioners who sat to try his son's appeal, and when the sentence of banishment against both parties was pronounced at Coventry, on the 17th September 1398, this Roman father, who had concurred in it, thus sought to console his son:—

> "All places that the eye of heaven visits
> Are, to a wise man, ports and happy havens.
> Teach thy necessity to reason thus:
> Think not the king did banish thee,
> But thou the king: woe doth the heavier sit,
> Where it perceives it is but faintly borne."

On the 3d February following the duke died in his palace of Ely House, in London, a place of many historic memories. Although he had concurred in the sentence, his son's banishment weighed deeply on his heart, and with almost his dying lips his grief found utterance in these passionate words of warning to the king, as he stood beside his bed:—

> "This royal throne of kings, this sceptred isle,
> This fortress built by nature for herself
> Against infection and the hand of war,
> This happy breed of men, this little world,
> This precious stone set in the silver sea,
> This blessed plot, this earth, this realm, this England,
> Dear for her reputation through the world
> Is now leased out (I die pronouncing it),
> Like to a tenement or pelting farm."

The duke was interred with great pomp in St. Paul's Cathedral beside the body of Blanche, his first wife, and beneath a sumptuous monument, surmounted with the ducal arms, which he had erected after Blanche's death. On this monument there was a long and laboured inscription, which, lengthy as it was at first, must have been renewed and lengthened at a later period.[1] By his will, dated the 3d February 1397, the duke directed that his body should not be committed to the tomb for 40 days, and on every day in the interval, and on the day of his funeral, large alms were to be given to the poor. There was to be a profusion of great wax tapers and mortars, and many minute directions are given as to the order of the funeral. Cloth of gold, tapestry, and arras, rich dresses, and an infinite variety of articles of gold and silver plate, as chandeliers, hanaps, basins, saucers, cups, ewers, wine-pots, spoons, and jewels, are disposed of. A gold chalice and other church plate are given to "our Lady of Lincoln," and two chantries, one at Lincoln and the other at Leicester, are directed

[1] Hist. Lanc. i. 152-3.

to be founded out of his estate. Walter Blunt, the same probably who appears afterwards in Shakspeare's Henry IV., was one of the witnesses to the will.[1]

The duke is said to have founded the chapel of St. Nicholas, now the parish church of Liverpool. But this chapel arose out of the necessity of providing a place of burial for the dead after the pestilence which visited Liverpool in 1360,[2] and it was probably the offspring of the cemetery, and if so the duke, who was not then of age, could hardly have been its founder, though he may have subsequently founded a chantry in it where masses might be said for him and his ancestors and successors. By his patronage of Wickliffe, however, he lost the favour of the clergy, and this, or some other cause, disinclined him from following the example usual in that age of founding and endowing a church or a religious house at his death to commemorate his piety. But as we have seen him providing venison for the house at Norton, so at a later period, 21st Richard II. (1397), he showed a like desire to improve the pittance of the religious house of Beauvale by granting it a tun of Gascoign wine yearly during his life.[3] If the wine and the venison had gone together, it might have been said of the receivers, *Implentur veteris Bacchi pinguisque ferinæ*. Within the castle at Halton there were doubtless from the first a chapel and a chaplain, for our ancestors never failed to provide for their people the ordinances of religion. William, the chaplain who witnessed Fitz Nigel's charter, was the castle chaplain, but no chaplain is mentioned in the duke's will, nor has any list of those who have officiated in the chapel from time to time come down to us. The chapel stood on the same site as that which in late years has risen phœnix-like from its ashes to supply its place with a beauty far surpassing all its predecessors, and standing like a city upon a hill, that cannot be hid.

The duke, who from his early infancy had lived with his royal father and the Black Prince, his brother, under them, had had large opportunities of gaining experience in the arts of war and government, but his after life does not show that he had profited as he might by his opportunities. After King Edward's death his position as regent gave him an ascendant over his brother, and made him, during his nephew Richard's minority, the first man in the kingdom, but he was neither popular nor enterprising.

---

[1] Nichols' Royal Wills, 145.   [2] Picton's Memorials of Liverpool.
[3] Madox's Formulare Anglicanum, p. 327.

A Coriolanus in his contempt for the people, he lost their favour and good opinion, while he was proud and passionate, and of a temper which was not engaging. In contrast with the Black Prince, his conduct as a commander appears to great disadvantage, for while the latter rarely fought a battle or engaged in an enterprise in which he did not succeed, the duke, who from his early years to the close of life rarely sheathed his sword, could scarcely claim a single victory, if we except Navarete, where he led the van, but did not command the host. It seemed to be his forte to follow rather than to lead.

The powerful support he afforded Wickliffe saved that reformer from the fate with which the Church in that age almost always visited such as dared to question her doctrines or pry too closely into her abuses. Wickliffe was a few years the duke's senior, and, as a native of the neighbourhood of Richmond, he may have lived on his patron's estate and paid him fealty. If so, he paid not only that service, but made his patron a sharer in the same glorious light of truth which had blessed his own eyes. The poet Chaucer, who was also by a few years the duke's senior, like him was an early adherent of the reformer, and by his writings did more than even the duke by his high power to support the "evangelic doctor," and spread his opinions. And, "as like inclines to like," we therefore do not wonder to find the poet, as well as Wickliffe, under the duke's patronage. But the poet, besides a community of opinions, had another reason for attaching himself to the duke, for in his house he had the good fortune to find a fit helpmate in Philippa Rouet, his wife, who was the sister of Catherine Swinford, the duke's third wife, and was probably at the time of her marriage, in 1360, in the household of Blanche, the duke's first wife. His biographers, in seeking for the origin of the poet's name, seem to have overlooked the probability of its being derived from *Chaud cire*, the name of a chancery officer who had charge of the chaff wax used for sealing patents.

Chaucer, who died on 25th October 1400, having survived the duke not many months, amply repaid his patronage by the interest he took in his patron's circumstances and his notice of them in his poems. The duke and his affairs are the subject of no less than four of his poems:—1. "The Book of the Duchesse." 2. "Chaucer's Dream." 3. "The Assembly of Fowls." 4. "The Duchess's Prayer." The Duchess Blanche—or the duke's grief for her loss—are the subject of all these poems, some of which are of considerable length. To have been the first Baron of Halton to receive a poet's notice, and to have been the friend and patron of the father of English poetry, was a great honour to John of Gaunt, but the greatest of our poets, by introducing him as one of the characters in his historic drama of "Richard II.," and so making his name immortal, has done him far greater honour.

The arms borne by John of Gaunt, as Duke of Lancaster, are those now used in the present duchy seal, which nearly resemble those used by Edmund Crookback in 25 Edward I. The present Halton court seal is probably copied from that used there in the time of John of Gaunt.

While on the subject of heraldic arms, on the principle of *suum cuique* we must not pass over here the origin of that ancient badge of honour which has given the heralds and antiquaries almost as much trouble as that of the origin of the knee-badge of the knights of the garter; the motto on which has lately received a new application in this inscription over a roadside seat for wayfarers at Knutsford—

> For public use at my expense,
> Et honi soit qui mal y pense !

The rival badge, the collar of SS., which adorns the monumental effigy of many a mediæval knight and noble, and which may still be seen round the necks of the three chiefs of her Majesty's Superior Courts of Common Law, Sir William Dugdale thought had its origin in the brotherhood of Simplicius and Faustinus, a society instituted to commemorate two Roman senators who were put to death for their faith under Diocletian, and the members of which society adopted a collar of double SS. ; but though this is carrying the origin very far back, later antiquaries have not acquiesced in Sir William's opinion.

Some of the dissentients have suggested that the collar had a religious origin, and that the double SS. were meant for the words Sanctus Sanctus, used in addressing the Deity. Others have supposed the SS. to be nothing but the form of the lever of a horse's bit, and to signify that the wearer of the collar was of equestrian rank ; while others, again, have thought that the two s's refer to the Saints Crispin and Crispianus, on whose day the battle of Agincourt was fought, and that the collar was invented by Henry V. in their honour. Another opinion makes the letters to stand for signum or sigillum, the beginning of most of the legends of a mediæval seal; and lastly, it has been suggested that the letters stand for senescallus, and that the collar was first adopted by some one who held some such office. After examining with great attention all these opinions, Mr. Foss, in his Lives of the Judges, has demonstrated that the origin of the collar is to be traced to John of Gaunt, who adopted it as the livery of the house of Lancaster, and that the letters stand for *souvenez, souvenez*, "Remember, remember," and it is certain that the collar was never seen or used until his time.

CHAPTER XIII.

HENRY BOLINGBROKE, AFTERWARDS KING HENRY IV.,
FIFTEENTH BARON.

ON the death of John of Gaunt, his son, HENRY BOLINGBROKE, at once succeeded him as 15th Baron of Halton. The inquisition on his father's death finds that he held Halton under the Prince of Wales, that being the title by which, in pursuance of an act of the previous year, the new king had been called in Cheshire. Henry, who was Gaunt's son by Blanche, his first wife, was born in 1367, just one year after the birth of Northumberland's son Hotspur, and more than twenty years before the birth of his own son, Hotspur's great rival, Prince Hal. It was a bold stretch of imagination, therefore, that made the two rivals infants together, and led Bolingbroke to exclaim on hearing Hotspur praised above his son:—

> "Oh that it could be proved
> That some night-tripping fairy had exchanged
> In cradle clothes our children where they lay,
> And called mine Percy, his Plantagenet,
> Then would I have his Harry and he mine."

In the year 1378, when he was only eleven years of age, and seemingly too young for such a manly honour, he was supposed to be old enough to take upon him the order of knighthood, and for that purpose his father levied the usual aid for making him a knight, upon which occasion Sir William Butler, Lord of Warrington, one of his father's feudatories, paid, as his aid, for two knights' fees, and a third of a knight's fee in Warrington, the sum of xlviiis. iiijd.[1] In 1384 the young knight was created Earl of Derby, and his father, being about to leave England to prosecute his claim to the kingdom of Castile, made the new earl his lieutenant in his absence, and, in consideration for his youth, gave him an able council of advisers to assist him. Scarcely any man has become great without a good mother, and Henry must indeed have had a good mother, if she deserved half the

[1] Dodsworth's MSS.

character which Froissart gives of her in his own peculiar manner. "I never saw," he says, "two such noble dames, so good, so liberal, and so courteous, as this lady and the Queen of England, nor ever shall, were I to live a thousand years, *which is impossible.*"[1] Henry married Mary, one of the two daughters and co-heiresses of Humphrey, late Earl of Hereford and Northampton, and constable of England, whose rent-roll amounted to 50,000 nobles a-year. There was a little romance in the way in which the marriage was brought about. Thomas of Woodstock, Earl of Buckingham, the husband of Mary's sister, Eleanor, anxious to secure the fortunes of both sisters for himself, took Mary under his own care, and with the view of making her a nun of St. Clare had her attended everywhere by two sisters of the order, who were to instruct her and to teach her the duties of the sisterhood, and in especial to inveigh against matrimony. The pupil seemed apt and willing, but at this crisis, the Earl of Buckingham being called abroad on the king's affairs, the quick eye of John of Gaunt saw the advantage of such a match for his son, and having engaged Lady Arundel in his interest, she invited the young lady from the earl's house at Pleshy, where she was staying, to come and visit her at Arundel Castle. There the young people met, and, as Henry was young and handsome, and the young lady rich and fair:—

> "Soon they loved, and soon were buckled,
> None tak time to think and rue:
> Youth and worth and beauty coupled,
> Love had never less to do."

They were married at Arundel, and afterwards, when the young wife died in 1394, she left behind her four sons—Henry, afterwards Henry V.; Thomas, Earl of Clarence, who fell at Beaugé; John, Duke of Bedford, afterwards regent of France; Humphrey, the good Duke of Gloucester—and two daughters, Blanche and Philippa.[2] Bolingbroke was one of the five great nobles who in 1388 formed the design of controlling and coercing the king, and who with that object appealed to his ministers. The part he took in this matter must have shown the king how very early "he wanted his cousin's love."[3]

Having, in September 1390, obtained the king's leave to travel, he took his journey into Prussia, Lithuania, and Barbary, in each of which places he served as a volunteer against the infidels, and gained renown, no

[1] Chronicles, ii. 166. [2] Froissart, i. 628. [3] Capgrave de Illustribus Henricis, 98.

less by his military exploits than by the display of piety and virtue in his conduct. He returned home from this foreign adventure on St. Mark's day (25th April), 1391.

In 1392, with a retinue of 300 followers, he was again in Prussia, from whence he went on to Venice. From that city he proceeded to Jerusalem, where he relieved the poor with alms, ransomed some Christian captives, and paid his devotions as a pilgrim at all the holy places. He afterwards visited Mount Sinai, Hungary, Poland, Austria, Candia, Rhodes, and Cyprus. He honoured the memory of his uncle Clarence by making a pilgrimage to his grave at Milan, and he showed his reverence for philosophy by a similar visit to the grave of Boethius at Padua, and finally, after long wandering, he returned again to England.[1]

On his return home after his long travel, the fame he had acquired and the renown of his skill in arms and valour made Bolingbroke justly popular with his countrymen at home.

In 1397, when his wife was then dead, and he was in possession of her vast inheritance, he was created by the king Duke of Hereford, from which time he began to be known as Harry of Hereford.

It will be remembered that Thomas of Lancaster claimed, as Baron of Halton, to have the water of Mersey always kept free and open for a barge of eight oars from Freshpool to Thelwall. For a similar reason his successor, Bolingbroke, when seated on the throne as Henry IV., issued his orders to remove all obstructions from the river Dee, and directed that all nets that might be taken should be conveyed to Chester Castle.[2]

On the 27th January 1398, the king having met his Parliament at Shrewsbury, Bolingbroke made his well-known charge of high treason against the Duke of Norfolk, Thomas Mowbray. The king, after attempting in vain to appease the anger of his two wrath-kindled nobles, thus takes his farewell of them both:—

"Be ready, as your lives shall answer it,
At Coventry, upon Saint Lambert's day;
There shall your swords and lances arbitrate
The swelling difference of your settled hate."

The appeal thus unwillingly allowed left the two opposing parties to decide their difference by engaging in mortal combat, and fighting it out from sunrise to sunset, unless or until one of them should either be killed or should cry "Craven."

[1] Capgrave de Illustribus Henricis, 98.   [2] Chester Records.

On St. Lambert's day (the 17th September), 1398, the two combatants entered the lists armed *cap-à-pie*, prepared for their deadly encounter. But now—

> "Being mounted and both roused in their seats,
> Their neighing coursers daring of the spur,
> Their armed staves in charge, their beavers down,
> Their eyes of fire sparkling through sights of steel,
> And the loud trumpet blowing them together:"

at this critical moment the king threw down his warder and arrested them in mid career, acting by the advice of the Parliamentary Commissioners, of whom John of Gaunt was one. The king now sentenced Bolingbroke to banishment—

> "You, cousin Hereford, upon pain of death,
> Till twice five summers have enriched our fields,
> Shall not re-greet our fair dominions,
> But tread the stranger paths of banishment."

To which, in the spirit of an ancient Roman, the banished man replied—

> "Your will be done: this must my comfort be,
> That sun that warms you here shall shine on me."

Bolingbroke's father had concurred in the sentence of banishment, perhaps because he thought his son had been wanting in honour when he revealed a private conversation to the ruin of the person who had entrusted him.[1] But the sentence was no sooner pronounced than at his intercession the king takes off three years from the term of his son's banishment.

Bolingbroke's departure into exile bore the resemblance of a triumph. He was attended by great numbers of his friends to Sandgate, from whence, on 3d October 1398, he sailed for France, where the Dukes of Orleans, Berry, Bourbon, and Burgundy, met him on his landing. The Duke of Bourbon, who had been his fellow-soldier in Barbary in 1390, knew him as a brave and gallant knight. To the other dukes, if not personally known, he was well known by the fame he had acquired in the crusade in Lithuania in 1392, and by his pilgrimages to Mount Sinai and the Holy Sepulchre at Jerusalem. It was owing to his frequent absence in the east that Bolingbroke appears but seldom in the pages of Froissart.[2]

But as he who has once drunk Nile water thirsts to drink it again, so when Bolingbroke was sentenced to exile by the king, he importuned his

---

[1] Hume's Hist. Eng. iii. 35.   [2] Traison et Mort Richard II. 44.

father in his last illness to allow him to go again upon the crusade, but his father refusing his consent, he remained in France and went no farther.[1] He knew from personal experience what the crusade was when at a later period of his life he professed to his friends his readiness to go as far as to the sepulchre of Christ.

On the 16th April 1399, the king being about to go to Ireland, made his will, and on the 19th of the following month he set out. But as the wolf, watching his opportunity when both the shepherd and his dog are away, easily leaps into the fold, so the Royal sails were hardly loosed to the wind before a cabal of discontented nobles met to concert the king's overthrow. To inflame their mutual discontent, they discuss their grievances together, and lay a plot, when Northumberland, one of the party, at length communicates to the rest this piece of intelligence:—

"I have from Port le Blanc, a bay
In Britany, received intelligence
That Harry of Hereford,
Well furnished by the Duke of Brotagne,
Is making hither with all due expedience."

Amongst the nobles and knights in his retinue the poet mentions Sir John Norbery, possibly a Cheshire knight, of whom we shall hear again.

Bolingbroke, who was no laggard, having landed at Ravenspurg, on the coast of Yorkshire in July 1399, immediately on landing despatched letters to his friends in all parts of England, some of which no doubt reached his retainers in Lancashire. He had wisely selected for his descent that part of the coast of England which was nearest to his greatest possessions, from which he might have the most ready access to his friends, and they to him. His first march after landing was to that old possession of his family, the Castle of Pickering, where, as we have seen, the Countess Alice, the widow of Thomas of Lancaster, resided and kept her state. Two days afterwards he passed on to Knaresboro', another of his castles, and thence to Pomfret, a great stronghold, which had come to his family from the Lacys, and which had proved fatal to Thomas of Lancaster. Here he was met by Percy, Earl of Northumberland, his son Hotspur, the Earl of Westmorland, Lord Willoughby, and a great number of knights, esquires, and gentry of Lancashire and Yorkshire. But amongst these Bolingbroke missed Sir John Butler of Warrington, the tried friend of his

[1] Froissart.

father, who was now no more, but whose place, it is likely, was supplied by his son, Sir Wm. Butler, with a large body of retainers. His next halt was at Doncaster, where his force was found to amount to 30,000 men, and it was then thought best, in order to provision them more conveniently, that they should divide into two bodies, one of which, taking the left-hand road, should march through Lincolnshire, and the other, under Bolingbroke, should take the right, and pass southwards by his castles of Leicester and Kenilworth to Evesham and Gloucester. Hitherto his flag had floated on every tower unchallenged anywhere or of any man, and he had met no enemy, but as he drew near to Berkley, being then in Gloucestershire, he inquired of Northumberland the distance to that town, and the latter having quickly learned to be a courtier, thus replies :—

> "I am a stranger here in Gloucestershire;
> These high wild hills and rough uneven ways
> Draw out our miles and make them wearisome,
> Yet your fair discourse hath much beguiled
> The tediousness and process of my travel."

At Berkley, "the castle where the madcap duke his uncle kept," he was met by that uncle, the Duke of York, whom the king had left guardian of the kingdom in his absence, at the head of a large force; but weak and timid at all times, and now perhaps treacherous, the duke, proved quite unequal to the present occasion. He first admitted his nephew, Bolingbroke, to a parley, and then declared his intention of standing neuter between him and the king. From Berkley Bolingbroke advanced unopposed to Bristol, and having taken that city, and there put Bushy, Green, and the Earl of Wiltshire to death, he began to retrace his steps, and having passed through Gloucester, Ross, and Hereford, he came on Sunday to Leominster, and from thence, passing through Prees, he marched on to Chester, which he reached on the 9th of August.[1] On arriving in that city he caused peace to be proclaimed at the market cross, but the next day he showed that by peace he did not mean safety, for there, without any form of trial, and for no fault but holding fast by his allegiance to the king, he cut off the head of Sir Peter Legh, and showed his true policy to be what the poet says it was—

> "To cut off the heads
> Of all the favourites that the absent king
> In deputation left behind him here,
> When he was personal in the Irish wars."

---

[1] Traison et Mort Richard II. 293.

On the same day, by a warrant, omitting none of his titles and calling himself Duke of Lancaster, and Earl of Derby, Lincoln, Leicester, Hereford, and Northampton, and Seneschal of England, he issued his safe-conduct to the prior of Beauvale (the same to whom his father had granted the tun of wine) freely to come to him or go elsewhere, with horses, harness, and goods, at his pleasure, and without let or hindrance from any one.[1] Probably the prior was grieving over the sudden termination of his grant of a tun of wine, which had expired with the life of John of Gaunt, and desired to approach his patron's son to obtain a renewal of it for a fresh term.

On the 19th of August, having obtained possession of the king's person by stratagem, and having conquered England without a battle, Bolingbroke proceeded to conduct his Royal prisoner from Flint to Chester Castle. But Cheshire was all loyal and devoted to the King, and he decided not to linger on the way, but to set forward at once to London. On the 21st of August he was at Nantwich with his charge, and the next day at Newcastle. On the 24th he was at Lichfield, and on the 29th at Northampton. On the 30th he reached Dunstable, and the next day St. Alban's. On the 2d of September he and the captive monarch made their well-known entry into London, and then occurred that scene which our immortal bard has described with such inimitable pathos.[2] The end was now at hand. On the 28th September a Parliament, summoned under Bolingbroke's management, and prepared to second his purposes, deposed Richard II., and declared Bolingbroke his successor, who forthwith ascended the throne by the style and title of King Henry IV. In 4 Henry IV., the chamberlain of Chester was respited £20 : 8 : 7 of the subsidy granted by the county to the king as well in the demesne of Halton as in other vills that were held of the king, because the said demesne was in the king's hands, and the collectors could not distrain there.[3]

In the year 1409, there being a lull in the sea of troubles of the king's busy life which the crown had brought him, he had leisure to think of setting in order his worldly affairs and making his will. By his will, written in English, and bearing the date of the 21st January in this year, he directs

---

[1] Madox Formulare Anglican. p. 327.   [2] Traison et Mort. Richard II. 215 n.

[3] Cheshire Records ; and on 22d August 5 (Henry IV.), we have this entry on the same records—"Fait Remembrer que mons^{r.} William Swynburne, lieutenant and justice de Chestre ad deliv'ée en nom de mons^{r.} Hen duc de Lancastre (i.e. the Prince of Wales), a Johan de Copenhurst meir de la citée de Chestre une charete liez de fer et deux chilvalx p. la salve garde decelles."

that his Queen Joanna shall be endowed out of his Duchy of Lancaster, so that Halton, which was a part of it, became included in the Royal dowry. But some parts of the will, for their style and sentiment, deserve more particular notice. It begins thus :—" In the name of God, Fadir, and Son, and Holy Gost, thre persons and on God, I, Henry, sinful wretch, be the grace of God, Kyng of England, and of Fraunce, and Lord of Irland, being in myne holl mynd, mak my testament in manere and forme that sayth : First, I bequeth to Almyghty God my sinful soul, the whiche had never be worthy to be man but through his mercy and by hys grace, which lyffe I have mispendyd, whereof I put me whollily in hys grace and hys mercy with all myn herte; and what tym hit liketh him of his mercy for to take me to hym, the bodye for to be beryed in the chirch at Caunterbury, after the descrecion of my cousin the Archbyshopp of Caunterbury. And also, I thank all my Lordis and trew peple for the trewe servise that they have done to me, and y ask hem forgivenes if I have missentreted hem in any wyse. And als far as they have offendyd me in wordis, or in deedis in any wyse, I prey God forgeve hem hit and y do. Also I devys and ordeyn that ther be a chauntre perpetuall of twey preestis, for to sing and prey for my soul in the aforesayd chirch of Caunterbury, in soch a place and aftyr soch ordinaunce as it seemeth best to my aforesayed cousin of Caunterbury. Also y ordeyne and devys that of my gooddis restitution be made to all hem that y have wrongfully greyvyd, or any good had of theirs without just tytle. . . . . . Also, I wyll that all my officers, both of household and other, the which nedeth to have pardon of enything that touch here offices, both of losse and oder thing they have pardon thereof in semblable manere as y of my grace have be wont to do befor this tym."[1]—Neither in this nor any other part of the will, except his founding of a chantry, is there anything to which a strict Protestant could object. His profession of a sound faith, the absence of all mention of the Virgin or the saints, the king's deep humility and selfabasement, the grateful acknowledgment of his subjects' service, his prayer for their forgiveness, and his forgiveness of them, his anxiety to make restitution to whomsoever he had injured, and the pardon of his servants' shortcomings, are all points to be admired. There is so little that is peculiarly Romish in the will that, did not history tell us of his persecution of the Lollards, we might suspect the king to have imbibed some of their views

[1] Nichol's Royal Wills, 203.

from Wickliffe, his father's friend. One of the witnesses to the will is John Norberry, probably the same person who is mentioned to have sailed with him from Port le Blanc, when he was, in Hotspur's language,

"A poor, unminded outlaw sneaking home."

If so, his continuing with his master through good report and evil report to the end, is alike honourable to the king and his faithful retainer.

On the 10th April 1409, Sir Richard de Aston was appointed the king's seneschal at Halton. In making this appointment the king was rewarding the faithful services of one of his father's servants in Spain, where Sir Richard had proved himself a valiant soldier, who could face death fearlessly in the field. He had come back, however, to confront him in a far more hideous form at home, for the plague broke out in his house at Ringey in Aston, and at one fell swoop carried off not only "all his little ones," but his wife also.[1]

In 1847, when the church at Runcorn was rebuilt, two grave-stones were discovered. One of them was inscribed to the memory of a descendant of the seneschal who bore the same name, who died in 1493, and the other was to the memory of Matilda, his wife. On the husband's tombstone were the words, "Jesu Mercye," and on the wife's "Ladye helpe?" both let into the stones with lead.

In old times making a will was often the sounding of its maker's death knell; the king, however, survived this prudent step more than three years, and before he died, having been covered with a hideous leprosy, and bent almost double with sickness, he breathed his last on the 20th March 1412, and in him, its first crowned head, expired the long and honoured line of the barons of Halton.[2]

[1] Hist. Ches. i. 533; and Duchy Records.
[2] Stanley's Westminster Abbey, 374, where there is the account of the king's being carried into the Jerusalem Chamber to die.

CHAPTER XIV.

HALTON UNDER KING HENRY V.

HERE we may shortly recall the barons in their order, from their rise to their ending.

(1.) Of Nigel the first (who lived *ante Agamemnona*), except that he was the founder of the line, that he chose Halton for the head of their barony and built the castle, and probably died in fighting for the earl against the Welsh, little is known.

(2.) William fitz Nigel rescued the earl when he was interrupted and hard pressed by the Welsh, and for that service the earl made him hereditary constable and marshal of his host.

(3.) William fitz William removed the canons of St. Augustine from Runcorn to their beautiful home at Norton, and was present at the dramatic scene which has been described as taking place at the bedside of Hugh fitz Odard.

(4.) Eustace fitz John greatly increased the family fortunes by his two rich marriages, and fell with honour in the discharge of his marshal's office fighting against the Welsh.

(5.) Richard fitz Eustace married the sister of Robert de Lacy, and in the end enriched the barony of Halton with the Lacy name and estates.

(6.) John fitz Richard, in a dark age, became the patron of science, and maintained in his service an astronomer, who wrote a book on the planetary conjunctions. He established the ferry at Runcorn, and built Stanlaw abbey as the burial-place of his family, but dying at the siege of Tyre during the Crusade, his own body did not rest in the family mausoleum.

(7.) Roger, who had gained by his sternness the ill name of "Hell," assumed for his family name the great name of Lacy. He took the cross, and served with distinction in the Holy Land under Richard Cœur de Lion.

(8.) John Lacy was one of the nobles who deserves honour for having assisted to wrest from King John the great charter of Runnymede. When

King Henry III. was married, the Earl of Chester carried the sword of state before him, and John Lacy attended as his constable.

(9.) Edmund Lacy, having been educated at Court, was married by the king to a foreign wife, to the great dissatisfaction of the English nobles. He first assumed the bearing of three garbs, afterwards so popular on the Lacy shield of arms.

(10.) Henry de Lacy became Earl of Lincoln, and as the soldier, minister, and friend of Edward I., was distinguished as a valiant leader and enlightened statesman. Through him the great name of Lacy became intimately linked with our English annals.

(11.) Thomas of Lancaster rose in rebellion against Edward II., who, having made him prisoner, beheaded him at Pomfret, where the people built a chapel to his honour and made him a (*pseudo*) saint.

(12.) Henry of Lancaster avenged his brother's wrongs, and took prisoner Edward II., and in the next reign had his brother's lands restored to him.

(13.) Henry, Duke of Lancaster, was at first called *Tort Coll*, but he ultimately deserved and obtained the better name of the "Good Duke." He served with very great distinction in the king's foreign wars, and wrote a book called " Mercy, Gramercy."

(14.) John of Gaunt, third surviving son of Edward III., became Duke of Lancaster, and filled the highest offices of the kingdom. He assumed the title of King of Castile and Leon, and though he was obliged to abandon it, he succeeded in seating two of his daughters on the thrones of Spain and Portugal. He was the patron of Wickliffe, and the friend of Chaucer.

(15.) Henry Bolingbroke, Duke of Hereford and Lancaster, is made the hero of three of Shakspeare's historic plays. He was an accomplished prince, and went upon the Crusade twice, and finally having dethroned Richard II., ascended the throne of England.

From this short retrospect it appears that the course the barons of Halton had held was ever "bold and forth on," and that from the first rise to the final ending, they were continually growing in wealth and importance. From simple barons, whose title was only by prescription, they rose to be earls, then dukes, then princes of the blood; and finally, having attained the highest of all dignities, the imperial crown and throne of England, their line may be said to have ended in a blaze of lustre; but from that time they lost their separate individuality, and their history sinks into and becomes part of the general history of the country.

And here, before we proceed to give the further history of the barony or honour of Halton, we must mention the steps which King Henry IV. took to secure his old inheritance in his family. Immediately upon his attaining the crown, his dukedoms of Hereford and Lancaster, and his earldoms of Derby, Leicester, Lincoln, and Northampton, with all his other titles, including the least but oldest of them all, that of Baron of Halton, became extinguished according to a well-known maxim of law, that all other titles meeting in the crown are extinguished and lost in that great fountain of all English honour.

Well aware, however, that while he held his duchy of Lancaster by an indefeasible title, and that his right to the crown was most questionable, one of his first royal measures was to obtain an Act that his eldest son, the Prince of Wales, in addition to his other titles, should have and bear the title of Duke of Lancaster, and that neither the king's inheritance of his said duchy nor its liberties should be changed, transferred, or diminished through his assumption of the royal dignity. This Act was followed by another, which ordained that after the king's decease, the right of succession to the duchy should belong to his said son and his heirs, and in default of such heirs, to his second son Thomas and his heirs.

After this re-grant of the dukedom, the Prince of Wales in all writs and official acts constantly styled himself Duke of Lancaster; and in the inscription on the beautiful seal of his lordship of Carmarthen he bears the titles of Prince of Wales, Duke of Aquitaine, Lancaster, and Cornwall, and Earl of Chester.

In the year 1417, being engaged in his French wars, and reminded by its dangers of his own mortality, the prince, now become King Henry V., made his will on the 21st July. This will, which like his father's, is in English, directed that his lordships and castles of Halton and Clitheroe, and all his other lordships in the north of England, should, after his decease, go to his brother John, Duke of Bedford, in tail male, with remainder to his own heirs, Kings of England, for ever. In this year Ralph de Radclif and Thomas Urswick were the king's receivers at Halton, and received from the chamberlain of Chester £86 : 13 : 4 by the king's command, as this entry shows :—De 86 : 13 : 4 solut Radulfo

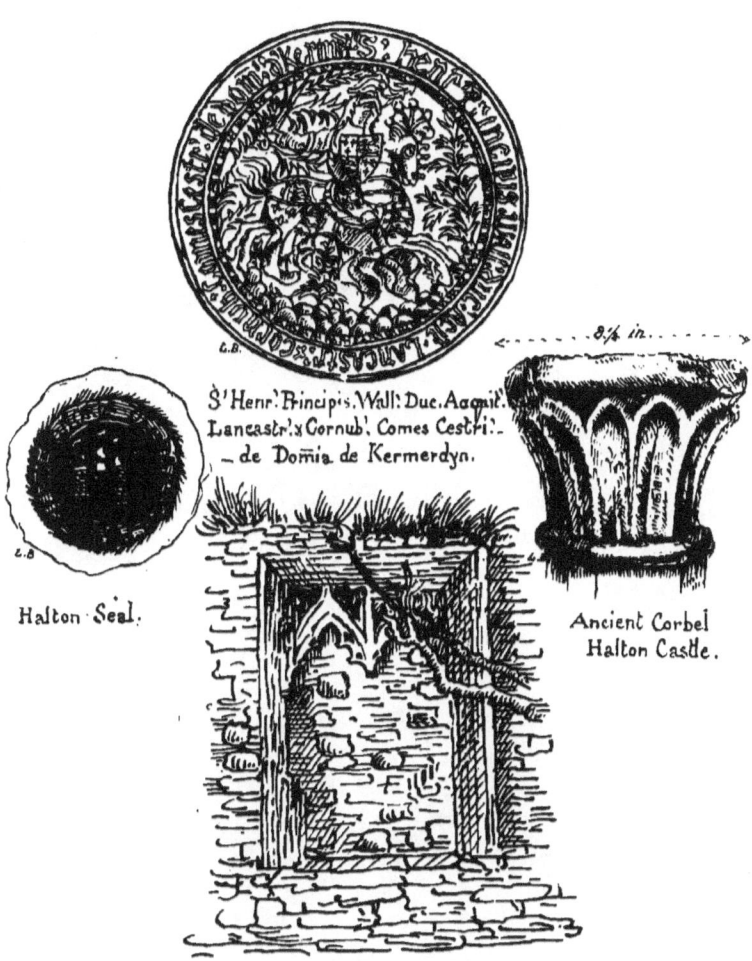

S¹ Henr¹. Principis. Wall¹. Duc. Acquit¹.
Lancastr¹. x Cornub¹. Comes Cestri:
de Domia de Kermerdyn.

Halton Seal.

Ancient Corbel
Halton Castle.

Window in the Ruins of Halton Castle.

de Radclif et Thomæ Urswick receptoribus castri manerii et dominii dñi.
R. de Halton p. mandat. dñi. R.¹

In the next year there occurs among the palatine records a curious claim and allowance of exclusive jurisdiction on behalf of the court at Halton. It appears that one Thomas de Nesse, of Runcorn, was presented by the jury of the palatine court for that of malice prepense he had assaulted his master, one Thomas de Chester, canon of Norton; whereupon he came, and being asked what answer he had to give, he said that our lord the king, as Duke of Lancaster, was seised of the manor and lordship of Halton, and held there a view of frank-pledge of all tenants and residents thrice a year—namely, the first between Michaelmas and Martinmas, the second between St. Hilary's Day and the feast of the Annunciation, and the third between the festival of the Holy Trinity and the Assumption, and that he also held there a free court-baron from fortnight to fortnight, in which court he took cognisance of all pleas of trespass and other pleas, and if a presentment were made by the king's bailiffs of any resident of the said manor and lordship of having broken the peace or made an affray, that then such bailiffs, by a process of attachment or distress out of the same court, brought the offender to his answer there, or if being presented in the aforesaid court-baron the offender confessed his offence or was thereof convicted, the same our lord the king was accustomed to inflict a fine or amerciament on him, and to have such fine or punishment levied by his own bailiff, and because the said Thomas de Nesse was a tenant of our said lord the king, and committed his said offence at Le Newstede, within the manor and lordship aforesaid, it was at the election of our said lord the king and his officers to punish his said offence in his view of frank-pledge, or other his free court aforesaid. And then the record goes on to state that at a free court-baron held at Halton, before Sir William Stanley, the younger knight seneschal of Halton, Richard del Wood, the king's bailiff of the said manor and lordship, presented the said Thomas de Nesse for the offence aforesaid, who then acknowledged the same, and throwing himself on the king's mercy, was fined forty pence; whereupon Matthew del Mere, who appeared for the king in his palatine court, in his proper person, came and confessed what the record averred, and admitted that the said Thomas de Nesse ought not to be called to answer further for his offence in the king's said palatine court.²

¹ Ches. Chamberlain's Accounts, 5 Hen. V.   ² Hist. Ches. i. 523.

On 29th August, 24 Henry VI. (1446), at a great return of the manor of Halton, held before Tho. Bylling, deputy to William, marquis and earl of Suffolk, and Sir Thomas Tudenham, chief stewards of the Duchy of Lancaster, for the northern parts, and William Coton, receiver-general, Thomas Westbury, abbot of Norton appeared, having been distrained for his relief of Middleton, his fisheries in the Mersey, the stallage of his tenants, and for the halmote and amerciaments of his tenants in the court of the manor of Halton (it seems to have been a sort of *quo warranto* proceeding); whereupon the abbot in full court produced a release for his relief of Middleton, and for his fisheries and stallage and halmote he showed the donation and foundation of his house, and the same were allowed, and the bailiff was directed to displace all the fisheries in the Mersey except the king's and the abbot's, and to allow no court or halmote in the manor except the king's and the abbot's, and as for the stallage and amerciaments of his tenants, the abbot was to hold them without impediment.[1]

Henry VII. again separated the Duchy of Lancaster from the crown, and entailed both it and the duchy on himself and his heirs for ever, and from that time until this day the duchy, although vested in the crown, has ever since remained a distinct and separate inheritance.[2]

Queen Elizabeth, who was no stranger to the importance of the Duchy of Lancaster, or of her barony of Halton, and had a high regard for both, in the year 1588 caused a survey to be made of the duchy, in which a full account of all its particulars is given. In this survey the receiver of Clitheroe and Halton is set down as paying to the receiver of the duchy the large sum of £1700 a year, and amongst the forests of the duchy enumerated in the same survey, express mention is made of the park at Halton.[3] Her Majesty, moreover, possibly in consequence of the entail created by her father, occasionally styled herself Duchess of Lancaster, of which, amongst others, one instance occurs in Sir Hugh Cholmondeley's Inquisition *Post-mortem* in 39 Elizabeth.[4] But besides these instances of Henry V., who, both when King and Prince of Wales, called himself Duke of Lancaster, and Queen Elizabeth, who, in the zenith of her power, assumed the title of duchess, no prince or sovereign since the time of Henry IV. has borne the title of Duke or Duchess of Lancaster. The

---

[1] See a copy of the record *penes me*.
[2] Hist. Lanc. iv. 747.　[3] Ibid. i. 176.　[4] Westminster papers.

creation by Shakspere's editor, Mr. Rowe, of that Prince John, whom Falstaff said he never could love because he hated sack, to be Duke of Lancaster, is of course apocryphal; and when the Lancashire men, jealous, like Judah of old, who shall show most loyalty to the sovereign, insist upon giving Her Majesty the Queen, who rules in all hearts, the title of Duchess of Lancaster, they are giving the sovereign a title which the heralds do not recognise. In reality there exists no such title, the Duchy of Lancaster and the Barony of Halton being both anomalies, each of them being a body without a head—a barony without a baron, and a duchy without a duke.

CHAPTER XV.

HALTON UNDER HENRY VI., EDWARD IV., RICHARD III., HENRY VII., AND HENRY VIII.

WHEN the barony lost its individuality by being merged in the Crown, Halton declined in importance; but its glory did not wholly depart. The grand old fortress, majestic and hoary, still remained; and, as might be expected, notices of it and the surrounding neighbourhood continue still to occur, and of these we propose now to give some account by way of continuing the history of Halton from the time when the line of its ancient barons ended.

In the 9 Henry VI. (1431) William Harrington, a stalwart warrior, who had borne the king's banner at Agincourt, and had been made seneschal of Halton on that account, issued his warrant to the keeper of Northwood Park, a dependency of Halton, directing him to furnish an oak for the repair of Farnworth church: the oak thus supplied would no doubt be one of the monarchs of the forest, and the stranger who now visits that quaint old church, and looks up at the work of its solid open roof, probably sees without knowing it some of these ancient spoils of the greenwood, which after four centuries, still fresh and sound at heart, look down upon him from the old roof-tree overhead.[1] William Harrington, the seneschal, was in the receipt of a pension of 40 marks a-year by grant from the Prince of Wales dated 11th May, 6 Henry IV.[2]

On the 11th June, in the following year, 10th Henry VI. (1432), Sir John Savage, another soldier then seneschal of Halton, was commanded to receive from Randle Brereton, sheriff of Cheshire, the bodies of Richard de Whelock and George de Wevre, and to keep them safely in the castle of Halton until they should be discharged by due course of law.[3] These persons were probably ordinary offenders sent to prison to await their trial.

[1] Hist. Lanc. iii. 722. Hist. Ches. i. 479. [3] Ches. Pat. Rolls.
[2] Ches. Recog. Rolls.

What was their offence, or before whom they were tried, and what was the result, we may know when the palatine records have been indexed. In the meantime we may conjecture that they were brought to trial either before the Justice of Chester, who until the time of Henry VIII. held at least three courts every year, or before the court of Quarter Sessions, which was held four times a year. The Justice of Chester was often some nobleman of rank, who was paid a salary of £100 a year, and did his work by deputy. In 1432, Humphry, Duke of Gloucester, the "good Duke Humphry," was Judge of Chester, and Sir John Savage often aided as his deputy. Coming down to a little later period than this, we find Humphry Stafford, Earl of Buckingham, and of four other earldoms—Hereford, Stafford, Northamptom, and Perch—filling the office of seneschal of Halton and Widnes. At this time, therefore, the office seems to have been one of great dignity.

On the 6th September, 20th Henry VI. (1441), this great nobleman appointed Sir Geoffrey Warburton his deputy, at a salary of C.s. a year for the life of the earl.[1] Our great bard more than once in his drama of Henry VI. (Part II.), introduces this patron of Sir Geoffrey, who stood deservedly high in that king's favour, for he had the rare merit in those unquiet times of holding fast by his allegiance. The king rewarded his fidelity by making him Duke of Buckingham, and he fell at last fighting on the king's side in the battle of Northampton, on the 9th July, 38th Henry VI. (1460). In the 17th Edward IV. William de Malbon, and James Alkok, appear as officers in Halton after Roger Dutton's death.[2]

The next notice of this neighbourhood which we meet with, and which seems strange, occurs on 15th April, 21 Edward IV. (1481), when the mayor and aldermen of Dublin received the king's command to make proclamation within their liberties that every Irish merchant ship charged with goods for Runcorn or any other place in Cheshire should first come to the port of Chester and there discharge, and then recharge her cargo, or be put under arrest.[3] The only object of this strange order must have been some intended benefit to Chester, in disregard of the interests of commerce, the safety or convenience of the trader, or the benefit of the general public. But, notwithstanding this order, Ed. Walshe, in April, 21 Edward IV., had a license to sail his ship direct from Runcorn to Ireland.

The Duke of Buckingham's deputy at Halton had been long dead

[1] Arley Deeds.   [2] Ches. Records.   [3] Chester Recog. Rolls.

before the day which proved so fatal to the Duke at Northampton ; but as the appointment of the deputy was for the duke's life, Piers Warburton, the son of Sir Geoffrey, stepped into his father's place, and afterwards, when the duke died, he was probably made chief seneschal, for we find him filling that office in 1490, and no other seneschal is heard of in the meantime. Piers continued seneschal until his death in 1496. In the family annals he has the cognomen of "Wise," which he owed in part to his rule at Halton, but still more to the prudence with which he steered his course in most critical times, when he managed to keep his head and save and increase his estates. Piers, who was the rebuilder and second founder of the house at Arley, was retained by the celebrated but unfortunate Sir William Stanley to serve him in peace and war at a salary of six marks a year. We know from their correspondence that Sir William and his retainer lived on the most friendly terms, and that they occasionally hunted and killed a buck together, which was sometimes, perhaps, in the park at Halton.

On the death of Wise Piers, his son, Sir John Warburton, succeeded to his office, and was made constable as well as seneschal of Halton. In one or other of these characters he was commanded, on 4th July, 2 Henry VIII., to receive into his custody the body of William Pull, Esquire, and to keep him safe in the castle of Halton until he should be thence legally discharged.[1] What was the prisoner's offence, how long he was detained, and when and by whom he was tried, and what was the result, are all points which have not been ascertained. It is singular, however, that an offender of the same name and rank, who was probably of the house of Pull or Poole in Wirrall, in 1441, had committed an outrage upon Lady Butler of Bewsey, for which he was proclaimed an outlaw, and declared to be held as traitor unless he should surrender himself by a certain day. It would indeed be singular if the William Pull, Esquire, now committed to Sir John Warburton's care, should be the same old offender who had been guilty of the abduction of Lady Butler. It would be satisfactory to find that such an offender met with his deserts at last.

Among the monuments in St. Peter's Church in the Tower there was formerly, and perhaps still is, one to the memory of Henry Southworth, of whom it states that he was born in the castle of Halton; that he became Yeoman of the Crown, and one of the Guard to Kings Henry VII.

[1] Cheshire Records.

and VIII., and held the office of Yeoman Bowyer and Surveyor in the Tower of London for the long period of 33 years.[1] The date of his death has been obliterated from the monument, but if we suppose him to have entered upon his office in 1st Henry VII. (1485), he must have died about the year 1518, and if so, he was probably born under the seneschalship of Wise Piers at Halton, and owed his skill in the use of the clothyard-shaft, which in yeomen's hands did such execution at Agincourt and Flodden, to his training under Wise Piers. Henry was of a good Lancashire family, one of whom, John Southworth, settled in Cheshire, and was a pensioner of Edward IV. The father of Henry was probably serving in some capacity at Halton when he was born.

In 10 Henry VIII. (1518), the day of Henry Southworth's supposed death, Thomas Butler, Esquire, son of the lord of the manor of Warrington, and himself a man of consequence, sued Thomas Aston, a gentleman like himself, for a trespass committed in the park at Halton.[2] Poaching and trespasses in pursuit of game were not then confined to the humbler classes, as they are now, when there has grown up amongst sportsmen a sort of game code of honour, and Thomas Butler, by his suit, was perhaps only asserting his sovereign's right, or his own, to the four-footed denizens of the forest at Halton. Two years afterwards, in 12 Henry VIII. (1520), Thomas Aston, as was not unusual in those times, retaliated upon Thomas Butler, and sued him and John Ffarington in a cross action for a trespass on the herbage and pannage of the park at Halton.[3]

But other officers besides the park-keeper were vigilant in the discharge of their offices at Halton at this time, for in 18 Henry VIII. (1526) William Brereton, the seneschal, prosecuted two persons for invading and trespassing upon the Halton fishery in the river Mersey.

On the 10th June, 22 Henry VIII. (1530), an inquisition being then taken as to the manor of Weston, William Brereton, who was still seneschal of Halton, was one of those who witnessed it.[4] Who appointed William Brereton to his office, and how long he continued to hold it, are points which have not yet been ascertained.

In 1536, when the dawn of the Reformation was reddening the horizon, and the religious houses were beginning to nod to their fall, the royal visitors came to Norton to take an inventory of the abbey plate and valuables. They had already inventoried and packed up such

---

[1] Weaver's Funeral Monuments, p. 286.   [2] Duchy Records, 127.   [3] Ibid. 128.
[4] Report on the Manor of Weston, p. 9.

articles as they meant to take away, and were about to take their leave when, the day growing late, and the weather foul, they determined to remain and pass the night in the abbey. But they were no welcome guests, and, in thus concluding to stay where they were, they were reckoning without their host, for the abbot had numerous friends outside, who assembled in hundreds round the abbey, and put the visitors in such fear that they betook themselves to a strong tower, and sent news of their alarm to Piers Dutton, the high sheriff, to beg him to hasten to their rescue, "else they were never likely to come out from thence alive." At two o'clock in the morning, when the high sheriff arrived, with a strong body of his tenants and retainers, he found great fires burning, both within and without the abbey gates, at which an ox was roasting whole, while other viands and provisions were being prepared for the abbot's people. The appearance of the high sheriff disturbed the anticipated feast, for on seeing him the people took to flight and fled in all directions, escaping as they could, some of them in their alarm even swimming across the abbey pools; but the abbot and three of the canons were made prisoners, and lodged in the King's Castle, at Halton, to be kept as the king's rebels, under a penalty of £1000.[1]

Sir Piers, by a letter of the 12th October 1536, informed the king what had been done, and by a letter from the king, of the 20th of the same month, he and Sir William Brereton (possibly the seneschal of Halton) were ordered to hang up the abbot and canons if they appeared to be traitors. What was the ultimate fate of the prisoners does not appear, but a Thomas Barkett, who is believed to be the last abbot, was living, and in the receipt of a pension, in the year 1553. It is probable therefore, that the king's clemency was extended to the prisoners.

In 35 Henry VIII. (1543), Sir Piers, who was still seneschal, held a halmote at Halton, when quarrels, breaches of the peace, and other disorders, seem to have been rife, for Margaret Norland was presented for having assaulted Robert Carrington, while Ellen Norland, another of the same family, was found to have lawfully undergone the punishment of the *theaue*, a sort of pillory for scolds. At the same time Alice Lesthwyte, widow, was presented for entertaining other men's servants, and the wife of Oliver Whitley, Joan, the wife of William White, and the wife of Richard Lightborne, were all presented as common liars and scolds.[2]

[1] Froude's Hist. Eng. ii. 424; Hist. Ches. i. 502, n.
[2] Chester Hist. Soc.'s Proc. pt. vi. 217.

CHAPTER XVI.

HALTON UNDER PHILIP AND MARY, QUEEN ELIZABETH, AND KING JAMES I.

IN 1 and 2 Philip and Mary, and also in 4 and 5 of the same reign, Sir John Savage was seneschal of Halton.[1]

On the 20th April, 2 Elizabeth (1560), when an inquisition was taken after the death of James Merbury, Sir John is again mentioned as filling the same office, and he still held it in 1570, when he is again mentioned.[2] In the same year Sir John, who had been three times sheriff of Cheshire—in the years 1550, 1560, and 1567—had the misfortune to lose his wife, the virtuous lady Elizabeth, as the Frodsham register calls her.[3]

On 16th October, 13 Elizabeth (1571), while Sir John was still seneschal, Richard Aston, gentleman, was the queen's attorney; William Hugh, gentleman, was the sergeant-bailiff; Thomas Kente, constable of the castle; and John Bayer, gent., bailiff of the burgh.[4]

In the 18 Elizabeth (1576), Thomas Grimsditch occurs as the name of the sergeant-bailiff of Halton,[5] and the office falling vacant that year, Thomas Cheshire was appointed to fill it.

The next year, when the Earl of Derby visited Chester in state, the event was honoured by the performance, before him, of a mystery or drama called the "Shepherd's Play," in which one of the characters indulged in this vaunt:—

> And brave ale of Halton I have,
> And whotte meat I had to my hire;
> A pudding may no man deprave,
> And a jannocke of Lankastershire.[6]

The ale-tasters, or ale-conners, at Halton, we must presume, then did their duty, and had established a high character for their brew of the national beverage. The audits of the barony, between which and the borough of Congleton, as we learn from an entry in the records of the

---

[1] Hist. Lanc. iii. 721.   [2] Arley Deeds, box 15, No. 33.   [3] Hist. Ches. i. 62, 528.
[4] Halton Rolls.   [5] Ibid. 30, 10.   [6] Stanley Papers, Chet. Soc. 25.

latter in 1578, which states that the borough paid, and had paid 26s. 8d. at the Halton audit for 100 years and more, were regularly kept up at this time, and the accustomed convivialties then indulged in had some share in maintaining the high character of its ale. The cobbler of Canterbury was an ale-conner, and it was said of him that

> He had a nose that gan show
> What liquor he loved, I trow;
> For he had before long seven year
> Been of the towne the ale connère.

It is not unlikely the officers of this class at Halton bore the same professional livery in their face, and had noses which were own cousins to Bardolph's.

At this time the beer brewed in great houses must have been brewed of unusual strength, and out of this practice arose the complaint which in 1586 was made to Burghley that, in order to save their wine, some of the nobles habitually brewed and used beer which they called by the name of "drowne beer," "courte beer," or "marche beer," all which was above the ordinary strength.[1]

The ale at Halton, which was so evidently above proof, was open to the complaint thus made to Burghley, while the queen's beer, on the other hand, sinned by a very opposite fault. It was notoriously thin and weak, as we learn from the following story:—Forget-not Tarlton, a favourite player of that day, whose religious ancestors who gave him his name never dreamt of seeing him embrace the stage as a profession, was a great favourite with the queen, who admired his wit and drollery, and often entertained him at the palace, until he lost her countenance and favour by publicly jesting on the thin and slender quality of the royal beer. This sarcasm, which was the more severe because it was well deserved, was resented by the queen, who forbade him entering the palace again. Fairholt, who, in his costumes, has represented Tarlton playing on the tabor and pipe, gives us no very exalted opinion of the actor's powers, but buffoonery was then more tolerated than now. Perhaps his chief forte lay in low comedy and in personating the character of clowns.

We have already seen Halton occasionally used as a prison for malefactors; but in the year 1579 its proud castle, once the chief seat of the constables of Cheshire, and which had given thrones to its possessors,

[1] Notes and Queries, Jan. 3, 1857, p. 7.

declined from its former high estate and became transformed into a prison for recusants, and Sir John Savage, its constable and seneschal, was ordered to receive such of this class of sufferers for conscience sake as should be sent there.[1] At this time it appears to have been thought necessary to repress with a strong hand offenders of this kind, and accordingly, on the 3d June in the following year, a letter from the Privy Council was received by the Ecclesiastical Commissioners at Chester, which gave them to understand that the penalties on recusancy were to be increased. The tender knees of the reformed faith, as yet but feeble and tottering, required to be strengthened, and Halton, of which Sir John Savage was governor, was deemed a proper place for receiving such persons as either wavered in adopting the reformed faith or obstinately resisted it. The Privy Council also directed the Commissioners to select some fit and godly person—a spiritual person or teacher was probably intended—who should take charge of them, and the prisoners were to have for their diet the same allowance that was made to prisoners of the same kind in the Fleet Prison in London.[2] Amongst those who habitually absented themselves from church and other places of public worship, and conscientiously adhered to the Roman Catholic faith, was Sir John Southworth, the representative of a long line of knightly ancestors. Sir John, who had obstinately refused to attend church, and had kept a seminary priest, one James Cowper, in his house at Samlesbury, not long after the queen's accession was summoned with others to sign his submission to her Majesty in the matter of religion, but he would only comply so far as to sign an undertaking not to maintain or countenance others in their recusancy.[3] In other respects he was loyal to the queen, and afterwards when a general muster of arms and armed men in Lancashire was made, Sir John furnished his quota of two light horse, two corselets, two coats of plate, two pikes, two long bows, two sheaves of arrows, two steel caps, and one caliver (the weapon which Falstaff bade Bardolph put into Wart's hand), and one morion.[4] In 1579, when an order was made that the leading Lancashire recusants should be imprisoned, Sir John Southworth and Campion, the Jesuit who had visited at his house, were amongst the number. To what place Campion was at first sent we do not know, but Sir John was sent, and possibly Campion with him, to Halton Castle, this same fortress, where

[1] Hist. Ches. i. 525. [2] Lanc. Lieut. Chet. Soc. p. 114, *in notis.*
[3] Hist. Lanc. i. 514. [4] Ibid. 525.

his kinsman, Henry Southworth, who, as has been mentioned, died in the still stronger fortress, the Tower of London, had been born. Sir John Southworth, who was among the first of those sent to Halton, was courteously received by his brother knight, Sir John Savage, the seneschal, who, no doubt, compassionated the condition of a prisoner committed to his charge for conscience sake. To his keeper's great relief, on the 22d July 1581 the prisoner was ordered to be removed from Halton, and on the 22d December following he was delivered to Mr. Robert Worsley, of Booths, an active public officer, to be kept in the New Fleet, at Manchester.[1] To the prisoner thus removed from Halton, with its healthy heights and its prospect of a rich valley watered by a noble river, and bordered by grand and majestic oak woods, to the flat and confined site of his new prison, the exchange must have been unwelcome. His new keeper, too, seems to have felt the full weight of his responsibility, and because Sir John neglected to attend grace when it was said by the rest of the prisoners, he denied him some of the indulgences to which he had been accustomed, until the 23d February 1584, when, at the intercession of Sir John's son, the Council ordered that the severity of the prisoner's restraint should be relaxed, and that he should be allowed to take exercise in certain walks of which he had been deprived.[2] In the same year the Council directed the Ecclesiastical Commissioners of Lancashire to learn from Sir John Southworth why he intended to disinherit his son [3]— a vain question, which they might evidently have answered for themselves. The son, who had probably not the father's constancy, had shown signs of wavering, and Sir John felt inclined to resent it. Soon afterwards Sir John was removed to the Fleet prison in London, and, consistent in his recusancy to the last, he died in 11 James I. (1613). In 1592 Sir John had in his possession a copy of the Rheims new Testament, which was only published in 1582.

On the 10th September 1586, the Council had information that Sir Richard Bannister, "an old priest, was receipted at the Carter's house near to Runcorne bote."[4] But we do not hear whether Sir Richard was apprehended, or, if he was, whether he also was sent to the recusants' prison at Halton, which was so near to his place of retreat.

About this time, however, it seems to have been the frequent practice to commit to Halton not only recusants, but offenders in other crimes,

[1] Hist. Lanc. i. 525.   [2] Ibid. 538-9.   [3] Ibid. 540.   [4] Ibid. 542.

from other and distant parts of the county. Congleton, it will be remembered, is affiliated with Halton in the plea to the *quo warranto*— (33 Edward III. 1359)—and from that place, in 1591, two offenders (Highfield and Rathbone)—were sent to Halton to be tried for felony, and the constables had 8s. for their conduct money. In 1595, when one Horton was brought from Congleton to Halton for a like offence, Vardon, the officer who brought him, received 6s. 8d. for his charges. But another Congleton entry is curious and more suggestive. It runs thus :—

 Pay'd for two cordes which whipped two rougs . jd.
 Pay'd Raufe Stubs for takynge sayd rougs to Halton
  Castle to be tryd . . . vijs. vjd.

Of that old judge Æacus it was said *castigat et audit*—he first punishes his prisoners, and afterwards tries them; and the Congleton justices appear to have taken him as their great exemplar, and administered justice after the same rough sort, when they first whipped their prisoners, and afterwards sent them for trial. The subsequent trial of the two rogues probably took place before the magistrates in quarter sessions. But where these sessions were held, whether at Halton or some other place, does not appear.

The officers who conveyed the above prisoners from Congleton to Halton, a distance of 25 miles at a time when there were no public conveyances, and when the roads were bad, the ways foul, and the company not select, must have well deserved their fees. On 15th October, 34 Elizabeth (1592), Sir John Savage being still seneschal, the Halton records give us these as the names of the officers under him,—Edward Savage, gentleman, constable of the castle; Robert Whitby, sergeant of the fee; and Wm. Ashurst, gentleman, bailiff of the manor of Halton and Over Whitley.

After his long rule as seneschal at Halton, and while he was serving the office of mayor of Chester, Sir John Savage was gathered to his rest on 5th December 1597. He was succeeded by his son, another Sir John, who became, like him, constable and seneschal of the old fortress at Halton.

In 1600, when there was a cock-fight at Congleton, this second Sir John attended on the first great day, and his worship the Mayor then spent 2s. in wine and sugar in entertaining him and the friend who accompanied him. Nearly at the same time when Sir John, attended by (Mr. Egerton) the lord keeper's son, paid another visit to Congleton, he was entertained still more expensively, a sum of 8s. 7d. being spent on the occasion. The following year, when Sir John again visited Congleton, 6s. 8d. was spent on his entertainment in " wine, cakes, and, sugar," and at the same time the Mayor extended his hospitality to the worshipful Mr. Warburton of Arley, and spent on his entertainment 3s. in "burnt sack and cakes."

In 1602 a great bear-bait, proverbially a very favourite amusement at Congleton, took place there, and was honoured with the company of Sir William Brereton, Mr. Warburton, and Mr. Egerton (the lord keeper's son), when the Mayor entertained the whole party with "wine, sack, spice, figs, and almond beer;" the feast, however, was not expensive, for the whole sum spent on all these varieties was only 1s. 10d.

The same year the constable of Congleton brought another felon to Halton, and received 4s. 8d. for his expenses. If we could trace the prisoner's crime, we might assign some of it to the practical instructions he received at those demoralising scenes—the cock-fight and the bear-bait.

At this time the office of bailiff was rising in importance at Halton, and in 1603 we find it filled by no less a personage than Sir Thomas Holcroft, the knightly owner of Vale Royal.

In 1608 Sir John Savage, the seneschal, being required to state what records there were at Halton, reported that there were under his charge there records from the time of Edward III. It is likely enough he would express his desire for their removal, but whether he did so or not, they were not removed; and, with the large additions made to them since Sir John's time, they remain at Halton still. They consist of plea and suit rolls, rolls of the court-leet and of the copyhold manor, annual court rolls and presentments, books of account, and steward's books. An examination of these shows how little the political changes of five centuries have disturbed the proceedings at Halton. From these records might be extracted curious traits of ancient manners, many local statistics, and a number of historical facts which would be useful to the historian and the genealogical enquirer. It were to be wished that these records were removed to some safer depositary, and were catalogued and indexed, so as to be made more easily accessible for reference. To their non-removal, however, we are indebted for these lines of counsel which some ancient court keeper at Halton has amused himself by writing in one of them:—

> Spare not, nor spend too much, be this thy care,
> Spare but to spend, and only spend to spare;
> Who spends too much may want, and so complain,
> And he spends best who spares to spend again.

In 1609 John Savage, the younger son of the first baronet, was murdered by Ralph Bathurst, who being arraigned for it and refusing to plead, was sentenced to the *peine forte et dure*, and was pressed to death on 13th July in the above year.[1] In 1610, when the Congleton officials dutifully met to pay their annual allegiance to the seneschal at Warrington, this entry in their books records their visit: "Spent by Mr. Mayor and the jury at Warrington, and on their return and at the audit, to deliver their verdict and rental before Sir John Savage and Mr. Auditor, in wine and horse hire, £1 : 2 : 8."

The appointment of Sir Thomas Holcroft as bailiff of Halton having been revoked on the 13th February 1611, Thomas Ireland, a rising young lawyer, who was afterwards knighted and made attorney-general of Chester, was appointed in his place; and the king having consented for a money consideration to convert the copyholders of Whitley lordship, a part of the honour of Halton, into freeholders, Thomas Ireland received the further appointment of bailiff of Whitley, with a view to assist his Majesty in carrying the design into effect. The king's object was satisfactorily accomplished about this time, and amongst the Whitley copyholders who were thus transformed was "the sailor bishop," William Lyon, Bishop of Cork. Drake, to whom he had been captain, it is said, presented him in such favourable terms to Queen Elizabeth, that she was pleased to promise him the first piece of preferment at her disposal. The Bishop of Ross dying soon afterwards, Captain Lyon reminded her Majesty of her promise, and pressed his suit so earnestly, that she, finding no obstacle either in his education or his character, in the year 1582 bestowed upon him the vacant bishopric, and the next year gave him also the sees of Cork and Cloyne, to be held in commendam with it, and he was at last confirmed bishop of all the three sees.[2]

On the 2d December 1611 Thomas Ireland was advanced to the still higher office of bailiff-sergeant of Halton, in the room of Thomas Cheshire, who had previously held it. This was that same ancient office which, as we have seen, Hugh de Preston, held in 1359, when he was called bailiff of the sergeanty of Halton. In the year 1613, for some reason that does not appear, the country being then at peace, Sir John Savage directed a beacon to be made and set up on Frodsham Hill.

In 1615 this entry occurs in the Congleton books:—"Payd for claret

[1] Lyson's Ches. 755. [2] Chambers's Edinburgh Journal, No. 285.

wine bestowed on Sir John Savage, 17s. 10d. ; and ordered a bushel of malt to be brewed against his next coming, 13s. 6d."

The last entry might serve to point a lesson. The beer was brewed and the welcome prepared, but, alas ! the expected guest in whose honour it had been prepared was not to share it.

Sir John was cut off by death on 14th July 1615, leaving all his honours to his son and successor, Sir Thomas Savage.

The family of Savage has been so often mentioned in connection with Halton, that a short notice of them may very fitly be permitted here. The family were originally settled at Scarcliffe, in Derbyshire.[1] It does not appear whether that Robert le Savage, who was the king's bailiff of his lands between Ribble and Mersey, in the time of Henry III., was of this family, but in the fourteenth century one of the family acquired Clifton by a marriage with the heiress of Sir Thomas Danyers. Clifton, which was very near to Halton, had been given by one of the barons there to Geoffrey, a younger son of Hugh de Dutton, and after descending by inheritance through several families in succession, it had at length fallen to Margaret, daughter and heiress of Sir Thomas Danyers the hero of Cresey. Since the time that they had first acquired Clifton the knightly race of the Savages had lived there in much splendour, and had given some memorable names to history. Margaret's son, Sir John Savage, fought and was knighted at Agincourt; and Sir John Savage, the younger, was killed at the siege of Boulogne in 1492.[2] Thomas Savage, who was successively Bishop of Rochester and London, and who died Archbishop of York in 1508, was of this house, and so also was that Sir John Savage who led the left wing for Henry of Richmond at Bosworth, and who, probably, mustered under the walls of Halton the forces which did such service on that great day. He was still living at Clifton in 1488, when he presented a clerk to the living of Barrow.[3] But clouds will at times hang over the best families, and in 1520 such a fate overtook the house of Clifton, and it suffered an eclipse, when in that year Sir John and his son, both of them knights, were implicated in a charge of slaying John Pouncefote.[4] What were the circumstances of the case we are not informed, but as the consequences which followed it were not capital, it is but charitable to suppose that their crime was unpremeditated, and only arose out of one of those sudden affrays so common

[1] Hist. Ches. i. 526 *in notis.*   [2] Lyson's Ches.   [3] Hist. Ches. i. 186.   [4] Ibid. 528.

ROCK SAVAGE, CHESHIRE. circa 1780.
The ruined Seat of the Savage family.

in those unsettled times. A little later another knight who bore the family name, Sir Arthur Aston, a soldier who stood high in the royal favour, in 1598 being sent by Queen Elizabeth with 4000 men to the assistance of Henry of Navarre, served with distinction at the siege of Amiens, and was present when that city was wrested from the Spaniards. Sir Arthur, a soldier of the old school, valued valour and bodily prowess so highly, and laid such stress upon these in opposition to walls and strategy, that he had almost a contempt for forts and fortresses, and was wont to say—

> Give me sinews and bones,
> Not castles of stones.

Another Savage, who is more known than *well* known, Bishop Bonner, came of the house at Clifton, but with a bar in his escutcheon, as did also in later times, with a like bar, the poet Richard Savage, whose biography has been written by Johnson. In 1565, Queen Elizabeth's early days, Clifton, the family manor-place, having fallen into decay through old age, Sir John Savage rebuilt it in a more stately style, and gave it the new name of Rock Savage, which has almost ever since supplanted Clifton as the name of the township. It has been said that the Queen honoured the builder by laying the first stone of the new house, and that she afterwards visited him at it, but there appears to be no foundation for either of these traditions, for in none of her Majesty's royal progresses do we find that she ever came so far north as Rock Savage. After the building of the new house at Rock Savage, Clifton was deserted, and at that hour it was said "she remained like an aged matron, well contented to go to her grave, having seen in her lifetime her daughter advanced to such a height of honourable dignity."[1]

What the new house of the Savages then was may be gleaned from this description, written by a contemporary, who says:—"We next behold the magnificent fabric of Rock Savage overlooking the waters and goodly marshes round about the skirts of it, and so contrived in the situation that from the lower meadows there is a fine easy ascent upon the face of the house, which as you approach it still nearer, as is the nature of true beauty, fills the eye with more delight; and to see now the late additions of delectable gardens, orchards, and walks, would make one say it longs to be the abode of so honourable a master as it doth service to."[2]

[1] An old author, quoted in Greswell's Runcorn. [2] *See* Greswell's Runcorn, p. 24.

And still later another writer thus speaks of the site:—" A comparison of Rock Savage with the house at Brereton will leave little doubt that Sir John Savage, and his son-in-law Sir William Brereton, employed the same architect in the erection of their sumptuous fabrics. The situation of Rock Savage is remarkably fine. Halton Castle rises behind it, at one side is the estuary of the Mersey, and the Weaver, also an estuary, descends in front to its confluence with the first-named river. Over the Weaver is a fine view of Frodsham and the Welsh hills—Overton Scar and Helsby Tor closing up one side of the picture, while the richness of the Lancashire shore makes a fine contrast on the other." [1]

Margaret Danyers, the heiress to whom the family were indebted for Clifton, bore her father's shield of arms, that is, *argent* a pale fusillé *sable*, and of these arms, which were then considered matters of importance, she made a formal grant to her husband. This shield the Savages continued to bear until they built Rock Savage, when it was discontinued, and the builder of the new house adopted instead on a shield *argent* six lioncels *sable*, with the crest of a lion's jamb. These whelps of the savage king of beasts, and the jamb of their sire as a crest, might be intended for a species of canting heraldry upon their family name. We will now, however, resume our notices of the family line at Rock Savage. A little later one of the Savages obtained from King James I. a lease of the whole honour of Halton, which lease, after being renewed from time to time, is now and has ever since been held by his descendants, and about this time one of the family seems also to have acquired from the Crown [2] a grant of the manor of Frodsham. Sir Thomas Savage, who has been already mentioned, who inherited the baronetcy from his father, and married Elizabeth, a daughter and co-heir of Earl Rivers, stood high in the king's favour, and on the baptism of John, his son and heir, on the 31st December 1606, Henry Prince of Wales honoured him by being the child's godfather, and presented him, instead of the usual gossip's spoons, with a quantity of silver plate, which was of more value and far more useful. [3]

In 1617, the king returning from Scotland to London passed through Lancashire and Cheshire on his way. At Hoghton Tower, in the former county, he halted, and was entertained in great state by Sir Richard Hoghton. To do honour to the occasion, the neighbouring gentry attended on the king's host at Hoghton Tower, and wore his livery. The king found

[1] Hist. Ches. i. 530. [2] Ibid. 31. [3] Issues of the Exchequer, 300.

his reception so gratifying, that he was moved to unusual hilarity, and at one of the feasts he is said to have raised the loin of beef to the honour of knighthood. The carcase, roasted whole, had long been dignified as a *baron*, and the loin was now dubbed *sir*-loin and made a *knight*.

On the 20th August his Majesty, in his progress, arrived at Bewsey, and rested for the night under the roof of his serjeant-bailiff of Halton, the vice-chamberlain of Chester, whom he now created Sir Thomas Ireland. On the day following he proceeded to Rock Savage, where he was received in fitting state by its owner, Sir Thomas Savage. After partaking of the goodly repast prepared for him and his suite, his Majesty, attended by his host, hunted and killed a buck in Halton Park. As we have already seen, Halton had been visited by Edward II. after the death of Thomas of Lancaster, and this visit of King James I. was the second royal visit with which Halton and its old castle had been honoured.

The drinking tastes of our ancestors had now undergone a change, and, as a sign of it, bards no longer sang the praises of Halton ale. A few symptoms of this change have been already seen in some of the hospitable entries which have more recently come under our notice. But an entry in the Congleton records of 1624 makes it still more manifest. In that year, when Thomas Parnell was mayor, he and the Corporation spent £1 : 4 : 2 in "sack and sugar" to entertain Mr. Savage of Woodtree, and some of the aldermen and officers of the Corporation. "Cakes and ale," one of the earlier entries, will call to mind Falstaff's regret over the dreaded disappearance of those dainties; but still his greater weakness for sack and sugar was so remarkable, that it obtained for him from Prince Hal the familiar name of "Sir John Sack-and-Sugar," which brings him more vividly before us. But what was this sack which thus supplanted ale, and which has itself now sunk into oblivion, and been forgotten, the usual fate of favourites? Sack could hardly, as has been supposed, have derived its name from the French word "sec," dry. The days of Elizabeth and James were days of flowing bowls, but our ancestors could hardly have drunk healths "five fathoms deep" in a wine of such strength as dry wines usually are, nor, if their taste was for such wines, would they have sweetened them with sugar. Though brought from the same place, sack was certainly not the same wine as sherry, for in a list of wines of which Queen Elizabeth granted the prisage to her favourite Leicester, sack, among many others, is expressly mentioned by its distinctive name. It was drunk and sweet.

ened with sugar, perhaps to correct its acidity, and it was often ordered and brought in by the gallon, and drunk in cups and bowls. Thus, in the scene between the hostess and the two idlers, in Withers' Canterbury Tale, we read—

> I used to drink no wine,
> Yet your best morning draught is muscadine.
> With that the drawer's called to fill a quart.
> (Oh ! 'tis a wholesome liquor next the heart.)
> Then one calls " Drawer !"   He calls " What d'ye lack ! "
> " Begone, bring up a gallon more of sack."

CHAPTER XVII.

HALTON UNDER CHARLES I.

IN 1625 the Cheshire antiquary, Sir Peter Leycester, visited and noticed the old chapel at Halton, which he calls a chapel of ease to Runcorn; but the foundation of the chapel goes back to a very ancient date, for our ancestors in their strongholds never omitted to supply them with a hold still stronger, a place of prayer and divine offices. In Baron Roger's confirmation charter to the convent of Norton, he grants them the chaplainship of his whole constableship of Chester, which must include the chaplainship of his castle at Halton. From the time of this grant, if not before, one of the canons, we presume, officiated and performed Divine service in the chapel at Halton. Probably William, the chaplain, the witness to Baron William fitz Nigel's Keckwick charter, Richard, the chaplain of Halton, witness to Baron Roger's confirmation charter, and John, the clerk of Halton, who is mentioned in one of the Arley deeds, were all canons of Norton, or if not canons, were clerks sent by the convent to officiate in the castle chapel at Halton.[1]

In 1629 the king sold the manor of Moore, which had hitherto been within the honour of Halton, and declared it to be thereafter no longer a part of that fee, but to be held of the manor of Enfield, in Middlesex.

Unwilling to forget their old attachment to the house of Clifton, the Corporation of Conlgeton found out a new and more substantial, though a less ceremonious or refined way of showing it, for in 1632, as their books show, they "paid for a fat cow which was bestowed on the Right Honourable Viscount Savage for a present at his being here." Viscount Savage was in fact our old acquaintance Sir Thomas, under a new title. Some difference exists among genealogists as to how he acquired the title. Sir Peter Leycester says he was created Viscount Savage on the 6th November 1626, but the Peerage has it that he became a viscount in consequence of

[1] Arley Deeds, box i. 34.

the earldom of Rivers being granted to Lord Darcy, whose daughter and co-heir, Elizabeth, Sir Thomas had married, with the immediate remainder to Sir Thomas.[1]

While Viscount Savage was in London, probably attending upon his duties as the Queen's Chancellor, he was seized with an illness of which he died on the 16th December 1635, when he was succeeded in his titles by his son, Sir John Savage, the young heir to whom the Prince of Wales had stood godfather. Jane, one of the deceased viscount's daughters, who married John Powlet, Marquis of Winchester, was honoured with an epitaph by Milton, upon her death in 1631.[2] The viscount's body was conveyed to the family burial-place at Macclesfield, and on its way through Congleton, these entries in the Corporation books show that it was treated with marked respect—

	s.	d.
"Mending Rood Lane against the coming of Lord Savage's corps	1	6
Sugar, 6 lbs.; cloves, 1 oz., at the entertainment . .	11	0
There was a horse-load of wine and many other items, particularly—		
Four links to light	5	0"

On the same day on which the Viscount was laid in earth, his mother, Lady Mary Savage, of Bostock Hall, was also borne to the grave, and laid probably in the same tomb with her son, in the family burial-place, the Savage Chapel at Macclesfield.

John, Viscount Savage, who on his father's death succeeded to the family estates and honours, soon afterwards became Earl Rivers.

Besides the castle of Halton, of which he was at the same time castellan, seneschal, and constable, as well as lessee, he had another residence, the sumptuous house of Rock Savage, with its splendid views of wood and water, hill and champaign. The prospects which dawned on him at his father's death were fair and bright. Almost from his birth he had enjoyed the favour of royalty. The lines had fallen to him " in pleasant places," and he was married to a noble lady of a rank equal to his own, Catherine, daughter of Lord Morley and Monteagle, the peer to whom was addressed the memorable letter which led to the discovery of the Gunpowder Treason. But these prospects, so bright, were too fair to last. Gloom and darkness were on the way, and the days were hastening on

When hard words, jealousies, and fears,
Set men together by the ears.

---

[1] Hist. Ches. i. 530 ; Collins' Peerage, ix. 400. [2] Collins' Peerage, ii. 379.

In 1635, John King, clerk, and probably the minister at Halton, who died on 28th February of that year, minding to improve the place morally and materially, gave £5 a year for ever towards maintaining a preacher at Halton chapel, and 8s. a year towards mending the ways there; and his wife, Ursula, at the same time gave £30 for a stock for the "poor women" of Halton.[1]

It would seem from this entry in the Congleton books in 1638:— "Banqueting stuff for Lord Savage, £2 : 0 : 0," that the Corporation, still loyal to the house of Savage, had been entertaining his lordship.

In 1642, when the sword of the great Civil War was first drawn and the scabbard thrown away, the earl found "he had fallen on evil days and evil tongues." Bound to the king by every motive of duty, loyalty, and gratitude, he cast in his lot with such of those nobles and gentry as at the outset of the struggle subscribed to find forces for his Majesty's service, among whom his name appears as engaging himself for a force of 30 mounted horse. But he and his family sent officers as well as men to serve the king, and Thomas Savage, who appears as a lieutenant-colonel in Colonel Osborne's regiment, was probably his near relation.[2] His opponents, not unnaturally, perhaps, taking umbrage at his proceedings, scrupled not to say hard things of him. Amongst others they said, as a parliamentary paper of July 1642 informs us :—"The Lord Rivers gives out many scandalous speeches against us, and strives by all the means he can to set the whole country against us."[3] Many mouths took up this story, and, whether he deserved it or not, his lordship had reason to remember an old incident of the same kind, which was attended with the like damaging consequences.

Hinc spargere voces
In vulgum ambiguas et quærere conscius arma.

Confidence amongst neighbours being now thrown aside, suspicion took its place, while trade was interrupted, and scarcity and want seemed almost at the door.[4] On the 30th December 1642, the county of Chester, availing itself of a seeming lull, tried to avert the storm from its borders by meeting and entering into a convention of neutrality at Bunbury; but this peaceful movement was annulled and set aside by the Parliament.

Meanwhile the king's commissioners of array, not disposed to remain

[1] Hist. Ches. i. 499.
[2] Hist. of the Siege of Manchester, p. 11.
[3] Army Lists, 1642, pp. 8 and 17.
[4] Hist. Lanc. ii. 18.

indifferent to the distractions of the neighbourhood, issued public notice to all soldiers not to seize or take up horses or property without authority, on pain of being heavily punished for such offences.

It has been said that on the 21st February 1643, Sir William Brereton seized both the castles of Halton and Beeston on behalf of the Parliament; but, as respects Halton, this is a mistake.[1] It is true that after the failure of the Bunbury convention Sir William seized on Beeston Castle; but its rival castle was already in the possession of Earl Rivers, who gave it a governor, and threw into it a sufficient garrison, and as a royal castle should hoist the royal colours, so these now floated over the old walls of Halton; and while sentries kept the gate, the portcullis was probably renewed, the warder resumed his place on the high turret, pikemen and musketeers, in half or whole armour, patrolled the courts, and some time elapsed after this before Sir William Brereton made any attempt to wrest the castle from its owner.

Meanwhile a spirit of distrust among the gentry was springing up, and gradually widening on all sides. In this neighbourhood it must have been very strong, for on 10th February 1643, when an indictment for misprision of treason was preferred at Chester against Colonel John Moore, of Liverpool, Weston, near Halton, was the place where the crime was alleged to have been committed.[2] While Norton, another adjoining township to Halton, but on the opposite side to Weston, was also arrayed against it, for we read that about the same time a reconnoitring party of the Parliamentarians, having heard that the royalists from Chester were doing damage between Frodsham and Chester, repaired to Norton Priory, and ordered that place to be fortified.[3]

One of the worst consequences of these disturbed times was the separation it caused between those who being nearest neighbours to each other, ought to have been the best friends. Earl Rivers, at Halton, and the Brookes, at Norton, the two nearest neighbours, espoused opposite sides in the struggle, and were directly opposed to each other. Colonel Henry Brooke, the then head of the house at Norton, was appointed by Parliament a commissioner for raising the assessment they had ordered, and he was afterwards for four years their high sheriff of Cheshire; and Major Peter Brooke, an active Parliamentarian commander, who, in January 1643, was

---

[1] Hist. Ches. pref. xxxvi. [2] Moore Rental, by Chet. Soc. xiv.
[3] Civil War Tracts, Chet. Soc. 92.

elected a member of what was afterwards called the Long Parliament, for the borough of Newton, was Colonel Brooke's brother. But, on the other hand, Edward Bridgeman, Esquire, who had married Dame Eleanor Brooke, their mother, was a zealous royalist, and suffered much in that cause.

The preparations for the defence of Norton, it appeared, had been taken none too soon, for on the 26th February 1643, the day being Sunday, a small force of horse and foot, with one field-piece from Chester, appeared before the house and summoned it to an immediate surrender, and the summons being refused, preparations were made to attack it. The besiegers with their one gun opened fire upon the house, but the cannoniers were either new at their work or did not intend to do serious harm to the house, if only they could awe or alarm the inmates into submission. But Colonel Brooke, a man of spirit, felt that he was defending his own hearth ; he had plenty of ammunition, and a force of eighty loyal men, many of them his servants, at his back, who, although they were not well disciplined, were all animated by a like spirit with his own. One of them, being ordered to the roof of the house, stationed himself on the highest tower to enable him from thence to observe the enemy's movements, and from time to time to telegraph them to the house below. An active fire from the one gun was for a time kept up against the house, and answered with spirit by discharges of musketry in return, until a chance shot having killed the cannonier and wounded several others, the besiegers drew off their forces and retired to Halton Castle, leaving Colonel Brooke and his brave little garrison in possession of the honours of the siege.[1] The historian of the siege informs us that the man on the tower made very merry with the enemy's bad marksmanship, and assailed their cannonier with many jibes and sarcasms upon it, from time to time calling upon him to take better aim. These domestic or country-house sieges seem to have been a distinguishing feature of our great civil war. Besides Norton, apparently the first instance in this neighbourhood, the houses at Crowton, Biddulph, Withinshaw, and, above all, Lathom, were thus attacked. But now the Parliament had higher aims in view, and towns and cities became their objects of attack. At the end of March 1643, Wigan was invested and fell before their arms, and the turn of Warrington came next. They sat down before this place on the 21st March 1643, and met with a vigorous resistance from the garrison under its gallant governor, Colonel

[1] Hist. Ches. xxxvii. and i. 504.

Norris. At the end of a week, during which the enemy effectually cut off their supplies, the garrison capitulated on honourable terms, and on Whit-Sunday, the 28th May, the enemy took possession of the town. The fall of so important a place, so near to Halton Castle, necessarily filled with alarm the little band of defenders of the fortress. They remounted their guns, secured their outposts, redoubled their watch and ward, and made such preparation as they could to resist the coming storm. Impressed with the importance of the occasion, and that the castle might be better prepared for defence, Earl Rivers, on the 24th June 1643, appointed Captain Walter Primrose governor of the castle, and commander of the forces within it.[1] It soon appeared that all these preparations had not been made too soon. The fall of Warrington had set free the Manchester forces, who were besieging it, and within a month of the new governor's appointment he found himself shut up in his fortress by a strong body of those forces under the command of one whose name at Halton sounded like that of a storm-bird. Little more than a century before, upon the dissolution of monasteries, a Sir William Brereton had been engaged in quelling the disturbance in Norton Park, and in seizing and carrying the abbot and his confederates to Halton Castle to be shut up in prison there, and to him and Sir Piers Dutton were addressed those prompt orders to have the prisoners put to death. It was another Sir William of the same family and name who now led the forces besieging the Castle. No royal chronicler like the industrious Burghall has left on record the particulars of the siege at Halton, or has told us the exact date when it began. We may suppose, however, that when the siege of Warrington ended, the troops, flushed with victory, would be anxious for more work, and would demand to be led to Halton. Certain it is, however, that no long time elapsed after Warrington fell before a besieging force appeared before Halton Castle, and summoned it to surrender, and that on the summons being refused they made their approaches before the place in military form. No plan of these has come down to us, but probably the plan adopted at Pontefract was that adopted at Halton. Lines were drawn around it, and a series of forts planted in the most advantageous positions to command it. While the siege continued, the castle chapel, which stood just outside the walls, "was demolished and totally destroyed."[2] Once

[1] Mercurius Aulicus, 25th June 1643.
[2] MS. Petition of the Inhabitants of Halton after the Restoration.

begun, the siege was steadily pressed on for several weeks, but towards the middle of July 1643, the defenders beginning to experience some want of provisions, listened to terms of parley, and on the 22d July 1643 the castle was surrendered on honourable conditions, and Sir William Brereton entered and took possession of it in the name of the Parliament. That the garrison had well performed their part appears from the account given by one of the enemy, who, in relating the surrender of the castle, tells us with a lingering sense of spleen that it would have fallen sooner if the garrison had not received supplies through the treachery of some of the Parliamentary commanders.[1]

Early in the following year (1644) Prince Rupert arrived in the neighbourhood, and his renown as a fiery warrior naturally filled the enemy with alarm; it was no longer safe for any small forces of the Parliament to keep the field. On the 18th March the force which was besieging Beeston, hearing of his approach, raised the siege hastily and withdrew to Chester. But that which filled the enemy with alarm, as might be expected inspirited and emboldened the king's friends. Halton again opened its gates to Colonel Fenwick, the new governor, and a party of Royalists who now entered it and again hoisted the royal standard, had their quarters beaten up by the garrison at Warrington, probably to divert the prince's attention.[2]

In the month of June of the same year, when the prince was meditating his attack upon Liverpool, and the enemy's forces were drawing towards that place for its relief, some of them, on the 15th June, attempted to pass over the river at Haleford within sight of Halton Castle, but they were met and defeated, and taken prisoners by two of Goring's regiments, under Blaickston; Sir William Davenant, the poet, was with the enemy on this occasion.[3]

Early in July, when Rupert had left the neighbourhood, and was on his way to the fatal field of Marston, Halton, no longer supported by the influence of his name, again succumbed to the enemy, and the royal flag was once more hauled down. The resistance it had formerly offered made Sir William Brereton aware of the full importance of the Castle, and he hastened to take possession of it and to place a garrison in it to hold it. A part of this garrison were with him on the 20th of August 1644, when he

---

[1] Civil War Tracts, Chet. Soc. p. 147.   [2] Memoirs of Rupert and the Cavaliers, 519.
[3] Ibid.

had a skirmish with the Royalists at Tarvin, and took 45 of them prisoners.[1]

Once more in the power of the Parliament, which had now reduced to submission most of the neighbouring garrisons, Halton Castle was easily kept by the small force which Sir William Brereton had thrown into it, but Rock Savage, its near neighbour, was now no longer a pleasant or a safe residence for Earl Rivers, its noble owner. It had suffered at the hands of the soldiery during the siege of Halton, and the ruin then begun had afterwards proceeded at so rapid a rate, that at length the proud pile, reared so recently at so much cost, was no longer a fit home for its owner, and he deserted it and removed to Frodsham Castle.

There were still soldiers scattered about the neighbourhood, and the burial of James Heyes, who was one of them, is recorded in the register of Aston Chapel on the 12th April 1645. Very probably this man died in the castle at Halton, and was carried to his last home by his comrades, with trailed pikes, muskets reversed, and a muffled drum.

The fall of Halton once more led Sir William Brereton to invest the castle of Beeston. But after he had "begun to raise a brave mount with a strong ditch about it, and had placed great buildings thereon," a rumour of the king's approach from Shropshire alarmed him, and he retired to Chester. After the rout of the king's troops at Rowton, however, he returned and again closely invested the castle. For eighteen weeks the garrison and its brave governor, Colonel Ballard, resisted all his attempts to take the place, until, pressed by a scarcity of provisions, a capitulation was agreed on, by which "the governor and officers, with horses and arms, and their proper goods, and the soldiers with their arms, their colours flying, their drums beating, matches alight, and a proportion of powder and ball, were to march out under a safe conduct to Flint Castle." After this treaty the castle was surrendered, and the enemy entered and took possession of it on the 16th November 1645, when they found in the place "neither meat nor drink, except a piece of a turkey pie, two biscuits, and a pair of pea fowls"—a convincing proof of the extremity to which the garrison must have been reduced. The condition of things at Halton Castle, when it was surrendered, was probably of a similar character.

On the 9th February 1646, a council of war assembled at Warrington,

[1] Hist. Ches. ii. 167.

at which Colonel Henry Brooke, Sir Wm. Brereton, Sir George Booth, Sir Thomas Stanley, Roger Wilbraham, Henry Delves, Philip Mainwaring, and Robert Dutton, Equires, were present, when an order was issued, and shortly afterwards obeyed, for dismantling Beeston Castle, and we can hardly doubt that a like order was then issued respecting the castle at Halton, Colonel Brooke's formidable neighbour. On the 1st October 1646 the names of John Earl Rivers and Thomas Savage were struck out of the commission of the peace for Cheshire by order of the Parliament.[1]

The cavaliers were now made to feel the iron heel of conquest. They had suffered in their persons; they were now to suffer in purse. A series of questions had been freely circulated, for the purpose of ascertaining the degree of each man's delinquency. The answers had been obtained, and now, as a consequence,

> Nobles and knights, so proud of late,
> Must fine for freedom and estate.

Fines were now exacted according to the measure of each man's malignancy, and the money was employed either in furthering the triumphant cause or in rewarding its friends. As might be expected, Earl Rivers and his family suffered heavily in this way. He was fined £1110; his mother, the Dowager Countess, £100; Thos. Savage, Esq., of Emling Castle, £1487; Thos. Savage, Esq., of Beeston, £557; and Thomas Savage, gentleman, of Barrow, £70; besides which the following persons amongst his neighbours were also fined—namely, Thos. Cheshire, gentleman, of Halton, £100; Richard Heath, gentleman, of Weston, £138; Robert Cooper of Runcorn, £80; Edward Bridgeman, Esq., of Warrington (of whom we have heard before) £100; and Ann Fearnley of Warrington, widow, £21.

The triumph of the Parliament party was now complete. Earl Rivers, the castellan, constable, and seneschal of Halton, had lost his office; his castle was dismantled, and Rock Savage was roofless. He retired to his seclusion at Frodsham, to live in quiet and wait for better times; but those times he was not to see, for anxiety and care had made him prematurely old, and on the 10th October 1654 he died at Frodsham Castle in the prime of life. The same night the castle was set on fire and burnt down. The incendiary who kindled the flame probably intended it to be the earl's funeral pile, but, if so, he was disappointed, for the body was rescued from

[1] Hist. Ches. i. 209.

the fire, and two days afterwards it was buried with due honour in the Savage chapel at Macclesfield.

In the lull before the outburst of the civil war, forty noblemen and others had joined in declaring their full belief that the king had no design to make war on the Parliament, and that he would use a constant and firm endeavour towards the settlement of the true Protestant religion, the just privileges of Parliament, the liberty of the subject, and the law, peace, and prosperity of the kingdom.[1] It was the concluding passage of this declaration which was echoed by the words *Relig. Prot.—Leg. Angl. Liber. Par.* which afterwards appeared on the royal coins, and have since proved a puzzle to some antiquaries. Amongst those who signed this declaration was John, Earl Rivers, whose body we have seen so narrowly escaped the funeral pile intended for it. Not very long after the signing of the above declaration a furious mob entered the house of his mother, the Dowager Countess, who lived near Colchester, and after destroying her furniture and curiosities worth £40,000, would, if she had not secured her safety by flight, have done her further violence, for no better reason than that she was a Roman Catholic.[2] When war seemed no longer to be avoided, the king associated Earl Rivers with Lord Strange in his Cheshire commission of array, but in this capacity the earl proved of little use, in consequence of his co-religionists, the Roman Catholics, having been previously disarmed. But his being named for this employment, and his joining those noblemen and others who came forward with offers of troops for the king's service, led to his being one of those who were especially excepted when a power was given to the Earl of Essex to pardon certain delinquents and others.[3] The earl, still bent on peace, was one of those who at a later period appealed to the Lords of the Privy Council in Scotland to stay the intended invasion of England.[4] Although his share in these various actions resulted in no benefit to his Majesty, it caused him to be classed as a delinquent, a recusant, and a malignant, and greatly increased the amount of the fines on his sequestration.

The castle of Halton having been dismantled, and ivy now streaming where banners once floated,

Her walls o'er desolation wept!

---

[1] Clarendon's Hist. Rebel. v. 233.   [2] Ibid. vi. 346.   [3] Ibid. 353-45.
[4] Ibid. vii. 440-1.

At different times it had been a garrison for both parties, and the survey which Cromwell now ordered to be made of it describes it as very ruinous, having a gate-house with five rooms over it, a great hall, with two ranges of buildings and nine unfinished rooms above them, with a prison to confine debtors and criminals within the honour of Halton.[1]

Colonel Henry Brooke was then made seneschal, and his son, Richard Brooke, Esquire, constable of the castle, which, however, was then only in a transition state, and was shortly again to change owners. Very soon afterwards, despite the existing lease to the house of Clifton, the honour, fee, manor, and castle of Halton (except only the park which had been granted to the Savage family in fee by King James) were put up to sale, and being purchased by Colonel Henry Brooke, became a most desirable adjunct to his silvan and picturesque domain.[2]

The castle had been for so many ages a fortress, to which arms and armour are a necessity, and where the noise had been so often heard

> Of armourers, accomplishing the knights,
> With busy hammers closing rivets up,

that a colony of smiths had grown up at Appleton, a dependence of Halton, on the other side of the Mersey—who had found employment in supplying jacks and hauberks, back and breast plates, bills, crossbows, and other arms offensive and defensive, to the inmates of the castle; but now that the castle had fallen, and fallen as it seemed for ever, the occupation of these workers in iron being gone, the smiths, who might be called "Milaners"—for the Milanese were once as famous for making iron and steel suits for our sex as their descendants in our own age are for adorning the heads of the fair sex, whence their English successors have their name of milliners—had to seek other employment. It seems strange, indeed, that while Milan has had the honour of clothing our sex in mail, and adorning the heads of the other sex with millinery, Mantua, a neighbouring city, and the home of Virgil, should give name to the "mantua-makers," who help the ladies to dress. It seems as if in later times, Italy, deserting arms and taking refuge in the arts, had so fulfilled the Druid's prophecy to Boadicea—

> Other Romans shall arise,
> Heedless of a soldier's name.

---

[1] Survey in the Augmentation Office. [2] Lyson's Ches. 701.

But arms and an armoury having now fled from Halton, the smiths of Appleton, after such a pause as a state of transition always causes, turned their skill in iron into another channel, and without beating swords into pruning-hooks, have become what they are, the busy and skilful makers of small tools and implements, and of those more delicate wheels and movements that animate our watches and clocks.

CHAPTER XVIII.

THE INTERREGNUM.

THE late war had bequeathed its usual legacy of distress to this neighbourhood, and entries such as this, which are common in the town's books of Frodsham, are an evidence of it, and at the same time show how part of it was relieved :—"1655. Gave to a woman who came with a certificate from Col. Brooke."

In 1656, when Webb, the author of the Vale Royal, visited Halton, his pencil drew a view of the castle, in which he indulged his fancy so largely that the picture is anything but like. But his letterpress account of the castle may be taken to be more trustworthy. In this he tells us that on every alternate Saturday a Court was held in the castle for all matters happening in Halton fee. It had its prison for thieves, who at every sessions were taken to Chester to be tried. He might have added that the fee had its own coroner, who took cognisance of all suspicious deaths occurring within its liberties, and also that it had a yearly fair on St. Bartholomew's day, to which, as to every fair, there was incident a court of pie powder (*curia pedis pulverizati*), so called from the jury being composed of suitors who had come there "stained with the variation of each soil between their homes and the fair." Madox, in his Formulary, has given us the record of a judgment at one of these courts, which, as such judgments are not common, I shall here give as follows :—

"New Sarum to wit.—At a court of pie powder there, holden in the canons' close in Pentecost week, in the 35th year of the now king, Clement Hegge was attached by his body for picking the purse of one John Thomas, of London, capper, of an account book of no value, wherewith the said Clement being charged, could not deny it, wherefore he was adjudged to the pillory, there to remain for two hours during the fair, and execution was done accordingly ; and there being nothing further against him he was forthwith dismissed and discharged. Witness, John Whittokesmede, bailiff to Richard, Bishop of Salisbury, for his city of new Sarum, on the 1st July, in the 35th year of the now king's reign (Henry VI., 1457). Given under a copy of the aforesaid roll whereto the seal of our office is attached."

We read of no punishment like this occurring at Halton, but no doubt, as it was often deserved, it may have been inflicted, though it is not recorded. Notwithstanding the humane ordinance of the Protector, which in 1654 abolished cock-fights and cock-pits—that very ancient but still most cruel sport,—which it was reserved for the present reign to see finally put an end to, still prevailed, and, with their usual perverseness, men were found secretly frequenting such scenes and places. An offender of this sort from this neighbourhood has recorded his being present at a cock-fight in 1658, and losing 13s. 4d. at it ; but, as if he had still a lingering sense of shame, and did not intend it to be read, he has recorded it in cipher.

On 3d September 1658, the anniversary of his birth and of all his great victories, Cromwell breathed his last, and his sceptre fell into hands which could not grasp it. His son, who was weak and amiable, which gained him the sobriquet of "Queen Richard," was not fitted for a throne which required a firm and vigorous rule. In Norfolk his sudden fall is irreverently commemorated by the tavern sign of "Tumble-down Dick." The vanquished and prostrate Royalists felt his feebleness, and thence took courage to raise their heads once more.

> They rallied in parades of woods,
> And unfrequented solitudes ;
> Convened at midnight in outhouses
> T' appoint new rising rendezvouses.

The Presbyterians, who had never wished the king's death, and felt some compunction for their share in it, now coalesced with the Royalists in their wish to see monarchy restored. Colonel Henry Brooke, the same who at the outbreak of the war had so gallantly defended his house, and many others of the same party, made common cause with Sir George Booth, the leader of the Royalists, when in 1659 he issued his manifesto from Chester announcing his intended rising and his reasons for it. It is evident that in Halton and the neighbourhood he did not lack sympathy. He had Colonel Brooke and his brother, Major Brooke, and the Rev. Wm. Finmore, the parish minister, with him. Earl Rivers might have been with him also, but he had no longer a home in the neighbourhood.[1] But to rise in rebellion is always a serious thing. Hotspur found it so before the battle of Shrewsbury, when, besides his father and his correspondent, the cowardly Scotch Earl of March, whom Shakspere miscalls Lord Mortimer of Scotland, he found himself deserted by a host of other nobles and friends. And

[1] Hist. Ches. pref. xli.

so it happened now, for Mr. Newcome tells us that "five hundred lords and gentlemen of the best in England who had engaged with him were all either prevented or failed in their trust, and none of them rose with him but Sir Thomas Middleton."[1] The fatal hour had not yet struck, but Sir George had gone too far to recede, and on the 18th August he and his little army set out from Chester and marched to Winnington, where on the very next day they were encountered and routed by Lambert. The battle has been often described, but we print the following letter respecting it, which has only lately been discovered :—

Dear Sir—I suppose ere this you have an account of the great victory obtained with little bloodshed upon Friday last. This day Chester was surrendered to my Lord Lambert without any termes but his owne. Some of the enimyc's horse went hence last night and this morning to the number of 300 to Chirk Castle, in Wales, under the command of Sir Thomas Middleton, the owner of it, to which place our troope and three more of my Ld's regiment and some foote are marchinge this afternoone. To-morrow, God willing, I purpose to be with them. They lye this night at Rixam. Lord Kilmorrey, Sir William Neale, and many other persons of quality, are taken.—I am, sir, your most affectionate and obliged brother,   J. PEASE.

Chester, Aug. 25, 1659.

Colonel Henry Brooke was made prisoner in the battle, and sent to Chester Castle, and Major Peter Brooke, who was also made prisoner there, was on that account expelled the House and committed to the Tower for high treason. Sir George Booth, who was discovered and taken at Newport Pagnell a few days after the battle, was also sent to the Tower, and ordered, like Major Brooke, to be indicted, and Mr. Finmore, the minister of Runcorn, who, like the fighting prelates of old, had given the sanction of his office to the cause, was taken in the battle and sent prisoner to Chester Castle.

But another revolution of the political wheel was now at hand, and this significant entry in the Frodsham book gives us notice of it :—"1660. Given to a company of Irish people, who had a pass from my Lord General Monk."

On the 21st February 1660, the Rump, so the remains of the Long Parliament which now re-assembled was called, gave orders that Major Brooke should be set at liberty, and on the 16th March following, the same Parliament, having given orders for a new one to be called, dissolved itself, after having sat nearly twenty years. There was now a general throwing up of caps. The king was recalled, and the whole nation seemed to be of opinion that Sir George Booth, in his rising in the previous year, had only risen a little too soon.

---

[1] Autobiography, Chet. Soc. i. 110.

CHAPTER XIX.

HALTON UNDER CHARLES II., JAMES II., WILLIAM III., AND QUEEN ANNE.

ON the 29th May the bells of Frodsham and Runcorn rang in honour of the restoration. The king's arms were set up in those two churches, and the royal standard once more floated over the shattered walls of Halton Castle, which was now restored to Earl Rivers, its rightful owner. Mr. Finmore, exchanging his prison for a parsonage, came back to Runcorn, and Mr. Thos. Woodfall, the curate of Halton, returned to his curacy at that place. In a few years more Mr. Finmore became first a prebendary, and then the archdeacon of Chester.

War resembles a great lawsuit, in which one side must lose, and as a consequence, is sure to have a large bill to pay for damages; but civil war is a suit in which neither party can escape loss, and both sides have often to suffer serious consequences. The war was now over, and from a petition issued in 1662 we learn some of the consequences which from it had fallen upon Halton. The petition, which is signed by Henry Ferne, who became Bishop of Chester in February 1662, and died the following March, is addressed to "all pious and charitable Christians, who have a due sense of the glory and honour of Almighty God," after setting out that theretofore there was a comely chapel in Halton wherein the petitioners and their forefathers had worshipped and enjoyed the benefit of divine services until the civil war broke out, when such chapel (standing near to the castle in Halton, then besieged) was by the soldiers demolished and totally destroyed, to the great dishonour of God, the reproach of Christianity, and the prejudice of the neighbourhood, the petitioners proceed to state that since this sad misfortune they had been compelled to celebrate public worship and offer up their joint devotions in a small building erected in Halton, which had been erected for a schoolhouse, which as they were of opinion that time and place were circumstances necessarily required in conjunction with the more essential conditions of public worship, they accounted a diminution of the divine honour: they then state that this consideration had prevailed with them to endeavour the rebuilding of the said chapel, and that according to their endeavour they had cheerfully contributed towards effecting the same, and had collected in the neighbourhood a sum of four score pounds, which had raised up the walls into great forwardness and provided most of the timber necessary for the roof, but a considerable share of the work being yet unpaid for, and materials being wanting to perfect the design, which would require at least £60, the petitioners requested the aid of all charitable persons towards completing the good work, and they promised to be ready to contribute to the necessities of others when engaged in a like good work, and to pray that all happiness here and hereafter may attend those who help them. The petition was signed amongst others by Elizabeth Savage, Willoughby Aston, Richard Brooke, and Thomas Woodfall, curate of Halton.

The effort seems to have been successful, for the chapel was rebuilt, and it remained until its present new and more beautiful successor, which stands like "a city on a hill, which cannot be hid," arose, to challenge the admiration of all who behold it.

The Restoration, though it had brought back the King, and restored to the Savages their possessions, did not immediately bring them into this neighbourhood. Their castle at Halton was a ruin, Rock Savage was almost in the same state, and their castle at Frodsham had perished by fire. Thomas, Viscount Savage, who on the death of his father, the late earl, had succeeded as third Earl Rivers, having no longer a Cheshire home, removed his residence to London. Halton, however, being once more his own, he appointed his constable to take charge of the prison, his steward to administer his affairs, and his bailiff to execute processes at the castle as before. His family had suffered much for their constancy in the king's cause, but the new earl, who was no bigot, showed that when there was good reason he was open to conviction, and had courage to change his opinions. In 1680, when the Duke of York's devoted adherence to popery gave rise to a cry through the country to exclude him from the throne, and a struggle between the court and the popular party began, and ran so high that liberty seemed to be in danger, Earl Rivers cast in his lot with the popular party, and in 1682, when the Duke of Monmouth made a progress through Cheshire to aid the cause of the exclusionists, Earl Rivers and his eldest son, Lord Colchester, though they were not implicated in any of the rival plots which were the spawn of those unquiet times, joined the duke and received him as a guest at Rock Savage, which had now been repaired and restored. For taking part in this proceeding, Lord Colchester was presented by the grand jury at Chester Assizes on the 17th September 1683, and ordered to find sureties of the peace.[1]

In June 1684, when, at the instance of the Duke of York, an order was given by the Secretary of State to the Lord Lieutenants to seize all guns and muskets that might be found in the possession of persons not qualified by law to hold them, we may be sure that the order was rigidly carried out at Halton and Rock Savage, where the Duke of York was known not to be in favour. But this inquisition discouraged neither Earl Rivers nor Lord Colchester, and accordingly, in the year 1688, when the Prince of Orange arrived in Exeter, Lord Colchester, then a lieutenant in Lord Dover's troop of guards, was the first nobleman who waited on him with an offer of his service.[2]

An old statute, made so long ago as the 56th year of Henry III. (1271), in order that bread and ale, two necessaries of life, might always be made and sold unadulterated, at a proper price and of a right quantity, regulated the price of these articles by the current price of corn and barley. This statute, which was called the assize of bread and ale, and which, so far as bread is concerned, had, until lately, its parallel in force in France, was jealously guarded by our ancestors. In France, the price of the loaf was regulated by a list published at stated times at the *mairie*, and something similar was also formerly in use in England, but here the trade in bread has been released from its fetters, and is left to be adjusted by the ordinary balance of demand and supply. At Halton, however, which seems to have been jealous of its name for good ale, the Halmote jury of the court, sitting on the 18th April 1692, presented six persons by name for breaking the assize of that article. The punishment by law for this offence was carting in the tumbrel, but it does not appear in the records whether any of the six offenders suffered the penalty they had incurred. But the jury were in a genial mood, and immediately afterwards proposed that, as they met but thrice a year to hear and redress grievances, it would promote brotherly love and good neighbourship if they at these courts always dined together, and they so resolved accordingly. After passing such a resolution they would be in no hurry to be severe with the offending

---

[1] Hist. Ches. pref.   [2] Macaulay's Hist. ii. 495.

brewers, who were, probably, dismissed with no other punishment than an admonition not to offend again.

About the year 1693 Earl Rivers sustained a severe loss in the death of his eldest son, Lord Colchester, a young nobleman who had given promise of great usefulness. Lord Colchester married Charlotte Maria, daughter of Charles, sixth Earl of Derby, by whom he left issue an only daughter. The next year Earl Rivers, whose own death was probably accelerated by grief for that of his son, died at the age of 67. He was buried in the family burial-place at Macclesfield, leaving behind him the character of a modest patriot, who, while he had welcomed the revolution of 1688, had mixed but little in public affairs, remembering the early misfortunes of his house in the cause of Charles I.

Upon the death of Thomas, Earl Rivers, in 1694, his eldest son, Lord Colchester, having died before him without male issue, the Rivers title and estates, including the family interest in the ancient castle of Halton, devolved upon Richard Viscount Savage, his second and now only surviving son, who thereupon became Earl Rivers. Although the Castle now no longer possessed its old importance, or was a fit place of residence for the family, the Savages had still their old home, Rock Savage, in the same neighbourhood, which they had now restored and made once more habitable, as formerly. About this time, or a little earlier, the family had reason to be proud of the commendatory notices they had received from the poets. The Marquis of Winchester, who had married Jane, the daughter of John, Earl Rivers (not Thomas, as Collins has it), was honoured with an epitaph by Dryden, while Jane herself had the still higher honour of a beautiful epitaph from the pen of Milton.[1] Richard, Earl Rivers, the new owner of Halton, following the example of his late brother, took an active part in public affairs, in the conduct of which, and in the military profession which he had adopted, he showed equal ability and skill. In 1692, when the present land tax was first imposed, and the amount to be paid by each township was fixed as it has ever since remained, the loyalty of the several townships to the new government, or the reverse, is said to have been measured by the liberality or the want of it, with which they assessed themselves for the new tax. At Halton, where Earl Rivers, a well-known favourer of King William, was the proprietor, the sum at which the township returned itself was likely enough to be liberal. In

[1] Collins' Peerage, ii. 380.

the year 1698, six years after the tax was first introduced, the halmote jury at Halton, still holding to the vestiges of their ancient traditionary power, taking upon them the part of assessors, divided and distributed the amount of the assessment among the several inhabitants. They chose to do this by the *mise*, an old mode of rating which was peculiar to the county of Chester, and by which all local rates were at that time collected, and in a copy of the Halton mise for 1700, still preserved in the court-books, the amount of each person's quota at that day is given with his name at full length.

At another Halmote, held at Halton on 20th August 1703, we find the jury again legislating, and this time their subject was the village causeways. These causeways, pavements about three or four feet wide, some of which still remain in remote places, were originally laid out when the general traffic of the country was carried on by means of pack horses, and were the ancestry of our present paved cartways, those rough roads which Miss Berry, when travelling in this neighbourhood at the beginning of this century, so appropriately called *chemins ferrés*. At this period these, the only paved roads at that time, were vigilantly watched at Halton, where a law was enacted by its little local parliament that every person who should drive any waggon or cart upon any of the town's causeways should be fined 3s. 4d., one-third to be paid to the informer, and the remainder to the surveyors of highways, who were directed to sue all offenders at the town's cost.

On the 3d December 1705, when the Duke of Argyle,

> Argyle, the state's whole thunder born to wield,
> And shake alike the senate and the field,

was raised to the rank of an English peer by the title of Earl of Sundridge, the office of introducing him by his new title to the House of Lords was assigned to Earl Rivers.[1] Argyle, who has had the good fortune to be celebrated as a statesman and warrior by two poets, appears to advantage as a man in Scott's "Heart of Mid Lothian."

In the year 1707, when the nation determined to support the claims of the House of Austria to the Crown of Spain, in opposition to the house of Bourbon, and an army of 13,500 men was despatched to Spain, the queen appointed Earl Rivers to command it. The earl sailed with the forces, and safely disembarked them at Alicant about the 8th February,

---

[1] Collins' Peerage, vii. 445.

but there being some conflict between his commission and that of Lord Galway as to which of them was to command in chief, the two generals came to a timely agreement, and in order to prevent detriment to the service, Earl Rivers generously yielded up the chief command to Lord Galway, and soon afterwards returned to England. By this timely concession Earl Rivers escaped the discredit of being present in the disastrous battle and defeat which the allies sustained shortly afterwards at Almanza.[1]

In 1709, Earl Rivers, who stood high in the royal favour, was sworn of the Privy Council, and in the following year the queen sent him as her minister and plenipotentiary to Hanover, with instructions to satisfy that court that the Protestant succession was of all things the object which the Court of England had most at heart—a task which, in the face of the hundred addresses presented against it, all of which had been most graciously received, was one of considerable difficulty, requiring great adroitness and skill.[2]

On 1st January 1712, Earl Rivers was appointed Master-General of the Ordnance, an office for which he was eminently qualified, and he brought to its discharge the large amount of skill and experience, which he had acquired by his long service.

[1] Oldmixon's Hist. Eng. iii. 389.   [2] Ibid. 455, and Smollett's Hist. x. 54.

CHAPTER XX.

CONCLUSION.

In the 43 Elizabeth (1601) there was passed the memorable Act for the relief of the poor, by which all such persons were entitled to needful relief wherever they were living, and no one but the rogue or vagrant was liable to be removed to his domicile. In the 14 Car. II. (1662), however, another statute altered the humane provisions of this law, and gave the overseers of the township power to remove any person who might ask relief from the place of his actual residence to his place of settlement, which last he might derive in many ways, some of which were—1, birth; 2, parentage; 3, marriage; 4, hiring and service; 5, apprenticeship; 6, renting a tenement; 7, holding an office; 8, owning an estate; or 9, paying parish rates.

This statute, by giving the overseers of every township an interest not in affording but in withholding relief to the poor, and authorising them instead to remove every applicant for relief to his place of settlement, not only gave an invitation to selfishness, but interfered with the free exercise of industry, put fetters upon labour, and opened a wide field of strife and litigation.

In 1714, the time at which we are now arrived, the new statute having been more than fifty years in operation, had had ample time to produce its evil fruits; the dragon's teeth had been sown, and the crop was ripe. In construing and administering the poor law, where above everything simplicity should have been aimed at, in order that common sense might prevail, the judges, in deciding such questions, became more than usually astute, and the result was a complex system which led to the expenditure in litigation of vast sums of money which should properly have gone to maintain the poor. In some years more than £100,000 a year of this money was thus spent.

On so serious a subject there was little opportunity for a joke or any indulgence in humour, but on one occasion a reverend judge on the bench repeated the decision of the court in verse. The question was, whether a woman who had a settlement had lost it by marrying a man without one, and this is the record of the case and the decision :—

> A woman having a settlement,
> Married a man with none ;
> The question was, he being dead,
> If that she had was gone ?
>
> Quoth Justice Pratt, "The settlement
> Suspended doth remain,
> Living the husband, but him dead,
> It doth revive again !"

This short notice of the poor law will serve to introduce an entry on the subject which we meet with at this time in the records of the little legislature at Halton. The statute of Charles II. had enacted that any person coming to settle upon a tenement under the value of £10 a year might be removed to the place where he was last legally settled, and an entry of the Halmote Court shows that if the jury were vigilant they heeded little whether their orders were or were not *extra vires*. This is the entry:—"April 26, 1714. No person in Halton shall let any person belonging to another town any house under the value of £10 per annum the person not bringing a certificate before he enters on the premises, the burgess offending to forfeit £5 for every offence."

This order, which was tantamount to a prohibition against any stranger taking a house in Halton at a less rent than £10 a year, then a much more considerable sum than now, was sufficient to exclude others beside paupers, and its harshness requires no comment.

Richard, Earl Rivers, was the father, and Anne, Countess of Macclesfield, was the mother of Savage the poet. Savage was born on 10th January 1698, and soon afterwards the Countess, by Act of Parliament, was divorced from her husband, the Earl of Macclesfield, and married to Colonel Brett. Earl Rivers, who was anxious to make the best reparation in his power by acknowledging his base son as his own, became his sponsor at the font, and called him Richard Savage, after himself. A few years afterwards, while the son was still young, the earl, lying on his death-bed, and, being minded so far as he could to make him further reparation for the injustice of his birth, sent anxiously to the Countess of Macclesfield to find him, and when he was falsely assured by her that he was dead, he left to another person the legacy of £6000 which he intended for him, and thus the mother robbed her child of what might have made him independent. But this was only one of the many acts of cruelty she inflicted on him at a time when he was too young to have done anything to deserve such treatment. Justly, therefore, in his poem addressed to her in after life did the poet complain—

> "No mother's care
> Shielded my infant innocence with prayer."

The fate of Savage was indeed hard. "Born," says his biographer, "with a legal claim to honour and affluence, he was in two months (by an *ex post facto* law) illegitimated by Parliament, and disowned by his mother, doomed to poverty and obscurity, and launched upon the ocean of life only that he might be swallowed by its quicksands or dashed upon its rocks."[1]

In 1714 (or, according to Dr. Johnson's account, in 1712) the Earl's busy career drew to a close, and on the 14th December in that year he breathed his last. He had married Penelope, the daughter of Roger Downes of Wardley, in the county of Lancaster, Esquire, by whom he had an only daughter and no male issue. Upon the Earl's death, the title for a short time rested in his cousin, John Savage, a Roman Catholic priest, who died without issue, when the direct male line of the Savages, which had flourished for so many generations in great splendour, first at Clifton and afterwards at Rock Savage and Halton, expired and went out.

John Savage, to whom the title had descended on the death of his cousin the late earl, Earl Rivers, acting under a deep sense of the obligations of his sacred calling, for which we must honour him, or leaning secretly to the fortunes of his fallen master James II., and too honest to yield a divided allegiance to the new government, declined to take the title which belonged to him, preferring to remain in a private station, and when he died without issue, in 1728, the title of Earl Rivers became extinct. In the meantime Halton Castle, Rock Savage, and the rest of the large estates of the family, passed to, and were enjoyed by, Earl Richard's daughter, and only child, Elizabeth, Countess of Barrymore, wife of James, fourth earl of that name.

While Lord and Lady Barrymore inhabited Rock Savage that fine old house saw some of its palmiest days. They repaired and enlarged the

---

[1] Johnson's Life of Savage.

house, added to it large stables and outhouses, and kept up the family honour with its accustomed hospitality, and more than its usual splendour. The countess, however, did not long survive her acquisition of the estate, for though she outlived John Savage, she died before the earl, her husband, leaving to succeed her an only child, the Hon. Penelope Barry, who, about the year 1730, married the Hon. James Cholmondeley, second son of George, second Earl of Cholmondeley, then a major in the army. In 1731 her husband became a lieutenant-colonel. Having seen much service in the interval, he served in the campaign in Flanders in 1744, and the next year he served and distinguished himself at the battle of Fontenoy. Upon the news of the Pretender's victory at Prestonpans, Colonel Cholmondeley, now become a brigadier, was despatched in command of two regiments to Scotland, where he greatly signalised himself at the battle of Falkirk, when he and General Huske are said to have saved the fortunes of the day.[1]

The Halmote Court, who were a sort of Vigilance Committee at Halton, for which they deserve praise, in the year 1721 very properly directed their attention to a matter quite within their province. There were in the village, as formerly in most other country places, large undivided fields which were common to all the farmers of the township, and which therefore could only be employed profitably by the observance of some general rules. This year the court employed themselves in drawing up the necessary rules as to the time and manner in which these fields should be enjoyed.

In 1732 the old appetite for interfering in the question of parish settlements again took possession of the Halmote. On the former occasion they passed a law to prevent persons from coming into the township; their aim now was to exile an inhabitant from it, and this entry shows the plan they took to do it:—

"Aug. 12, 1732.—I acknowledge to have received from Christopher Meesom, one of the overseers of Halton, by order of the inhabitants of the said township, the sum of £3, in consideration whereof I promise to repay the said sum of £3 to the overseers for the time being, if at any time hereafter I come to settle in the said township of Halton, or put the said township, or any of the inhabitants, to any further expense, or cost, or charges.—In witness whereof, I have hereunto set my hand, the day and year above written. Humphry Lowis, his X mark.—Witness, Richard Wicksted."

---

[1] Collins' Peerage, iv. 32; and Aytoun's Lays of the Cavaliers, 196.

At this period Halton derived reflective honour from one of her sons, who having been born almost under the shadow of the old castle, achieved distinction and became a benefactor of his native place.

John Chesshyre, the second son of Thomas Chesshyre, was born in 1661 at Hallwood, the house which his father had built. After the usual education at school and the university, he entered himself at one of the inns of court, and in Hilary Term, 2 William and, Mary, 1689, was called to the bar. In a copy of Cardanus Rider's British Merlin, of 1688, a very popular almanac of that time, which Mr. Chesshyre used, he has entered among other particulars the fact of his call. Almost the earliest entry in this book records that he had attended four moots (it is presumed before he was called), and that he had spent upon them and the incidental expenses two guineas.

But what, it may be asked, were these moots, the very name of which is now almost forgotten? They were a kind of practice or exercise in which students for the bar engaged before the benchers of their inn, when difficult points of law were debated and discussed in order to make the students more proficient in their profession. As these moots are now obsolete, the following curious account may be given of them from Dugdale:—

"Immediately after supper," he says, "which then took place in the inn or hall at six o'clock, the benchers assembled in the bay window at the upper end of the hall, where, standing in order according to their antiquity, there repair unto them two gentlemen under the bar, whose turn it is to recite the pleadings, who, after a low obeisance, demand whether it be their pleasure to hear a moot, and depart with an affirmative answer. All parties being ready, the two benchers appointed to argue, together with the reader elect, take their places at the bench table, the ancient bencher sitting in the midst, the second on his right hand, and the reader elect on his left. Then the mootmen also take their place, sitting on a form close to the cupboard, and opposite to the benchers; on the one side of them sits one of the students that recites the pleadings, and the other on the other side. The pleadings are first recited by the students, then the case is put, and argued by the barristers (mootmen), and lastly by the reader elect and benchers in manner aforesaid, who all three argue in English; but the pleadings are recited, and the case argued by the other barristers (mootmen), in law French. The moot being ended, all parties return to the cupboard, where the mootmen present the benchers with a cup of beer and a slice of bread; and so the exercise for that night is ended."[1]

There is much doubt amongst our legal antiquaries as to the exact time when these moots, as a means of legal education, were discontinued, but Mr. Chesshyre's entry seems to show that they were then a substantial thing. Part of his two guineas probably went to pay for the bread and beer presented to the benchers.

[1] Jeaffreson, about Law and Lawyers, ii. 178.

In his first term Mr. Chesshyre's whole receipts are put down as amounting only to £7, a very small return for his long training and the expense of his education: Let no young man who embraces a profession, however, despair, "for by patience and perseverance the mulberry leaf becomes satin," as an Arabic proverb has it, and Mr. Chesshyre persevered, and in the end reaped his reward.

In Trinity term—4 Anne, 1705—he was called to the degree of the Coif, which conferred the right to wear that round patch on the crown of a barrister's wig, which is the diminished effigy of the judge's black cap. On attaining this rank he gave the usual rings which marked the ceremony by which a serjeant is wedded to the law. But he distinguished the occasion in a manner more beneficial to Halton, by giving the chapel an augmentation of £200, which he afterwards increased to £600, towards the increase of the minister's stipend.

In 1714 he was made the king's serjeant, and being thereupon knighted, became Sir John Chessbyre.

In 1718 he went the northern circuit, and attended the York Lent Assizes, where his clerk's fees on each brief were 1s. 6d. The great rise in the scale of payment for this service—at least 40 per cent—shows the difference between the value of money then and now.

Success now flowed fast upon Sir John, and from 1719 to 1725 his fee book shows that he received year by year nearly £3250, a very large income for any man to make at the bar at that time, and which shows the great extent of his practice.

At this time, at the request of the benchers of his inn, he had his portrait painted, and a memorandum in his diary mentions that 30 guineas were paid for it to Sir Godfrey Kneller, with £4 paid for the frame and £1 as a gratuity to Sir Godfrey's servant. Portraits had risen since Cromwell's time, when Lely, afterwards Sir Peter, painted the Protector's likeness, and received 20 guineas for it.

When Sir John was 63, and in the full career of his success, he determined, with commendable moderation, to contract his business and to confine himself exclusively to the Court of Common Pleas, leaving the rest of the forensic arena to younger men. The effect of this self-denial was to reduce his income to the more moderate sum of £1320 a year.

He must have been in great favour with royalty and the great, for his book is a constant record of his presents of venison, and of the vails

T

to the bringers. A buck, with shoulders and umbles (those umbles, the inwards of the deer, which give name to *humble* pie), comes from the king, and the bearer is rewarded with a guinea and a half, while for half a buck each from Sir Robert Walpole and the Duchess of Marlboro', the messenger is rewarded with half-a-guinea.

His house was furnished with that now antiquated piece of music, a spinet, and he paid half-a-crown for tuning it.

Sir John, whose grateful feeling for his native village had been shown more than once on previous occasions, was shown still further in the year 1733 by a new and graceful act, when he erected there, at his own expense, a building for a public library, and furnished it with several hundred volumes of standard books, amongst which were a valuable edition of Rymer's Fœdera, an original edition of Dugdale's Monasticon, Walton's Polyglot, with very many works of the old divines. The whole was dedicated to the public, and placed under the care of the curate of Halton for the time being. To Sir John's sagacious forethought, and his care for learning, belongs the honour of being among the first to found a free library in a country village. Sir John's foundation still remains, and above the entrance is this inscription :—

HANC BIBLIOTHECAM,
Pro communi literatorum usu
Sub curâ curati capellæ de Halton
Proventibus ter feliciter augmentatæ
JOHANNES CHESSHYRE MILES,
D.D.D.
ANNO MDCCXXXIII.

But Sir John's earthly career was now drawing to a close, and on the 15th May 1738 we have the following announcement of his death :— "Sir John Chesshyre, Knight, Serjeant-at-Law, and the King's Prime Serjeant, died suddenly this day as he was getting into his coach. He was aged 77."[1]

His memory is honoured with this monument in the church at Runcorn :

IN MEMORY
OF SIR JOHN CHESSHYRE,
Who Departed this Life
On the xvth May,
MDCCXXXVIII.
" A wit's a feather and a chief's a rod,
An honest man's the noblest work of God."

---

[1] Gent. Mag. 1738.

The addition of the two lines from Pope were surely intended by the epitaphist as a protest against the vulgar belief that a lawyer cannot be honest.

After a long interval, in which no mention has occurred either of the seneschals, stewards, or other officials, or of the castle prison at Halton, a record of all of them appeared on the walls of the Court-house in 1737, where the old officers, with a change of name, are found in very good company, but their offices had declined in honour since the old times, or Sir John Chesshyre's name would have found its place amongst them as seneschal. This is the inscription :—

"7th Dec. 1737.

"At a court of revenue held for the duchy of Lancaster, before the Right Hon. George, Earl of Cholmondeley, chancellor of the councell of the same court, it was ordered by them that £500 be forthwith raised and paid for the rebuilding of this court-house, gaol, and court-yard.

"Commissioners to survey the same :—L. S. Cotton, J. Lee, H. Legh, R. Leicester, P. Davenport, and W. Tongue, Esqs.

"The Honorable James Cholmondeley lord of this manor.

"T. Pickering, Esq., steward; W. Middlehurst, deputy; H. Sephton, J. Orme, undertakers."

In 1743 an order was made by the Halmote prohibiting any person from gathering boulders between the Hempstones—a place afterwards famous in the Bridgewater Acts as one of those places where the canal was to end—and Linnish-pool-rails. The object of the law was, perhaps, to prevent or stay the encroachments of the river at that place ; and any person infringing this law was to pay a sum of £1 : 6 : 8.

In 1747 the dangerous spectre of parish settlements again rose up before the mind of the court, for they then ordered that no person should mow gorse upon the common to make ashes to sell, but that the same should be for the use of the inhabitants to heat their ovens and furnaces with, and it was added that *no certificate person* was to get any; offenders to be prosecuted.

The certificated person thus tabooed was a man residing in the township as it were on sufferance, under a certificate from some other township owning him to be settled elsewhere, and this man was not to have the privileges of the other inhabitants.

But there was a divine as well as a lawyer who flourished in the neighbourhood about this time—the Rev. John Free, D.D., who was presented by the Dean and Chapter of Christ Church, Oxford, to the vicarage of Runcorn, on the 22d February 1740, at which time he was pro-proctor of the university. The new vicar coming to Runcorn was apparently well satisfied with the place, and he recorded his satisfaction in this Latin verse on a rock at the top of the Beacon hill—

> Tusculum hic esset placidumque Tibur
> Hic mihi cuperem senectæ
> Hic modum lasso strepitu scholarum
> Militiæque.[1]
>
> J. FREE,
> Æd. Christ. Oxon., A.M.,
> Academ. Pro Proc.
> v. v.

The "militiæque" at the end was a metaphor, probably a covert allusion to the tithe suit in which he found the parish engaged; but every one standing on the commanding spot where the vicar stood, and looking from thence on the broad Mersey and its bounding shores, with the distant prospect of the hills beyond them, would have joined in his satisfaction.

While he was at Runcorn Dr. Free wrote and published, in 1749, "An Essay towards a History of the English Tongue."

In 1756 he was presented to the living of East Coker, in Somersetshire, a poor living, and his resigning Runcorn for it shows either that the latter was still poorer, or that the tithe suit had wearied him. The endowment of Runcorn, which is small now, was still smaller then.

---

[1] Another copy of the inscription, made fifty years ago, when the inscription was more perfect, is here given with the unknown copyist's paraphrase:—

> TVSCVLVM HIC MIHI
> PLACIDVM ESSET
> TIBVRQ. HIC SEDEM
> VTINAM SENECTÆ
> HIC MODVM LASSO
> STREPITV SCHOLARVM
> MILITLÆQ.
>   J. FREE.
>
> Could on this beauteous hill be placed
>   Such halls as those which Tully graced
> In Rome's all glorious days;
>   Halls, such as echoed to the spell,
>   Which from the lips of Horace fell
> In most harmonious lays.
> When time had silvered o'er my hair,
>   Wearied with toil, oppressed with care,
> Here would I wish a place of rest;
>   Where sophists' wildering lore
>   Should perplex my brain no more,
> Nor thoughts of war again molest.

In 1756 he published a volume of poems on various occasions, from which the following, from a parish clerk to his absentee rector, is extracted, as a specimen of the Dorsetshire dialect :—

> Measter, an't please you, I do zend
> Theaz letter to you as a vriend,
> Hoping you'll pardon the inditing,
> Becaz I am not us'd to writing,
> And that you will not take unklud
> A word or so from poor George Hind,
> For I am always in the way,
> And needs must hear what people say.
> First of the house they make a joke,
> And zay the chimneys never smoak.
> Now, the occasion of these jests,
> As I do think, were swallows' nests,
> That chanc'd the other day to vall,
> Into the parlour, zut & all.
> Bezide the people, not a few,
> Begin to murmur much at you,
> For leaving of them in the lurch,
> And letting strangers zerve the church,
> Who are in haste to go agen,
> Zo we han't zang the Lord knows when.
> And for their preaching, I do know
> As well as most, 'tis but zo, zo.
> Zure if the call you had were right,
> You ne'er could thus your neighbours slight.
> But I do fear you've zet your aim on,
> Nought in the world but filthy mammon.

In 1766 the Doctor again appeared in print, and published an original scheme for founding a university and a universal liturgy.[1]

In 1768 he preached and published a sermon on the death of William Allen, who was killed in one of the Wilkes riots. Allen was one of several innocent persons who were killed by the firing of the military when the mob assembled in St. George's Fields to see their hero, Mr. Wilkes, in the King's Bench prison.[2] And in the same year the author was chosen lecturer of Newington, Surrey.

In 1788 he completed his Essay towards a History of the English tongue, of which a fourth edition then came out, to which was added a catalogue of all his very numerous literary productions, and in the May of that year he addressed a long letter to Dr. Moore, the Archbishop of

[1] Monthly Review, vol. xxxv. 472.   [2] Notes and Queries, ii. 333.

Canterbury, pleading for some preferment in consequence of his long services in the church. The archbishop listened to the plea of the old divine, who was now 77, and gave him some preferment. He did not long survive it, however, for he died at his chambers, in Lyon's Inn, on the 9th September 1791, with the character of a well-read and learned divine.[1] That his taste was not always grave, but sometimes relaxed into humour, his letter of the parish clerk sufficiently shows. The volume from which it is taken contains poems in many languages, and amongst the rest in Hebrew, Greek, and Latin.

General Cholmondeley died at Rock Savage on the 13th October 1775 and his wife, the owner of Rock Savage, survived until 1786, and then died at the same place, leaving her great estates to her husband's nephew, George James, Earl and afterwards Marquis of Cholmondeley. After her death, Rock Savage being deserted fell to ruin, and so rapid was its decay that a gentleman who was born in the house lived to follow a pack of hounds through its ruins in pursuit of a fox, and of it Dyer's words might be repeated—

> 'Tis now the raven's bleak abode,
> 'Tis now the apartment of the toad;
> And there the fox securely feeds,
> Concealed in ruins, moss, and weeds,
> While ever and anon there falls
> Huge heaps of hoary, moulder'd walls.

The Castle at Halton necessarily suffered somewhat from the desertion of Rock Savage and the withdrawal of its noble proprietors from the neighbourhood; but though over its walls the ivy now waves instead of the banners of Fitz Nigel, Lacy, or Plantagenet, the old ruined fortress has associations which Rock Savage has not, and its story may be fitly concluded with the reflections of an American traveller :—" To see every day the walls on which our forefathers, ages ago, patrolled in armour, or from which they aimed the crossbow, to walk and study and repose habitually under their shadow, to have always, in sport and in toil, in sorrow and in joy, such monuments of time and history about one; how ought it not to refine and mature the character, and make a man feel his place between two eternities, and inspire him to live well the short and evil day which, if ever, what he does for futurity must be done quickly and with might."[2]

[1] Gentleman's Mag. 1788, 1791   [2] Coxe's Sketches of England.

NORTON Priory, or Abbey, reduced from the Engraving of S & N. Buck. A.D. 1727.

PART II.

What other yearning was the master tie
Of the monastic brotherhood—on rock
Aerial, or in green secluded vale,
One after one collected from afar,
An undissolving fellowship? What but this
The universal instinct for repose ;
The longing for confirmed tranquillity
Inward and outward, humble yet sublime.

NORTON

CHAPTER I.

HAS ÆDES SACRAS PIETAS CONSTRUXIT AVORUM.

OF this religious house the history still remains to be written, for the meagre notices to be found of it in the works of Dugdale and Tanner are scarcely deserving of the name; besides which much that we now know of it was unknown to them, having only been brought to light by inquiries made since their time.

There were several other houses besides this at places of the same name in different parts of England, which seems to show that the *villare* of the names of places in England, like the Christian names of women, is but limited in number. One of these houses was at Norton, by Stockton, in the county of Durham, another at Norton-super-Cors, in Norfolk, a third at Cold Norton, in Essex, and a fourth at Norton, by Malton, in Yorkshire, and, which is not a little singular, all these houses, except the last, were of the same religious order as the Cheshire house of Norton. It is to be hoped, however, that their historian was better informed as to their history and geography than the historian of the Cheshire house who, although a native of the county, informs us that it was founded in 1210, instead of more than half-a-century earlier, and that it was situated in Wirrall, opposite Liverpool, from both of which places it was many miles apart; but, after all, he possibly mistook Birkenhead for Norton. The brethren of the house of Norton were canons regular of the order of St. Augustine, and wore a white tunic with a linen gown under a black cloak, and a hood which covered the neck and shoulders, while they wore on the head a five-pointed cap. Their white tunic led to their being called White Monks, to distinguish them from the Black Monks, or Benedictines. Of this habit of the canons, which was picturesque and becoming, there is a description and a drawing in Fosbroke's "British Monachism." Canons, as a sort of order in the Church intermediate between priests and monks, seculars and regulars, had been known long before the 11th century, but so much corruption had found its way among them that the zeal of Ivo, Bishop of Chartres, was roused by it to undertake its reform. A sermon of the good bishop's, probably one of those which sounded an alarm to the canons, was once in the possession of Sir John Fastolf, and was given by him to William of Waynflete, who deposited it in the library of Magdalen College, Oxford, where it now is. By his earnestness and energy many houses of canons were induced to renounce their worldly possessions and devote themselves to a life of mortification and self-denial, after the manner of the monastic orders, and as by their reformer's suggestion they professed to follow the rule of St. Augustine, they came from thence to be called canons regular of that saint's order.[1] Ivo's reformation proving to be real, and not merely seeming, the new order soon afterwards became deservedly popular. Their rule binding them to have all things in common, the rich at their entrance were obliged to sell their possessions and to distribute the proceeds to the poor. Without leave of the superior no brother was to receive anything, and if, by persecution or otherwise, the brethren became scattered, or were driven from their house, they were to repair as soon as possible to the same place to which their superior had withdrawn. The first part of every week-day was to be spent in manual labour, and the rest, which was not occupied in the church or in the offices of religion, was to be given to reading. Saturday was to be allowed to the brethren to provide themselves with necessaries, and on Sundays only they were to have a small allowance of wine. They were religiously to observe all days of fasting and abstinence; were to be read to at their meals from a pulpit in the refectory; and, like our Lord's first disciples, were always to go forth in pairs whenever they went abroad. They were never to eat out of the monastery, except in cases of absolute necessity; were to receive neither letters nor presents in secret, and to vow and observe the strictest chastity. These, with some general directions on modesty and some other of the Christian graces and virtues, constituted the rule of the order, which was to be read once a week in the chapter-house in the presence of all the

[1] Mosheim's Eccl. Hist. ii. 538.

brethren. Guyot de Provins, when he wrote his satirical work, says that Ivo de Chartres was more courteous in his rule than Benedict, for he made it a part of it that the canons should be well shod, well clad, and well fed; that they should go out when they liked, mix with the world, and talk at table.¹ The satirist, when he thus wrote, might have had in view the humour of his brother satirist, who said of the men of All Souls, at Oxford, that they were all to be "bene nati, bene vestiti, et mediocriter docti." Before the year 1100, when Henry I. ascended the throne, the new order had attained such popularity that Edelwald, his confessor, afterwards Bishop of Carlisle, using wisely and well his influence with his master, induced him to found a priory of these canons at Nostell, in Yorkshire, which is believed to have been the first house of the order in England, though Tanner, who agrees that this was their first house, thinks that it was founded by Ilbert de Lacy in the time of William Rufus.² It is clear, however, that the foundation dates from about the year 1100, for Maude, King Henry's queen, following, it is said, her husband's example, in the year 1108 erected for the new order her priory of the Holy Trinity in London, in which, strangely attempting to combine a religious with the secular character, she ordained that the prior should always be one of the 24 aldermen of the city. The example which the king and queen had thus set was soon followed by other patrons, and the houses of canons regular of the order of St. Augustine increased so fast that before the reign of Edward I. there were no less than 53 such houses in the kingdom, where, while the poor were relieved, the ignorant instructed, and divine offices, celebrated, special provision was made for instructing the young. Morery is mistaken in claiming Erasmus as a canon regular of the order of St. Augustine, and, speaking of these canons as a body, Montalembert says they neither gained distinction nor rendered eminent services, but that they had attached to them the illustrious order of Prémontré, and the equally illustrious order of La Merci, which was established for the redemption of captives.³ The priory of canons regular of this order at Norton was placed at first by its founder, William fitz Nigel, the second baron of Halton, at Runcorn, on the river Mersey, the place where Elfleda, the daughter of the immortal Alfred, had built a castle, to check the piratical inroads of the Danes up the river. "In the year 913," says the Saxon

---

¹ Fosbroke's Brit. Monachism, 65. ² Tanner's Notitia Mon. 654.
³ Monks of the West, i. 14, n.

chronicle, "Ethelfleda, with all the Mercians, went to Tamworth and built the fort there in the fore part of the summer and before Lammas that at Stafford. The next year (914) that at Edisbury, in the beginning of the summer, and the same year, late in the autumn, that at Warwick. Then in the following year (915) was built, after mid winter, that at Cyricbyrig, and that at Weardbyrig, and the same year, before mid winter, that at *Rumcofan*."[1] Henry of Huntington calls the place Rumcoven,[2] and in an old inscription in Saxon characters in Leominster church it is called Runcofan;[3] but in the king's books, at a later period, it is called Ronchestorn. All these names probably had their origin in the word Roncaria, Runcaria, or Roncorn, which means a place overrun with brambles or briars,[4] and is itself derived from the Latin *runcare*. If this be a true etymology, it might be said of Runcorn in its origin, as it was said of Troy in its ruin—

"tota teguntur
Pergama dumetis."

As a vill, Runcorn, which now contains only 600 acres, at the Conquest probably did not contain more than 700 acres, which is an unusually small area for a Cheshire township; and this circumstance, notwithstanding the early Saxon importance of the place, may have led to its being overlooked by the compilers of the Domesday Survey, who have passed by it without a name, probably considering it part of Halton, with which its boundaries are strangely intermixed.

The charter by which William fitz Nigel first founded the house has not come down to our times, and our only knowledge of it is derived from the short notice of it which is contained in Henry II.'s charter confirming William fitz William's removal of the priory from Runcorn to Norton. From the mention there made of it, Runcorn church and seven carucates of land, which were probably the small carucates of one hundred acres each, comprising the then vill of Runcorn, constituted the whole of the original endowment.

We do not know, and are therefore left to conjecture, from what parent house the founder drew the first inmates of his priory. If, however, the canons of Nostell, the first English house of the order, who then owned the neighbouring church of Winwick, were possessed with the proper

---

[1] Ingram's Angl. Saxon Chron. 130. [2] Monumenta Britannica, 744.
[3] Weever's Funeral Monuments, Addenda, 583.
[4] Sir Ed. Coke's First Inst. fo. 5a; Ducange s. v. Runcalio.

missionary spirit, it is likely enough that they would send the new priory its first supply of canons, and, once arrived at their Runcorn home, they would proceed to elect their prior and take their respective places under him.

RICHARD, on whom their choice fell (for that is all we know of the name or family of the first prior), as soon as his election had been made and confirmed by the bishop, undertook the rule of his new family, and proceeded to set it in order. He appointed his subprior and his other officers, installed his canons in the church at Runcorn, which was dedicated to St. Bartholomew, and made provision for the daily performance of divine service there. The church, which was probably but a humble Saxon structure of wood, such as we see in the church of Greensted in Essex, has long since passed away, and left no traces of its architecture behind it. Several churches have occupied the same site since, and of one of these a view may be seen in Troughton's History of Liverpool, and of this or of some other church which had stood on the same site, a few fragments, which may serve to show the style of its architecture, were discovered when the present Runcorn church was built in 1856.

Runcorn had long been reclaimed from its state of wildness and neglect, the briars and underwood which gave it its name had been uprooted, piratical inroads upon it were at an end, and the resort to it of ships, with its fishery and its ferry, had now made it a little port. It is believed also to have attained to the dignity of having a mint, for there are some Saxon coins which have on the obverse, "Eadred Rex," and on the reverse, "Othbrim on Ring," which Camden, who gives a print of them, thinks may probably have been coined at Runcorn, or, as he says, Ringhornan, which by mistake he tells us is in Lancashire.[1] And in Mr. Thoresby's Catalogue of Saxon Coins there is one (No. 102) which has on the reverse the inscription, "Leodmer on Rinc," which he conjectures to have been also coined at Runcorn about the year 1017. If these coins were really from a Runcorn mint, the credit of establishing it must be ascribed to Elfleda.

But though the prior and his canons had found God's house, the church at Runcorn, ready prepared for them, they had scarcely had time to select even a site for their own, before William fitz Nigel, their friend, patron, and founder, died. Even before his death, however, which must have occurred in or about 1135, they had begun to sigh for larger bounds and

[1] Camden's Britannia, Gibson's edit. 1695, p. 143.

a quieter place of retreat, more suited to meditation and undisturbed devotion; and, no sooner had William fitz William, the baron of Halton, succeeded his father, than, their wishes having been whispered in his ear, he took counsel with Roger de Clinton, who was bishop of Chester from 1129 to 1149, and with Roger Gernons, his palatine suzerain, who reigned from 1128 to 1153, and then determined, out of a pious regard for his father's soul, which in that age was held to be assoiled by such services, to remove the canons from Runcorn, and to place them at Norton, beneath the shadow of the strong castle which had been lately built at Halton. At Norton there were great woods waiting to be cleared, which might profitably employ some part of the time which every day the canons by their rule were bound to spend in manual labour. In reducing the surrounding country to cultivation, he thought perhaps that they might help to humanise the manners of the neighbouring serfs and rustics, and by serving as his chaplains might at the same time reduce under better rule and order his rude soldiery and retainers at the castle.

Taste had hardly dawned upon lay eyes in that age, but in his estimate of the canons their patron no doubt found that he had neither misjudged them nor their qualifications. In one of the old chroniclers we read— "Norton prioratus fundatur per Willielm constabularium Cestrensem anno 1131."[1] And another, who has mistaken the name of the founder and given us the date of the removal instead of the foundation of the priory, writes as follows:—"Anno MCXXXV. monasterium de Norton in comitatu Cestriæ fundatur a Willielmo filio Nigelli constabulario Cestriæ."[2] The charter by which the removal to Norton was effected was as follows:—

"In the name of the Father, the Son, and the Holy Ghost.

"I, William, the son of William, the son of Nigel, do give and grant to the Holy Church of Mary of Norton, and to the canons regular serving God there, the vill of Norton in free alms, with all its appurtenances in wood, with forests and warren and in plain, with lands, pastures, and waters, and at the request and by the advice of Roger, Bishop of Chester, and by the advice of my own people I change the habitation of the said canons from Runcorn to Norton, which Norton I give and grant to the said canons in free alms and the exchange of three carucates in Stannings and one carucate and a half in Aston, in lieu of all Runcorn, except the church and four oxgangs of land and one fishery, which is called Pulcorpe, which belongs to the church of Runcorn, which church belongs to the aforesaid canons. Also I give and grant to them the mill of Halton, with a moiety of all the fisheries which belong to Halton; I also grant them and their tenants common in the woods, waters, and pastures which belong to Halton, and two oxgangs of land in Halton, with one dwelling there, and one moiety of my whole fishery of

---

[1] Harl. MS. 280, fo. 78.   [2] Hist. Aurea Joannis Tynemytensis, lib. xix. c. 41.

Thelwall, with one oxgang of land, and the fisherman there. Also, two oxgangs in Widnes, with common of the woods and pastures which belong to Pulton (probably Ap-pulton) for them and their tenants dwelling in Widnes. I also grant to them common of the woods and pastures of Cuerdley, and the mill of Barrow, and two parts of the demesne tithes of the same vill, and two parts of the demesne tithes of Sutton, and likewise in Stanney, and in Raby, and in Stanning, and one dwelling in Chester, and the church of (Great) Budworth, and the church of Dunnington (in Leicestershire), and the tithes of the mill of the same vill and of the parish itself, and Wavertoft, which is computed at half a carucate of land, and the church of Radcliffe (upon Soar, in Nottinghamshire), and the tithes of a fourth part of the mills, and the tithes of the remaining three parts of the same vill, and the church of Oneshall (in Nottinghamshire), and the tithe of the mills which belong to the same vill, which are near Sitella, and the tithe of the mill of Alretone and the church of Burtone in Lindsey (in Lincolnshire), and the church of Pirinton (in Oxfordshire). All these donations made by my people, or hereafter to be made, I grant for the health of their souls, and these things I have done on the suggestion, and with the confirmation, of Roger, Bishop of Chester, and with the consent of Earl Randle, the younger, for the health of Earl Hugh, Earl Richard, and Earl Randle, my own health and that of my wife, and for the health of the souls of my father and mother, my brothers and sisters, and all my ancestors and successors. And I grant these alms as free and discharged from all services and customs, pleas or plaints, as any alms can or ought to be granted. Whoso, therefore, shall augment or maintain this charitable foundation, may be, through the benefits of Holy Church, obtain the kingdom of heaven ; but whoso shall infringe or violate them in any respect, may he, unless he make restitution, be punished in hell with Judas and Pilate, Dathan and Abiram."

Witnesses—William (the chaplain), Roger de Angerville, Alfred fitz Humphrey, Nigel fitz Angot, Robert fitz Peter.[1]

No sooner did Prior Richard and his canons find themselves in possession of Norton, than, casting their eyes round,

> A shady grove not far away they spied,
> Whose lofty trees yclad with summer's pride
> Did spread so broad that heaven's light did hide,
> Not peaceable with power of any star.[2]

Having selected for the site of their house a sheltered and secluded valley, the prior and his canons set themselves vigorously to work to raise a fence round the priory, and form a close, within which their church, with the priory, its offices, and gardens, and perhaps a tank or stew for fish, should stand. For all these they found materials ready to their hands in the timber of the surrounding woods. The prior being their director, they laid the foundations of the chancel of their church, and built for themselves dwellings, which for the present they were content should be but a temporary abode of boards and shingles. Their next business was to clear some portion of the neighbouring woods, and convert it into a domain sufficient to support their few sheep and cattle, and perhaps raise a scanty

---

[1] Creswell's Runcorn, 41 ; Hist. Ches. i. p. 508.   [2] Fairy Queen.

crop of wheat, barley, oats, and peas. By their labours Norton soon assumed a park-like appearance, and in due time was converted into the beautiful and silvan place which it is and has now for so long time been.

Prior Richard had scarcely been installed in his new home and office before he was called upon to assert and defend the convent's rights against a powerful neighbour, who, in clearing his own boundary, was thought to have encroached upon theirs. But Adam de Dutton, the neighbour who was suspected to have thus acted, was just as well as great, and the prior being politic and not unreasonable, the dispute was accommodated without their having recourse to the law, a well-defined boundary was agreed to by Adam, and he was allowed to retain all the lands he had assarted within it, towards his demesne in Sutton.[1]

As there exists neither a drawing nor a description of the house at Norton as it came from the builder's hands, we are left to imagine what were its plan and elevation from the few particulars contained in the History of Cheshire, and from a comparison of the views given there and in the work published by the Messieurs Buck at the beginning of the last century, of Norton, Combermere, and the other religious houses in Cheshire, some of which have been republished in the History of Cheshire. These houses would appear to have had many features in common, and from the views given of them we may realise some idea of what was the original appearance of Norton. Each building had its foundations, its lower storey its corners and gables, and its one or more towers, built of stone, while the upper storey was constructed of timber and plaster. Each had its solars (sun chambers), rising up into the roof like small gables, while the face of the upper storey in each was decorated with a geometrical pattern in black and white, which gave a more domestic look to the building, and added to the picturesqueness of its outline. At Norton, as at Combermere, Vale Royal, and Stanlaw, the upper storey was approached by an external flight of steps, and at Norton and Combermere there are evident traces of cloisters.[2] There was, indeed, such a general similarity of outline and ground-plan in most of the religious houses in England that it is not difficult to conjecture what was the plan of Norton. We must suppose the gateway to have been under the tower which occupies the left of the view given in Buck's engraving, while a wall to form the close seems to have been carried across to the building at the opposite corner, where probably

[1] Arley Charters, Box I. No. 20.   [2] Hist. Ches. iii. 211.

the prior first, and afterwards the abbot, had his lodgings. The church and the chapter-house, standing to the east of the main building, were approached by a cloister which screened the church on the north, and served as a covered way by which the canons might pass to the church or the chapter-house when they were summoned to either place, either for prayers or other purposes, by night or by day. In the rear of the house, and having a stream running from them under the kitchen, were the tanks and fish-ponds so necessary to every monastery, where a fish diet was periodically enjoined, and which we know, from an incident which occurred when the royal visitors arrived there before the dissolution, existed near the house at Norton.

But though the house, with its refectory, its dormitory, its school, its infirmary, and its other offices, has passed away and left no trace behind them, though neither the canons nor any lively chronicler like Joscelin de Brakelond have left us any annals of Norton, the few fragments of their works in stone which still remain sufficiently attest their skill as artificers and builders, and prove them to have been men of taste. A beautiful doorway and some very fine vaultings which go back to the first foundation of the house, and than which nothing finer can be executed now, are still preserved in the present house. The semicircular arches of this doorway are enriched with elaborate foliage and other ornaments, and rest upon pillars with sculptured capitals, and the vaults originally consisted of groined arches springing from short octagonal columns with capitals.[1]

> They dreamt not of a perishable home,
> Who thus could build.

Prior Richard, who had shown his prudence by the way in which he had accommodated the dispute with Adam de Dutton without resorting to a lawsuit, and who well knew that gifts to a religious house were unsafe without the king's confirmation, again showed his prudence by applying to King Henry II. for a confirmation of the gifts which had been made to the house at Norton; and in or about the year 1155, a date which we are enabled to approximate from the charter being witnessed by Richard de Beaumis, Bishop of London from 1152 to 1163, who was one of the witnesses, he obtained the following grant of confirmation:—

"Henry, &c., King, &c., greeting. Know ye that I have granted, and by the present charter confirmed in perpetual alms to God and the canons of Norton, whatsoever has been

---

[1] Hist. Ches. i. 5.

duly given to them; videlicet the whole manor of Norton, with all its appurtenances, which William the younger, Constable of Chester, gave them in exchange for seven carucates of land (a carucate must here have meant a hundred acres, as it did in some other parts of England),[1] which the father of the same William had before given them in alms, and the church of Runcorn and the church of Budworth, with all their appurtenances; and the half of Barrow and the mill of Halton, and two oxgangs of land in Halton, with one dwelling and the half part of all the fisheries that belong to Halton, and common of woods and waters and pastures belonging to Halton, as well to the canons as to their tenants; and the half part of the whole fishery of Thelwall, with one oxgang of land, and with one fisherman, and two oxgangs of land which are called Widnes, with common of woods and pastures belonging to Appleton and Kuerdley, both to the canons and their tenants, and two parts of the demain tithes of Steinings, and two parts of the demain tithes of Barrow, and two parts of the demain tithes of the half part of Sutton, near Chester, and two parts of the demain tithes of Stanney, and of Rabey and of Sutton beyond the water of Mersey; and the Church of Radclive, with all its appurtenances, and the tithes of the mills of the same vill, and the tithes of the remaining three parts, and the Church of Cucshall, with all its appurtenances, and the tithes of the mills of the same vill, and the tithe of the mill of Alreton, and the Church of Dunington, with all its appurtenances, and the tithe of the mill of the same vill, and one carucate of demain land in the same town, and half a carucate of land near Dunington, which is called Wavertoft, and the Church of Burton in Lindsay, with all its appurtenances, and the Church of Pirinton, with all its appurtenances, and one dwelling in Chester; and in the same city two dwellings, which they themselves have bought, and the half part of the vill which is called Sutton, near Chester, with all its appurtenances, and the Monastery of St. Michael, in Chester, with one dwelling in the same city, with two oxgangs of land in Stanney, and the tithe of the mill of the same vill, and the mill of Waleton, and one parcel of land between Weston and Runcorn, which is called Gorst's Acre, and of the fee of Warren de Vernon two oxgangs of land in Surnalethe, and of the fee of the Bishop of Chester one plot of land without the gate of the city of Chester, and of the fee of Robert de Stafford one oxgang of land in Calvedon." Witnesses—F. Cantuar, " Archiepiscopo " Ric. London. Joceline Sarum, " episcopia " R., Earl of Cornwall, etc. Dated at Warengford.[2]

From the foundation of the priory until the palatine jurisdiction of the Norman Earls of Chester ceased, the Prior of Norton, as one of their spiritual peers, was an important personage. He occupied a seat in their local parliament, was styled the Lord Prior, appeared on many public occasions, and whenever a charter was to be witnessed, to him, if present, was assigned the place of precedence. Prior Richard continued in office until the year 1159, and it was in his time, as it would seem, that Hugh de Cathewick (probably Hugh de Kekwick) contracted to build a church at the priory to be dedicated to the Blessed Virgin. Like many a contractor since, Hugh proceeded with his work so very slowly, that Eustace fitz John (de Burgalia), the fourth baron of Halton, sharing the prior's anxiety to see the work finished, and in order to stimulate the con-

---

[1] Planché's Corner of Kent, p. 43 in notes.   [2] Greswell's Runcorn, 48.

Sepulchral Slabs — at Norton.

tractor to greater diligence, granted him pasturage for a hundred sheep, upon condition that he proceeded at once with the new church, and finished it in all respects according to William fitz Hugh's first foundation.¹ Though church work is proverbially "a cripple at going up," yet it is but reasonable to presume that after this stimulus to his diligence, the contractor for St. Mary's church at Norton would proceed rapidly with his work, and that the baron's eye might be gladdened by seeing it finished and consecrated before A.D. 1157, in which year his own eyes were closed. The church which the baron was thus instrumental in building stood a little to the east of the present mansion, at Norton, where, from the time of the dissolution of abbeys until quite recently, its site had lain buried under the greensward. Then, however, by reverent hands, it was unearthed and exposed to daylight, when a series of handsome sepulchral slabs, most of them doubtless the memorials of the former heads of the house of Norton, each lying *in situ*, were disclosed for the admiration of the reflecting spectator.²

¹ Tanner's Notitia Monastica, Nasmith's edition, *in notis*; and Hist. Ches. i. 504, *in notis*, and 508; and Kuerden's MS. Chet. Library, 274.

² In the garden at Norton there is an incised sepulchral slab, and a few other sculptured fragments which were dug up before 1856 towards the north-west corner of the house. This slab has a cross florée upon it.

CHAPTER II.

HENRY, the second prior of Norton, who succeeded to his office about the year 1159, having seen the priory church completed, was stimulated probably by that circumstance to provide an additional church for Daresbury, an outlying portion of the parish of Runcorn, in which divine ordinances might be ministered by the canons of Norton, and having there built and dedicated such a church to All Saints, he thought it prudent to seek a confirmation of the priory's title to it, and he accordingly obtained from Albert Grelley the younger, a son of that Albert who had married William fitz William's youngest sister, the following charter of confirmation :—

"Aubert Grelley to all men sends health and greeting. Know ye that I have granted and confirmed to the blessed Mary of Norton all the gifts within my fee, which William, the Constable of Chester, my grandfather, and William, my uncle, gave them in free alms—that is to say, the whole church in Piriton in Oxfordshire, and the chapel of Daresbury, in Cheshire, with all its appurtenances which belong to the church of Runcorn ; and this confirmation I have made to the aforesaid canons for the souls of my father and mother, and all my heirs."—Witnesses : Robert de Bury, William, son of Wulfric, and Richard, son of Henry.[1]

Few grants in that age were supposed to have inherent vigour enough not to require being confirmed from time to time, and such charters of confirmation were very often sought from persons who were either not at all or only remotely interested in the subject matter ; and here, notwithstanding the grant which the prior and convent had had from the great man, their founder, they sought and obtained the above confirmation from Albert Grelley, a collateral, who could have had little or no interest in the matter.

Daresbury—whose name, unique in the *villare* of England, probably came from some of the early possessors of the place—has not in later times had any great family of its name, though Hugh fitz Geoffrey de Deresbury, the homicide, whose lands at Scroby in Yorkshire, escheated to

[1] Sir P. Leycester, liber B. p. 202, No. 18. Hist. Ches. i. 539. Sir Peter says this charter was made in the reign of Henry II.

the Archbishop of York in 1235, may perhaps have been a descendant of some of its ancient possessors.[1] Until 1870, when it was taken down to be rebuilt, the church at Daresbury, after having succeeded more than one former structure since Prior Henry's, besides the usual admixture of styles contained a good deal of churchwarden's Gothic. Its north and south doorways, both of a good pointed character, had internally square trefoil heads of this form— 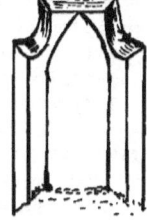 and the same construction was to be seen in some parts of the tower, though that as a whole was Perpendicular work, and not earlier than the time of Queen Elizabeth. The four-light west window of the south aisle had mullions running to the head, and was but very slightly pointed. The south window of three lights, immediately on the left of the porch, was good, though rather late Perpendicular work, and a window on the north side of the chancel and the great east window were of the same pattern. Outside the church, on the south wall, between the porch and the south chapel, was a stone with the base of a cross incised upon it, and near it were two other stones having portions of mouldings, evidently the remains of a former structure. The respond at the east end of the north aisle was semi-octagonal, with an Early English capital, and the chancel arch was acutely pointed and chamfered. The scraping of some of the walls showed the remains of black-letter inscriptions, and some ornamentation in colours, and on the chamfer of one of the arches there was a running pattern which seemed to be meant for vine leaves and fruit in red and yellow colours. The four pillars supporting the south arcade of the church had common Perpendicular caps, all of the same pattern. The first arch at the east end of the north arcade sprang from an Early English capital, with the usual stiff trefoil foliage, and under this capital the pillar was octagonal. The base of the fifth pillar was Early English. On the south side of the tower there was, and there is still, a stone on which, within a border, the date 1110 in figures of the middle of the seventeenth century has been cut. The probability is that the date was originally 1550, but the figures being in relief, and decayed, the workman who altered the date in the seventeenth century

[1] Archbishop Gray's Reg. p. 245.

mistook the fives, which were but slightly curved, and so made them tell a great falsehood, and antedate the steeple several centuries.

Round the east end of the church there was some very beautiful wood carving of the Decorated period.

Under the church were found two sepulchral crosses, one of which was of the twelfth century, some tiles, and many fragments of stained glass. The tiles were of early pattern, and if, as a late writer says, we owe to the Normans the early use of tiles in our churches, some of which have the figure of a Norman arch upon them, these Daresbury tiles may have belonged to Prior Henry's church.

The fragments of stained glass once, no doubt, were part of the painted windows in the church, of which we have this account in the Harl. MSS. (2129, f. 111):—

"2d window.—Aston de Aston. Partie per $\wedge$ sa. et ar.

3d window.—Daniel. *Ar.* a pale fuselie *sa.* Dutton. *Ar.* 2 $\wedge$ *gules* on a canton *gules* a mullet pierced. Starkye de Darley. *Ar.* a $\wedge$ three storks *sable.*

Another window.—Daniel *ut supra* et Norris, quarterly *ar.* and *gules* sur le gules a frett *or*, a barulet *b.*

And on a small tomb, without arms, there lieth Grimsditch."

The original church at Daresbury was probably, like that of Runcorn, a modest structure of wood, built in frame, with its intervals filled in with plaster, and painted white, which may have given rise to its being traditionally called the "white church of Cheshire," and this may also account for the fact that while there were abundant proofs of the existence of an Early English church there, no remains have been found of any Norman masonry or carving.

Although Daresbury is not mentioned in the taxation of Pope Nicholas, in 1291, a short notice of it occurs in the ministers' accounts of Norton, where also there is mentioned the grant of a payment to provide a light in the abbey, from Keckwick, which is within the chapelry of Daresbury.

Prior Henry continued in office from 1159 to 1190, and during that time he was present and took part in many important ceremonies. In 1178 he witnessed John de Lacy's grant of tithe salt in Northwich to Stanlaw Abbey.[1] In 1166 he was present and assisted at the founding of Burscough Abbey, a house, like his own, of canons regular of the order

---

[1] Whalley C. Book, Chet. Soc. 484.

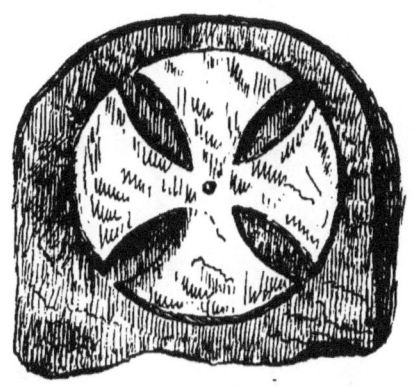

From Daresbury.
Slabs, Tiles, and moulding.

St. Augustine, and to which probably Norton contributed some of its inmates, and about the same time he witnessed Richard de la More's grant to Stanlaw Abbey.[1]

Richard de la More, who about this time helped to confer an important benefit on the neighbourhood in general, and Runcorn, Norton, and Halton, in particular, deserves a passing notice. To John fitz Richard, the sixth baron of Halton and constable of Chester, as we learn from the two charters, both specimens of the simplicity of the times, is owing the first establishment of the ferry at Runcorn, at which Richard de la More assisted. By the first of these charters Richard granted to his son W'goon two bovates of land in Roncover, late the lands of Beatrix of Higher Roncover, and a toft and croft in Widnesse, which John the constable had given him with the lands he had acquired from others, rendering yearly to God and St. John and the holy house of the hospital at Jerusalem ijs. on Saint Mary's day, and finding half the necessaries for the passage of the ship of Widnesse (the ferry boat) for ever, for all who should pass over there in the love of God.[2] By the second charter which explains the first, and is dated in 1190 (a time when it was not common to find dates in deeds), Garnier de Naplouse, grand prior of the English brotherhood of the knights hospitallers, granted lands in Platt and elsewhere to Richard de la More and his heirs, in consideration that he paid ivs. yearly at Michaelmas, and kept in repair on the river Mersey, at Runcorn, the vessel which John the constable for the love of God had provided to carry such persons as desired it across the stream, and that a third part of the chattels of Richard and his heirs in succession came back to the brotherhood for the good of his soul.[3]

About the time of the founding of Burscough, Prior Henry was party to an agreement by which, after reciting a controversy between his priory and the house of Stanlaw respecting certain tithes, it was agreed that the latter convent should pay the canons of Norton, every year on St. Mary Magdalen's day, five shillings for the tithes of two bovates of land in Stanney, the tithes of the demesne there, and the tithes of Aston. The high rank of some of the witnesses to this agreement shows its importance. Amongst them were John, the constable of Chester; Hugh de Dutton, Adam, his brother; Bertram, the chamberlain; Richard de

---

[1] Hist Ches. i. 562. Whalley C. Book, Chet. Soc. 530.
[2] Hist. Ches. i. 498. [3] Hist. of Birch, appendix, 189.

la More; Wronou Punterlynk; John, the chaplain; Gilbert, the monk: Richard de Combermere, and the whole chapter of Chester.[1] The prior who thus consented to receive a perpetual fixed money payment, the value of which was always diminishing, for the tithes which would always maintain their value, must have wanted the usual cleverness of the religious in that age, and have been very short-sighted. Prior Henry was also a witness to Roger the Constable's grant of one half of Combermere to the hospital of St. John of Jerusalem—

"The hospital that night and day
Received the pilgrims of the west."[2]

Canon Reginald, Henry's sub-prior, who was the corrector of the morals and behaviour of the inmates of the monastery—held an unenviable office, which resembled in its functions that of a university proctor.[3]

[1] Whalley C. B. Chet. Soc. 533.   [2] Hist. Ches. i. 454.
[3] Arley Charters, Box I. Nos. 54, 74, and 89.

CHAPTER III.

Roger, who about this time succeeded as third prior of Norton, seems to have held his office only a short time, for before the year 1193 he was either dead or had resigned it.

Peter, the canon, one of the witnesses to Adam de Carinton's grant to Adam de Dutton of one half of Sala, which seems to have been part of Appleton in 1191, was probably one of Prior Roger's brethren.

Very many religious houses in old time were in the habit of elevating and setting up some saint as their special protector. In most seaports Saint Nicholas, as the popular saint, to whom sailors paid their homage, had the pre-eminence. This saint, who chiefly as their patron, had not less than 376 churches dedicated to him in England. The sailors' devotion to him, and the reason of it, are thus alluded to by Vincentius and Mantuanus in the fifteenth century:—

> "Cum turbine nautæ
> Deprensi Cilices magno clamore vocarent,
> Nicolai viventis opem, descendere quidam,
> Cœlituum visus sancti sub imagine patris,
> Qui freta depulso fecit placidissima vento."[1]

At Norton, however, which from its first foundation looked out upon a great and stormy river, St. Christopher, whom the ignorant believed to have the care of such a stream, was chosen as the second patron of the house.

This saint was one of those of whom there were formerly many, who, though never born, were created saints for the sake of their good names, as others for the same reason were deified in heathen times. Potina, "quæ infantibus bibentibus præerat," was one of these old deities. And St. Veronica, whose beautiful legend is so well known, is one of these Christian saintesses who were made and not born, and so also was St. Hypolite, the patron of horses and leechcraft, to whose altar in Hertfordshire sick horses were led to be cured. The legend of St. Christopher, or the Christ-bearer, was meant to allegorise the Christian's passage over the stormy waves of

[1] Journ. Arch. Inst. 1863, p. 69.

this troublesome world. According to it he was a countryman of Goliath, and some of the other gigantic Philistines of whom we read, and was sent it is said, to live near a wide, deep, and stormy stream, which overflowed its banks, and where people in attempting to cross it were often drowned. One night he was startled in the hut where he dwelt by the shrill cry of a child, calling to him to come and help him over the water. The cry, like that heard by the infant Samuel, having been repeated thrice, he took his lanthorn, and looking out into the dark, there saw a little child sitting on the bank and waiting to be carried over the stream. Having lifted him on his shoulders, and taken his staff, he entered the water, but the wind blew, the waves rose and roared, and the child's weight grew every moment heavier and heavier, so that Christopher began to fear that he and his burden should both be carried away by the current. He nerved himself, however, to fresh efforts, aided his tottering steps by his staff, and at length reached the opposite shore, where, laying down his young burden gently on the bank, he said to him, "O child, whoever thou art, thou hast placed me in great peril by thy weight." To which the child answered, "Wonder not, Christopher, for be it known to thee that thou hast borne Him who bears the sins of all the world;" and to prove his words, he bade him plant his staff in the ground, and he would see it immediately take root and grow. The giant obeyed, and a miracle attested the truth of what he had heard, and made him from that time a saint.

At Norton, within sight of the broad estuary of the Mersey, where then, as ever since, many have been found

Suspendisse potenti
Vestimenta maris deo,

St. Christopher was esteemed to be a saint peculiarly adapted to the place. There, as everywhere, he was represented as of gigantic size. Erasmus, in his dialogue of the Shipwreck, tells us that one of the passengers in a sinking ship vowed a wax candle to the saint, which should be as large as his statue in his church at Paris, which he says was rather a mountain than a statue. To recommend the saint to the homage of those whose business lay on the great waters, these comforting legends were ascribed to him:—

Christophori sancti speciem quicunque tuetur,
Ille namque die nullo languore tenetur.

Whoso of holy Christopher this image sees,
That day shall know nor sickness nor disease.

ST CHRISTOPHER. NORTON PRIORY.

> Christophori faciem die quocunque tueris,
> Illo nempe die malâ morte non morieris.
>
> Whoso the face of Christopher shall see,
> From sudden death on that day will be free.

The saint's gigantic figure at Norton was placed under a canopy in front of the house, and looking towards the river, obtained the offerings of many a votary who knew nothing of his legendary story.

It is not known at what exact period his image was there set up, but the canopy under which it stood, and which looks as if it had been a part of the original house, seems to show that the figure must have been placed there much about the time when the house was built.

CHAPTER IV.

EGIDIUS, who, about the year 1193, succeeded as the fourth prior, between that time and the year 1208 was witness to an important charter respecting Warburton Priory, and it was probably he who received the grant of an assart which Richard fitz Adam de Bold made to the priory in the time of King John.[1]

It was probably also this Prior who obtained from Earl Roger this confirmation of the priory charter:—

"To all archbishops, etc., Roger, constable of Chester, sendeth greeting. Know ye that I have granted, and by this my charter have confirmed, to God and the church of the blessed Mary of Norton, and to the canons regular there serving God, all the donations, grants, and confirmations which William, the son of Nigel, constable of Chester, and William the younger, constable, son of the aforesaid William, and John, my father, constable of Chester, have made in pure, free, and perpetual alms, and confirmed by their charters to the before-named church and canons of Norton—that is to say, the whole of Norton with all its appurtenances; and the church of Radcliff-super-Soram, in Nottinghamshire, with all its appurtenances, and the fourth part of the mills of the same vill, and the tithes of the remaining three parts; and the church of Kneshal[2] with all its appurtenances, and the tithes of the mills of the same vill; and the tithe of the mill of Alreton; and the church of Dunnington, in Leicestershire, with all its appurtenances, and the tithe of the mill of the same; and one carucate of demain land in the same vill; and half a carucate of land near Dunnington, which is called Wavertoft; and the church of Burton, in Lindsey, with all its appurtenances; and one dwelling in the same Burton which Roger fitz Alured gave to the aforesaid canons for the soul of Leceline, his wife, and another in Derby which the same Roger gave them for the soul of Matilda, his wife; and the church of Pirinton in Oxfordshire, with all its appurtenances, with common of all issues and pastures belonging to Pirinton; and the monastery of St. Michael in Chester, with one dwelling in the same city; and the whole chaplainship of my whole constableship of Chester as well *ultra limora* as *infra* plenarily, and entirely with all its appurtenances; and the half of Sutton, near Chester, with all its appurtenances, with two parts of the demain tithes of the same half of Sutton, and one carucate of land between the same Sutton and the bridge of Stamford, which is called Dunnescroft, with a meadow, which is called Witaker, as far as the aforesaid bridge; and two bovates or oxgangs of land in Stanney, with two parts of the demain tithes and the tithe of the mill of the same; and two parts of the demain tithes of Raby, and likewise of Barrow, with the mill of the same, and the tithe of another mill which my father John afterwards built on the

---

[1] Kuerden MS. Chetham's Library, 32.
[2] Nottinghamshire, Thoroton, iii. 132.

Part of an Elk's horn. found at Norton.

Fragment of Glass.

Tiles from Norton Priory.

dam of the same Barrow; and the mill of Halton, which is near the church of Runcorn, with all its appurtenances; with the tithes of the other mills which my said father built in his territory of Halton; and two oxgangs of land with a dwelling in the same Halton; the half part of all the fisheries which belong to Halton, and the common of woods and waters, and pastures belonging to Halton, as well to the canons as to their tenants; and the half part of my whole fishery of Thelwall, with one oxgang of land and one fisherman in the same town; and one oxgang of land in Calvedon; and two parts of the demain tithes in Staininghes-ultra-Ribble; and the tenth part of the profits of the ferry at Runcorn; and the half of the demain tithes of Widness; and all the land which Gilbert Follis held, which is before the gate of the before-mentioned canons, and one parcel of land which is called Roger's Croft, which is between the fishpool of the canons and the wood which is called Estmor. I grant also to the before-named canons every year, for ever, at the Assumption of the Blessed Mary, two deer from my park at Halton;[1] and that all their demain swine may be with my demain swine in all my woods, and wherever else I may have mast for the same. I grant to them, moreover, whatever by the concession and confirmation of my ancestors, their knights, have given to the aforesaid canons, viz. two parts of the demain tithes of Sutton-ultra-Mersey, and one oxgang of demain land in Torboc, with all its appurtenances; and two parts of the demain tithes of the moiety of the town of Warburton-super-Mersey, which belongs to my fee; and two parts of the demain tithes of Eaton held by Roger fitz Alured, and the third part of the tithe of the fisheries, which belong to the same Eston-upon-Weaver; and the mill of Mulinton, with all its appurtenances, and one parcel of land which is called Mulincroft, with all the commons and easements which belong to the same Mulinton; and the mill of Waleton, with all the appurtenances, and one parcel of land between Weston and Runcorn, called Gorst's Acre. I will, therefore, and grant from my heart, that the often-mentioned canons have and hold all these donations before mentioned in pure, free, and perpetual alms; in wood and in plain, with warren, in meadows, in fields, in waters, and pastures, freely dischargedly and acquittedly from all secular service; and that they may hold as plenarily their own court with soc, sac, and infanganthef, and all other liberties and free customs, as any other alms may and ought to be better and more freely granted. Witnesses: Stephen de Muschamps, Hugh de Dutton, Peter de Goincourt, Adam de Dutton, Richard, Chaplain of Halton; Richard, Chaplain of Runcorn; Hugh Dispensator, Gaufridus Pincerna, Hubert de Waleton, Europius; Willielmus Venator."[2]

---

[1] The canons did not fail to profit by this hospitable grant, for, in excavations made near the house, bones and horns of the deer have been found. One fragment of a head and horn was so large that it might almost have belonged to the extinct Irish elk, though, as it was but little fossilised, it may have been part of the antlers of a red deer.

[2] Greswell's Runcorn, p. 44.

CHAPTER V.

RANULPHUS, about the year 1210, succeeded as fifth Prior of Norton.[1] In the time of King John, Richard fitz Gilbert de Aston gave to God and Saint Mary, and to Randle, Prior of Norton, all his land in Henley, with all its appurtenances.[2] This prior in 1211 had the melancholy office of burying in the priory, Richard, the brother of Roger, Baron of Halton, and Constable of Chester, who, though a great man by birth, was unhappily a leper, and was probably on that account denied the honour of being carried to the family burying-place at Stanlaw. It was probably in this prior's rule that John Lacy, Earl of Lincoln and Baron of Halton, granted to the prior and convent a confirmation of Middle Aston, by the name of Middel Aston "quam habent ex dono dñæ Matildæ quondam uxoris dñi Collini de Loches," and granted them at the same time an acquittance from all wardship and services due in respect of that land.[3]

JOHN, the sixth prior, obtained a charter from Earl Randle Blundeville, which must have been made in or before 1232, as in that year the earl died. This charter exempted the priory from all gelds, aids, and works in castles.[4] He also obtained from King Henry III. two charters, one of which granted the convent sac, soc, toll, and team, and exempted them from being summoned to attend the shire and hundred courts, and from all secular services whatever, and the other exempted them from all salt passage and customs.[5]

ANDREW, the seventh prior, was in office in 1233, 1234, and 1237, when Richard Phyton was justice of Chester,[6] but his rule was neither active nor eventful.

[1] Arley Charters, Box. I. 93; Harl. MSS. 2074, 179; Hist. Ches. i. 502, citing Sir P. Leycester.   [2] Hist. Ches. i. 500, citing Sir Peter Leycester.
[3] Ibid. i. 532, citing Sir Peter Leycester.   [4] Harl. MS. 280, fol. 78.
[5] Hist. Ches. i. 502; Harl. MSS. 2060, 142, 144, referring to the pleas of *Quo warranto*, 24 Edw. III., and 14 Hen. VII.
[6] Hist. Ches. i. 468; Whalley Coucher B. Chet. Soc. p. 7; and Arley Charters, Box I. Nos. 21, 93.

HUGH afterwards occurs as eighth prior in the time of Henry III.[1]

Sir Thomas de Dutton, in the time of Henry III., having built a chapel at Poosey, in Dutton, which Sir Peter Leycester says has its name from its lying between the Park pool and the river (ee or ey meaning water), obtained from the prior of Norton "liberam cantariam suam in capellis suis de Norton et Weston infra limites paroch. de Budworth et Runcorn," and in 20 Henry III., 1236, the prior covenanted with Hugh fitz Hugh de Dutton to find him a chaplain there for ever;[2] and on the 3 non. of June in the same year, Hugh de Norwico (probably Northwich) was instituted to the church of Kneshall, on the presentation of the prior and convent of Norton, the archbishop reserving power to ordain a vicar there if the parson should be non-resident.[3]

ROGER DE MAMECESTRE, the ninth prior, was the first head of the house who occurs with both a Christian and a surname. Every bishop now drops the latter name and takes that of his see instead; but in early times the heads of a religious house observed a different rule, for they dropped their family name and retained only their Christian name, as if desirous to lose their family personality on being married to their office. Prior Roger's surname is sufficient to indicate the place from which he came. He was of a busy family, and bustle and activity seem to belong to their name-place. One of them, Hugh de Mamecestre, born in the time of Henry III., was a preaching friar, who, with a brother friar, was sent in 1294 on rather a hazardous embassy, to renounce the King of England's allegiance to the King of France, and in 1305 he, with others, received a commission to attend the parliament, and he was also named as a commissioner to treat with the Scots. He was a great scholar and detector of impostors, and he wrote *Compendium theologiæ contra Fanaticorum Deliria*, and other works.[4] A Henry de Mamecestre appears as a party to a fine in Neston, 10 Edward II.;[5] and a John de Mamecestre was shortly afterwards one of the lessees of Warrington rectory. In 1328 there was a Geoffroy de Mamecestre, who was a trustee of the estates of the great family of Boteler, lords of the manor of Warring-

---

[1] Hist. Ches. i. 471. Sir P. Leycester, lib. c. 156. [2] Not. Cest. Chet. Soc. i. 357.
[3] Archbishop Gray's Regr., Surtees Soc. p. 9.
[4] Hist. Lanc. ii. 356; and Foundations of Manchester i. 26 n, in the former of which works there is a memoir of him. [5] Hist. Ches. ii. p. 29.

ton. Between the years 1249 and 1261 Prior Roger was a witness to the grant of Peter de Dutton to Adam fitz William fitz Hamund de Waleton.[1]

In 1262 he and his convent granted to Sir Geoffrey de Dutton a license to have divine offices celebrated by his own chaplain in his house at Sutton, except on the great festivals of the church, when the family were to resort to their parish church at Runcorn, and there to make their offerings, but at all other times the chaplain was to say masses for Sir Geoffrey and his family in their manor house at Sutton. The chaplain at his first entrance was to swear to be faithful to the church, and in no way to defraud her, and Sir Geoffrey and his wife, in the chapter-house at Norton, and before the whole convent and many others, swore faithfully to observe the agreement.[2]

ROGER DE LINCOLN, whose predecessor must have made his Christian name popular, succeeded about the year 1270 as the tenth prior. The abbot and convent of Vale Royal being at this time the owners of the chapel of Middle Aston, in which they were bound to perform divine offices on three days in every week, and the chapel being much nearer to Norton than to Vale Royal, the abbot and his convent proposed to transfer it to the priory of Norton, and in the above year, while Roger or his predecessor was in office, an agreement was come to between the two houses, by which the former granted to the latter the two bovates of land in Middle Aston which had been formerly granted to the rectors of Frodsham to provide a chantry for the lords of that manor in the chapel of the same; and the said abbot and convent also granted to the prior and convent all the predial and personal tithes arising within the said township or manor of Middle Aston by reason of the said chapel, or in any wise belonging to it, with all the fisheries, commons, and other rights, advantages, and immunities, which had at any time belonged either to the said land or the said chapel (except the small tithes, oblations, and mortuaries of people resident in the said village of Middle Aston). And for the said two bovates of land, tithes, liberties, commons, and rights, the said prior and convent agreed to pay the said abbot and convent forty shillings sterling yearly, and also at their own charges to cause mass to be duly celebrated

[1] Whalley Coucher Book, Chet. Soc. 397. Arley Charters, Box I. Nos. 41, 87.
[2] Arley Deeds, Box I. No. 38.

in the said chapel three days in every week throughout the year—that is to say, on Sundays, Wednesdays, and Fridays for ever; and the said prior and convent, for them and their successors, solemnly bound themselves to the said abbot and convent to pay the said rent, as well as to sustain the burden of the said chantry, and subjected themselves to the absolute jurisdiction of the Archdeacon of Chester for the time being, so that he or his official without judicial contention might compel them to the observance of the premises by ecclesiastical censures if (which heaven forbid!) they should chance to fail, or cease in part or in whole in the premises; and both the said parties, for themselves and their successors, renounced all deceit and fraud, and especially the rescript called *Bague de bonis*, obtained, or to be obtained, as well as all and singular indulgences, constitutions, or statutes, which might infringe, weaken, or obstruct the aforesaid gift, grant, and demise, or the said annual rent and chantry. Witness the Lords Simon, Abbot of Chester, Robert, Abbot of Stanlaw, and Reginald de Grey justiciary of Chester; the knights, William de Venables, Ranulph de Vernon Hugh de Dutton, and Richard le Mascy; Robert Grosvenor, Sheriff of Cheshire, Sir Alexander de Hamvyle, Randle Starkey, John de Marbury, Henry le Norres, and Alan de Walton.[1]

The livings of Runcorn and Great Budworth would seem hitherto to have been served by the canons of the house, sent there from time to time, which may account for the ancient stalls still to be seen in Great Budworth Church. It was now, however, thought necessary that at each of these churches a vicarage should be endowed, and on this subject we have the following entry in the Lichfield Register: "Ordinationes vicariarum de Budworth et Roncorne fact. per dñum Rog. Merland Cov. et Lich. epūm. Dat. apud Sallow 4 Id. Maii 1277."[2] But notwithstanding this we shall find that to both these churches the canons continued to be presented, "The practice of the religious houses appointing their own canons to do the duty of their parish churches crept in with William the Conqueror, and in a few reigns it became such a custom that above a third part, and those generally the richest benefices in England, became appropriated, and in these cures the monks did for some time reside, and officiate by turns, by lot, and even by penance, with many other ways of shifting off the duty upon one another; until at length such changes and intermissions

[1] From the original in the possession of Sir Richard Brooke, Baronet; and see Hist. Ches. i. 475, 598.   [2] Notitia Cest., Chet. Soc. i. 377.

in the pastoral care becoming very scandalous, the bishops did by degrees restrain the monks from a personal cure of souls, and confined them according to rule within their own cloisters, obliging them to retain fit and able capellans, vicars, or curates, with a competent salary paid to them. But then again they oppressed these stipendiary vicars with such sorry allowances and such grievous service that the bishops at last brought them to the presentation of perpetual vicars, endowed and instituted, who should have no other dependence on their convents than the rectors had upon their patrons."[1] But notwithstanding the rule which the bishops had thus made, and which was confirmed by an Act of 4 Henry IV., the churches of Runcorn and Great Budworth still continued for a time to be served by the Norton canons. Benefices given *ad mensam monachorum* sometimes escaped being appropriated. Had Runcorn and Budworth been so given that notwithstanding the bishops' rule and the act of parliament, they continued to be served by the canons ?[2]

In 1281, Roger, "the lord prior of Norton," was a witness to Hugh de Dutton's grant of one bovate of land in Aston,[3] and in 1286 he was witness to Geoffrey fitz Hugh de Dutton's grant of the Mill Pool in Aston,[4] and about the same time also he witnessed the chirograph or agreement between Peter de Dutton and Robert de Mascy.[5]

[1] Dr. Burn, quoted in Penwortham Priory, pref. xxxvii. Chet. Soc.   [2] Ibid.
[3] Whalley Coucher B. Chet. Soc. 23.   [4] Ibid. 399.   [5] Ibid. 403.

CHAPTER VI.

JOHN DE OLTON, who, after the year 1285, succeeded as eleventh prior of Norton, on the 24th January, 18 Edward I., 1290, had a license from the king that he and his convent might receive from Peter de Dutton a messuage and fourteen acres of land in Newton near Preston (on the Hill) and at the same time the owner had license to grant them this property without incurring any forfeiture under the acts against mortmain.[1]

In the taxation of Pope Nicholas the church of Runcorn occurs, and is valued at £20 and the tenth at £2, but no mention is made either of the priory church of Norton or of its dependent church at Daresbury, which, as both of them were certainly then in existence, is remarkable.

On the 4th October 1302, the Prior and his convent presented William de Rodyerd to the rectory of Grappenhall. This being the first mention of this living as a possession of the priory, we have endeavoured, but without success, to ascertain how or when it was acquired.

On the 2d September 1306, William Deyners of Daresbury, in making his will, remembered the prior and convent of Norton, and left them a legacy of xx. s. *in nomine principalis*.[2] This, which was then a considerable gift, was no doubt in acknowledgment of the services they had rendered him in their chapel at Daresbury. On the 10th February 1311 they presented Richard fitz William de Doncaster to the rectory of Grappenhall, Rodyerd having probably ceded it on accepting an Irish preferment.

Sir Hugh de Dutton, knight, cited the prior and convent of Norton before Adam Burum and Nicholas Grundchundeléc, the Bishop of Lichfield and Coventry's commissaries, in the year 1315, for not providing a chaplain and a lamp at Poosey chapel, according to the agreement which they had made for that purpose, and of which Sir Hugh produced the original charter. Prior Olton, who was present, confessed the charge, and

[1] Calr. Patent Rolls, p. 54, No. 41.   [2] Hist. Ches. i. 539.

was ordered by the commissaries to repair his neglect of the services.[1] It is not to the credit of the *religious* that there should be occasion thus to remind them of the duties they had intermitted, duties which were the very object for which they were associated, and to which they had bound themselves by a solemn agreement. The vicarage of Great Budworth had belonged to the priory from the first foundation, but, either because the records have perished, or for some other reason, we do not find any presentation made to that living until 6 Kal. May (26 Ap.) 1320, when Thomas de Colton was presented by the Prior of Norton to be vicar of Great Budworth, void by the death of Thomas Middleton, whom we may suppose to have been presented by them some twenty years before.[2] About 1322 the prior witnessed an agreement as to the tithe of Moor Marsh,[3] in which it is expressly stated that the prior and convent held Runcorn church to their proper use as rectors.

On the 30th October 1323, King Edward II., who had come to Liverpool to put down the adherents of the late Thomas, Earl of Lancaster, sailed up the river from that place to Ince, from whence he came to Halton, the castle of the rebel earl, where he remained from the 1st to the 3d November, visiting the priory of Norton and the abbey of Vale Royal, in the meantime. The visit being one of policy, the king no doubt made offerings at the shrine of St. Mary of Norton, and also at her altar at Vale Royal, and prudence and policy, if not piety, would incline him to be liberal at both places; but no lively chronicler, like Jocelyn of Brakelond, who saw King John make his offerings at the shrine of St. Edmund at Bury, and has recorded how very parsimonious they were, has left us a record of what King Edward did at Norton, and it must therefore remain for our imagination to conceive it.

On the 21st December 1325, the prior appointed Robert de Stapleford to the rectory of Runcorn.[4]

In the year 1326 there appears to have been some controversy between the prior and monks of Lancaster and the prior and canons of Norton, respecting the tithes of Slanyngness, which was then settled by a charter drawn up at a chapter held in the chapel of Gayrstang.[5]

The house of Norton having recently obtained grants of several addi-

---

[1] Sir Peter Leycester, Lib. C. fol. 146 m.   [2] Hist. Ches. i. 452.
[3] Whalley Coucher Book, Chet. Soc. 410.   [4] Hist. Ches. i. 500.
[5] MSS. at Thurnham Hall; Hist. Commission, Third Report, p. 247.

tions to their property, and being about to acquire others, the prior thought it prudent to fortify himself against incurring a forfeiture under the Mortmain Act by obtaining from King Edward III. the following two charters of license :—

Edward, the king, etc., greeting (after reciting the first charter of Henry II., the charter thus proceeds :)—

" We do confirm the grant and confirmation before mentioned ; and also the donations, grants, and confirmations which Wronou Punterline made by his charter to God and the aforesaid canons of the mill of Mullington, and one parcel of land which is called Mulnecroft, before the publication of the statute set forth concerning lands and tenements not to be placed in mortmain ; and the donation, etc., which Hugh de Dutton, son of Hugh de Dutton, made by his charter to the before-mentioned canons of two shillings and eightpence from the rent of Pulescy ; and four shillings from the land of John the Digger of Halton, and of timber from the wood of Kekwic to repair the mill of Kekwic ; and of land in Frodsham with its appurtenances ; and of land in Pulescy with the chapel, and all the assarted land and pasture there for sixty beasts, granted, as it is said, before the publication of the above-mentioned statute ; ratifying and approving them." Given, etc., at Gloucester, 30th Aug. 3 Ed. III. 1329.[1]

And the second runs thus—

" Edward, the king, sendeth greeting. Know ye that of our especial grace we have as far as in us lies given and granted for us and our heirs to our beloved in Christ, the prior and convent of Norton, in the county of Chester, our license to acquire lands and rents to the full value of ten pounds a year, as well of their own fee as of any other except lands holden of us *in capite*, to have and to hold to them and their successors for ever, the statute against placing lands and tenements in mortmain in any wise notwithstanding, provided that inquisitions of *ad quod damnum* thereof be duly made and returned to our Chancery. Dated at Westminster the 20th March, in the 5th year of our reign " (1331).[2]

---

[1] Greswell's Runcorn, 48 *et seq.*   [2] Calendar of Patent Rolls.

CHAPTER VII.

ROBERT BERNARD, who about the year 1340 succeeded as twelfth prior, seems, like his predecessor, to have had a just dread of incurring a forfeiture under the statute of mortmain, and being about to sell the Bishop of Lincoln a part of Wavretoft, the oldest possession of his house, he took the precaution, on the 27th October, 17th Edw. III. (1343), to obtain from the king the following charter:—

" The king to all whom it shall concern, greeting : Whereas by the Common Council of our realm of England, it is enacted that it shall not be lawful either for *men of religion* or others without our license to enter into any fee so that it should become mortmain without our license, and that of the chief lord of whom it is immediately holden, yet for a fine which our beloved in Christ, the prior of Norton, hath given us, we have granted and given him license, so far as in us lies, that he and his convent may give and assign sixty shillings of annual rent, with the appurtenances of their manor of Waretoft, in the county of Leicester, to the venerable father, Thomas, Bishop of Lincoln, to have, hold, and perceive to the same bishop and his successors for ever, and the same license is given to the said bishop and his successors to hold the same as is aforesaid by the tenor of these presents, the statute aforesaid notwithstanding. Willing that neither the aforesaid prior and his convent, or their successors, or the aforesaid bishop and his successors, either by us or our heirs, or our ministers, shall be in any wise troubled or aggrieved, the services due to the chief lords of the fee excepted. Witness ourself at Westminster, 27th October, in the seventeenth year of our reign" (1343).[1]

In 1345 the prior presented John de Acton to the rectory of Runcorn, and the same year, his title to the advowson of Grappenhall having been disputed by William fitz William le Boydell, he had the spirit to defend his right, and having been successful, he presented Roger de Shipbroke to the rectory on the 10th August in that year.

On the 20th August 1347, the king being pressed for funds to carry on his wars in France, required from the Prior of Norton[2] the modest loan of two sacks of wool, a strange but not an immoderate demand for a king to make. If the loan was to help to fit out another Argo, the adventure was more likely to involve the king in debt than to bring him or the prior a golden fleece.

Prior Robert Bernard either died or his rule ceased very soon after

[1] Patent Rolls.   [2] Rymer's Fœdera, iii. 123.

this last transaction, and the king's debt to him and his convent probably remained unpaid.

JOHN DE WEVIRHAM, whose name bespeaks his birthplace, succeeded as thirteenth prior about the year 1350, and in 24 Edward. III. (1351), when a *quo warranto* was issued against him requiring him to show cause by what right he and his convent claimed soc, sac, and toll, and to be exempt from attendance upon the shire and hundred courts, and from secular services, and also to be exempt from all aids, gelds, and works in castles, and to be freed from tolls of salt, passage, and customs, the prior appeared and pleaded the charters made to his predecessors by King Henry III. and by Earl Randle Blundeville, and his claim was allowed.[1]

In the year 1354, probably in consequence of some dispute as to the claim of the house of Aston to a corody in the priory at Norton, a record was made under the hands and seals of twenty-four persons, testifying that Sir Richard Aston, knight, Hugh and Richard his sons, and also Sir Robert Aston, knight, father of Richard Aston, the then lord of Aston, had been possessed of such a corody in the abbey of Norton, and that each of them had had the finding of a yeoman and a page, with three horses, a brace of greyhounds, and a goshawk, according to their estate, with their chambers, and such easements as belonged to their degree; all which the priors and abbots of the said monastery (considering the great possessions that had been given them out of the lordship of Aston), had always consented unto, granted, and yielded as their right of old time granted.[2] A corody, a right which had been acknowledged by the law from a very early period, gave the king, or the founder, or benefactor of a religious house, a right to have either a sum of money or an allowance of meat, drink, and clothing, towards the reasonable sustenance of such one of his servants or valets as he should think good to bestow it on. The following grant of such a corody may better serve to show its nature :—

"Know ye that we, Ralph, abbot of the monastery of St. John of Haghmon, and the convent of the same, at the instance and special request of our most excellent and revered lord, Thomas Earl of Arundel and Surrey, have granted to Robert Lee for his life the corody of an esquire, to be with the abbot of the said abbey, with one page and two horses, and to take such sufficient meat and drink for himself as the other esquires take or receive, and for his page to take or receive such things as the other pages of the abbot and esquires take, and also to take hay and provender for his horse, and the said Robert to take such clothing as the other esquires take. Dated 3 Hen. V."[3]

[1] Hist. Ches. i. 502.　　[2] Ibid. 533.　　[3] Blunt's Law Dictionary, *sub voce*.

The existence of rights of this kind, by which an abbot or prior was bound to receive another's servant at free quarters, shows the simple state of the times when it began and when it continued to prevail. It is clear from internal evidence, the mention of Sir Robert Aston, knight, and his son Richard, and of the abbey at a time when the abbey existed only as a priory, that the claim of the above Aston corody, if made in 1354, must have been revived and renewed at a much later period.

In or about 1355, Prior John de Wevirham presented David Heles to the vicarage of Great Budworth.[1]

In the year 1358, the prior being desirous to acquire for his convent from John de Winwick, treasurer of St. Peter's at York, a yearly rent of 40s., issuing out of the vill of Burgh-in-Lonsdale, which he had by the gift of Sir William le Boteler, knight of Warrington,[2] thought fit to fortify himself in holding it by the following charter of license :—

"The king, to all whom it shall concern, greeting : Know ye that of our special grace we have granted and given as much as in us lies, license to our beloved clerk, John de Wynewyk, treasurer of the blessed Peter of York, that he may give 40s. of annual rent, with the appurtenances in Burgh Parva in Lonsdale, which are not holden of us, to our beloved in Christ, the prior and convent of Norton, in the county of Chester, to have and to hold to them and their successors for ever, and to the said prior and convent and their successors we have given the like license to receive and hold the same, the statute against mortmain notwithstanding, saving to the chief lords of the fee, the services therefore due. Dated at Westminster, 1st Dec. 32 Edw. III." (1358).[3]

THOMAS, who has been put down as succeeding as fourteenth prior in or about 1368, is thought to have been abbot of Vale Royal, and not prior of Norton.[4]

[1] Hist. Ches. i. 452.   [2] Close Rolls, 32 Edw. III.   [3] Patent Rolls.
[4] Hist. Ches. i. 149, 502.

CHAPTER VIII.

RICHARD, the fifteenth prior, probably succeeded to his office in 1373, for on the 10th July in that year, John of Gaunt, Duke of Lancaster, baron of Halton and constable of Chester, in appointing Mathew de Rixton as his seneschal at Halton, commanded him to deliver to the prior and convent of Norton the tithes of his herbage and underwood in their parishes in the same manner as their predecessors had held it, which seems like the renewal of a former grant, and as if it were meant to inaugurate the advent of a new prior to his office.

In the year 1374, the prior and convent let the corn tithes of Appleton to Sir Geoffrey de Werburton for a year, and it speaks little for the confidence which one man then reposed in another, that the prior could not take the word even of a great landowner like Sir Geoffrey in so small a matter as this, without requiring him, on the 10th August in the above year, before the bargain was completed, to enter into a bond with Randle fitz Richard de Holcroft, Thomas Percival, and John de Hulse, as his sureties duly to pay the rent.[1]

On the 13th February 1377, Prior Richard presented William Leversage, presbyter, to the rectory of Grappenhall.

On the 13th November 1379, when Sir Thomas Dutton founded a perpetual chantry in the friary at Warrington, and when the solemnity was made the occasion of a great gathering of notables in that house to take part in it, Prior Richard of Norton attended as one of them.[2] If history has not done him injustice, Sir Thomas, whose hands had not been free from blood, was one of those to whom Mr. Hallam's[3] words apply, when he says "the clergy failed not to inculcate upon the wealthy sinner that no atonement could be so acceptable to Heaven as liberal presents to its earthly delegates," which often led the murmuring family to exclaim—
"Timeo monachos et crucem ferentes."

On the 11th June 1381, the prior granted to Sir Geoffrey de Werburton, Hugh de Soudenhed, Ralph Richardson, and William his son, Thomas

[1] Hist. Ches. i. 140, 502; and Arley Deeds, Box IV. 7.   [2] Hist. Ches. i. 478.
[3] Europe in the Middle Ages.

Percivale, and William the crier, a lease of the tithes of Appleton for six years, if Sir Geoffrey should so long live, at the rent of xii. li. a year.[1]

The seals of the priory are rare, but the seal of this deed is preserved, but it is not in such preservation as to deserve to be photographed.

The arms of the priory were those of the founder—*gules* a pale fusillé; or, as Tanner gives them, three fusils in pale within a bordure.

In 1390, the Prior of Norton occurs in the Boteler Annals as holding land or a burgage in Warrington, but the prior's name is not given. The abbot and convent of Stanlaw, who had a burgage in the same place, leased it to a tenant for life at the rent of 8s. 6d. a year, reserving to themselves "in dicto burgagio hospitio ad hospitandum et ad res nostras ibidem recolligendas et conservandas cum necesse habuerimus,"[2] and probably the convent of Norton would reserve a similar right in their burgage.

In 1399 the prior presented Richard de Halton, who was probably one of his canons, to the rectory of Runcorn.[3]

In 5 Henry IV. (1403) there seems to have been some confused idea that Runcorn church possessed the privilege of sanctuary, and Robert Morysson, a felon, who had feloniously killed one Thomas de Bulde, fled there, and being afterwards allowed to escape, the parish was fined for it 8li., as we learn from this entry in the accounts of the Chamberlain of Chester. "De 4li. solut. Rico Castell uni servientium dñi de dono dñi de parte 8li. quam gentes de parochia de Runcorn ipso dño solvisse debuerunt ratione evasionis per Robertum Morysson, felon. de ecclesia ibid. factæ, qui quidem Robertus ecclesiam illam cepit eo quod felonice interfecit, Thomam de Bulde."[4]

On the 24th September (1411) the prior presented Richard Dunham, canon of Norton, to the vicarage of Great Budworth,[5] a presentation seemingly in direct violation of the Act of Parliament, which forbade the presentation of a regular to one of the convent livings.

It was in this prior's time also that the Parliament of 1414 entreated the king, who was meditating an invasion of France, to seize all ecclesiastical revenues, and convert them to his own use, which filled the clergy with great alarm until the king was ultimately appeased by their offer to confer on him all the alien priories.[6] In the year 1418, pro-

[1] Arley Deeds, Box V.   [2] Hist. Ches. ii. 222-4.   [3] Ibid. i. 500.
[4] Cheshire Chamberlain's Accounts.   [5] Hist. Ches. i. 542.
[6] Hume's Hist. Eng. vol. iii. 91.

bably while Prior Richard ruled the house, one Thomas de Nesse of Runcorn assaulted Thomas de Chester, a canon of Norton, his master, for which he was presented by the palatine jury at Chester, but the baron's court at Halton having claimed to have jurisdiction in the case, it was remitted there, and the offender was punished.[1]

JOHN SUTTON, who next succeeded to the government of the house as its sixteenth head, was no longer called Prior of Norton, but abbot, by which latter title, in the year 1423, he presented William del Hethe, chaplain, to the rectory of Grappenhall, void by the death of William Leversage.[2] It is probable that it was this abbot who also presented Henry de Wigan and Hugh de Golborne to be successively rectors of Runcorn.[3] If the abbot was a Lancashire man, we can understand his partiality for his countrymen, which from their names both Wigan and Golborne must have been. We do not know how this new title of abbot was first obtained by the head of the house of Norton. It may have been either bestowed by the Pope, the head of ecclesiastical honours, or it may have been a consequence of the king's having granted to the priory his charter of liberties and protections when the superior of the house would have the title of abbot, which explains what Geoffrey fitz Peter meant by his saying to the Prior of Walden after the king had made him abbot of that house: "O my lord abbot, you and your monks have disinherited me and my heirs by turning my priory into an abbey, and throwing me off by subjecting yourselves wholly to the royal power."[4] Regner, however, who asserts that there never was an abbot among the Augustinians until the time of Pope Eugenius IV., who did not assume the tiara until 1431, was clearly mistaken, since that title was certainly borne by the Abbot of Norton in the above year.[5]

It was probably in the time of this prior that the claim of the Aston corody was renewed by Sir Robert Aston, knight, and Richard, his son, and allowed by the prior.

In June 1425, the chapel at Aston being out of repair, and the services in it, except on Sundays, being intermitted, and having been so for years, Richard, son of Sir Robert Aston, made a complaint of this defect to Richard Stanley, archdeacon of Chester, at his visitation at Christelton, and having proved his complaint, the archdeacon, on the 25th August,

[1] Hist. Ches. i. 523. [2] Ibid. 445. [3] Ibid. 500.
[4] Fosbrooke's Brit. Mon. 83. [5] Ibid.

ordered the abbot and convent immediately to redress the wrong and evil complained of.¹ On this occasion, also, the head of the house is again called an abbot, and probably in the pride of his new elevation he would have resented being called by his old title.

This remissness and neglect of duty on the part of the religious houses must have been of frequent occurrence, for besides the constant complaints so often made against Norton, the same fault occurred elsewhere. In the 17th Edward II. the Abbot of Shrewsbury suffered forfeiture of a certain piece of land called Wyldgreave, near Thelwall, but on the opposite side of the Mersey, containing a carucate of land, with a rent of xxs., from the manor of Weston, and a certain fishery in Merse water, near Thelwall, by reason of its having been found that he and his convent, for more than sixty years before the 13th August then last past, had intermitted and withdrawn a certain chantry at Wyldgreave, founded for the souls of the king's royal progenitors, who had given the same lands and tenements to sustain it.²

On the 14th January 1430, John, Abbot of Norton, made a lease of the manor of Pulsaye in Dutton to Sir Peter Dutton, for the term of ten years.³

On the same day of the month three years later, the same Abbot presented Thomas Hole, one of the canons of his house, to the vicarage of Great Budworth.⁴ As this appointment of one of his own canons to the vicarage was directly contrary to the Act of 4 Henry IV. c. 12, by which it was enacted that "the vicar of every church should be a secular person, and not a member of any religious house, that he should be vicar perpetual, and not removable at the caprice of the monastery, and that he should be canonically instituted and inducted, and be sufficiently endowed at the discretion of the ordinary for these three express purposes—to do divine service, to inform the people, and to keep hospitality," it is difficult to see how Thomas Hole could be appointed vicar, or how, having been appointed, his appointment could be sustained. The times must have been lax when these irregularities could be allowed.

This abbot seems to have been a person in whom his neighbours reposed confidence, for Sir Geoffrey Warburton and others, and Thomas

¹ Hist. Ches. i. 532, citing Sir P. Leycester.
² Marquis of Westminster's Deeds.
³ Dodsworth's MSS.
⁴ Hist. Ches. i. 452.

Venables, of Comberbach, having a dispute about their claims to certain property, referred the matter to the abbot's decision, and he, on the 21st December 1441, calling himself John Sutton, "abbot of the house and kirk of Norton," made his award in the premises.[1]

A poet of the time seems to think that the monasteries were too much resorted to in law matters, for it is thus he sings of it:—

> There are handled pleadings and causes of the law,
> There are made bargains of divers maner things,
> Byings and sellings scant worth a hawe,
> And there are for lucre contrived false leasings.[2]

---

[1] Mainwaring Papers.   [2] Barclay's Ship of Fooles.

CHAPTER IX.

THOMAS WESTBURY, who became abbot about the year 1444, was the seventeenth head of the house of Norton. On the 29th August, 24 Henry VI. (1440), when a great return (a kind of *quo warranto* proceeding) of the king's manor of Halton was held before Thomas Bylling, the deputy (for the northern parts) of William, Marquis of Suffolk, and Sir Thomas Tudenham, chief stewards of the duchy of Lancaster, and William Caton, the receiver-general, the Abbot of Norton having been distrained for his relief of Middleton, his fisheries in the river Mersey, and the stallage, halmote, and amerciaments of his tenants in the court of the manor of Halton,—Thomas Westbury, the abbot, appeared, and produced in full court a release for his relief of Middleton ; and as to the fisheries, stallage, and halmote, he showed the charters of foundation and donation to his house, all which were allowed, and thereupon the court directed the bailiff to displace all the fisheries in the river Mersey except those of the king and the abbot ; and to allow no court or halmote in the manor except the king's and the abbot's, and as to the stallage and amerciaments of his tenants the court decided that the abbot was to have, hold, and take them, without impediment.

Westbury, it would seem, was still abbot when Sir Geoffrey Warburton made his will on the 1st September 1448 ; by which the testator desired to be buried at Norton, between the high chancel and the chapel of the blessed Mary, from which it would seem that the church then terminated in a lady chapel, and he left to the priest celebrating before his tomb for the year Cs, and to the Abbot of Norton he left his best horse, in the name of a principal. He also left to the Lord Thomas de Sutton (probably the priest of his oratory at that place, and a canon at Norton) Cs out of the farm of his church at Wrexham to celebrate for his soul for a year, and he gave the like sum for the like service to John Humbleton, chaplain.[1]

[1] Hist. Ches. i. 428 ; and Arley Charters, Box 8, No. 9.

Shortly after this the abbot resigned his office, and in 1475 the good Countess of Richmond, who loved to have always a few young men of promise about her, brought from Oxford a learned person of his name to Lathom, where he helped to instruct in the best learning of the time her young scholars, some of whom, as Hugh Oldham and William Smith, rose to the Episcopal bench. It seems not improbable that the Thomas Westbury whom she thus brought to Lathom was the former abbot of Norton.

ROGER PLEMOUTH, the eighteenth head of the house, became Westbury's successor upon his retirement. It was this abbot who for some reason, possibly either because of the poverty of the house or the need there was for expending money upon it, or their farms, sold the advowson of Grappenhall which the convent had never appropriated, though they had held it so long, to the Byrom family, one of whom, Thomas Byrom, they presented to the living in 1451.

ROBERT LEFTWICH, who succeeded Plemouth, and was a younger brother of Richard Leftwich, Esq., of Leftwich, became abbot about the year 1452, and was the nineteenth head of the house of Norton. To the great discredit of the abbey, the old complaints about Aston chapel in this abbot's time again broke out anew. The service had been again intermitted, the chapel was again out of repair, and Sir Richard Aston, the then head of his family, contemplated a renewal of proceedings to compel the abbey to do their duty; but by the mediation of Thomas Dutton, Esq., and Anne, his wife, dame Isabel Carrington, late the wife of Sir John Carrington, and Jenkin of Leycester, the dispute was adjusted, and the abbot undertook to make the necessary reparations of the chapel, and to perform the stipulated services.[1] William, Bishop of Sidon, a canon of the same order as the house at Norton, was at this time suffragan to the good William of Waynflete.

On the 24th August 1459 the abbot presented William Trentham, one of his canons, to the *rectory* of Runcorn, on the resignation of Hugh Golborne, and by it the ordinance as to the vicarage and the statute of 4 Henry IV. c. 12, to which allusion has been made before, was again violated.[2]

On the 13th August 1459, the abbot obtained an exemplification of the agreement respecting Middle Aston Chapel.[3]

---

[1] Hist. Ches. i. citing Sir P. Leycester.   [2] Ibid. 500.   [3] Ibid. 480.

RICHARD MALBORN, who was probably a member of the respectable yeoman family at Walton, which has only recently become extinct, succeeded as abbot, and became the twentieth head of the house of Norton in 1495.

JOHN, the twenty-first head of Norton, who became its abbot soon after the year 1495, again setting the law at defiance, on the 8th March 1497 presented Richard de Kingsley, one of his canons, to the *rectory* of Runcorn,[1] and in 14 Henry VII. (1498), when *quo warrantos* were resorted to as a means of replenishing the king's exchequer, the abbot pleaded to that issued against him in the same terms in which a former head of Norton had met a similar *quo warranto*, and the claims were again allowed.[2]

On the 23d August 1447, he presented William de Norton, one of his canons, to the vicarage of Great Budworth.[3] The eyes of their ecclesiastical superiors were blind not to see these violations of the law.

ROGER (or as he is sometimes called Robert) HALL, who was the next abbot, and the twenty-second head of the house of Norton, in 1503 was made, by Robert Redish, one of the overseers of his will.[4] The mention of this abbot formerly occurred also in the monumental inscriptions at Great Budworth,[5] where in a window of the church, which was made by him, there were the arms of Nigel, baron of Halton—*gules* a pale fusillé *or*, with another shield, probably intended for the abbot's official coat—*gules* a pale fusillé *argent*, and on a canton of the *second* a fleur de lis, *sable*.[6]

JOHN MALBORN, the next abbot, and the twenty-third who had held rule in the house, seems to have been a man in whom confidence was to be placed that he would do justice, for he was appointed with William Stretforth, the abbot of Vale Royal, to settle a law dispute, and they joined on the 14th August 1518 in signing a certificate, verifying certain depositions of witnesses which had been taken before them, as to Sir Piers Legh's entry upon some land in Burtonwood, after the death of Sir John Boteler.[7]

[1] Hist. Ches. i. 500.
[2] Hist. Ches. i. 502.
[3] Ibid.
[4] Ibid. 453.
[5] Ibid. 452.
[6] Ches. Recog. Rolls.
[7] Bold Deeds.

CHAPTER X.

THOMAS BARKETT, Birkett, Bricket, or Birkenhead, for he was called by all those names, who succeeded as the next Abbot of Norton, and so about the year 1525 became its twenty-fourth head, was probably of the old Cheshire family of Birkenhead, one of whom died Bishop of St. Asaph in April 1518. The abbot, if not the patron, was at least a relative of that John Birkenhead who held office in the abbey and was pensioned at the Dissolution, and is mentioned as residing at Halton Park in 33 Henry VIII.[1] Succeeding as he did to the abbot's chair after so long a line of ecclesiastical ancestors, and before that little cloud no bigger than a man's hand had arisen in the sky, he might well have felt elated with his position, had he not at the same time found in the sense of its great responsibilities a sufficient counterpoise to any feeling of pride. It was about this time, soon after his election, that the vicarage of Great Budworth, a living in the abbot and convent's gift, fell vacant, and the presentation to it of William Hardware was probably one of the new abbot's first acts. The Duttons and others of the neighbouring gentry, many of whom had probably received the rudiments of their education in the abbey, chose its precincts for their last resting-place. Amongst those of them who were there interred was probably Adam de Dutton, one of their greatest men. Another of them, Lawrence de Dutton, on the 4th October 1527, desiring to lay his bones in the abbey, when he made his will did not forget either the place or its claims to his remembrance. In the will he says, "I bequeath my soul to Almighty God, beseeching humbly our blessed lady, and all the holy company of heaven, to be mediators for me to the Holy Trinity, to receive the same to the eternal bliss of heaven. And I will that my body shall be buried and interred amongst my ancestors in the chapel of our blessed lady within the monastery of Norton. Also I will that every priest that shall be at my burying shall have, to

[1] Halton Records.

pray for my soul, xii d., and every clerk iiij d., and every poor man and woman j d."¹

For some time after Abbot Birkenhead's election the sky continued bright and clear, and gave no signs of any tempest likely to arise soon to disturb it. The kingdom was at peace and the church at rest, and even afterwards, when the lawfulness of the king's marriage with his brother Arthur's widow came to be questioned, not even the keenest sight could foresee the mighty consequences that were likely to arise from it. The first step which the king took to set the matter at rest was to assemble a body of the bishops, prelates, clergy, and canonists of the province of Canterbury to meet in convocation, and after due deliberation to give him their opinions upon it, and they were accordingly summoned to meet in the chapter-house of St. Paul's Cathedral in London. At their meeting on the 5th November 1529, it was found that of the bishops and clergy there were 75 prelates and clergy and 44 canonists actually present, and that amongst them they held the proxies of more than 200 others who could not, or at least did not, attend. Amongst those who came was Stephen Gardiner, Bishop of Winchester, a man of fiery zeal, whom a poet not inaptly imagines thus addressing the Jesuit Angelo :—

> "Think not thine order, brother, nor thy tenets
> Sublime as that unquestioning devotion
> With which God's seraphim perform his mandate.
> Unknown, unnoticed, unobserved, I lay
> The volume of this heart, that man ne'er read,
> Before thee. There is hate of heresy
> Deep, desperate as thine own. In the dead night,
> And in the secret prayers of my dark chamber,
> Like thee I cry, Holy and True, how long?
> O when shall they blaze up and gladden heaven,
> The glorious purifying fires, and purge
> The land of its pollutions; when the church
> In pure and virgin whiteness re-array,
> And its true sons shake off dissembling darkness!"²

To the convocation came also the saintly Fisher, Bishop of Rochester, and Standish, Bishop of St. Asaph, who both afterwards appeared as the queen's advocates before Wolsey and Campeius, and no doubt voted with the dissentients in the convocation, and with these came also Longland, Bishop of Lincoln, and the Spaniard George Attequa, Attica, or Attien, Bishop of Llandaff, who had come over with Queen Katherine, and was

¹ Lancashire and Cheshire Wills, Chet. Soc. i. 23. ² Milman's Ann Boleyn.

bound to be her champion. With the bishops there came many of the chiefs of the religious houses, and amongst them the Abbot of Norton, and with him came Thomas Roncorne, the canonist, who, if not one of his canons, certainly had his name, and probably came from his neighbourhood.

The arrival of this reverend and dignified body must have attracted crowds to the neighbourhood of St. Paul's, who watched its members with interest as they arrived from different and distant parts of the country. The bishops and prelates came in their mitres, wearing their copes and carrying their pastoral staffs; the abbots, priors, and other religious persons, came in the habit of their respective orders; the Benedictins wore their black robes and hoods, and the Augustinians their white ones; and while the Franciscans appeared in their grey habits with their sandals and rope girdles, the Canonists wore their academic gowns and their college caps, each varying in shape according to the degree or the college of the wearer. The great variety of these solemn dresses was an object of interest to the spectators. As they entered the cathedral in their sweeping and varied robes, attended by banners and tapers, the organ pealed forth its solemn notes, which echoed through the aisles, and all present were solemnised, and when at length they were seated in order in the chapterhouse the assembly had a most august and venerable aspect.

The two questions which were proposed to the convocation, and which were debated at great length, were first "An ducere uxorem cognitam a fratre decedente sine prole sit prohibitio juris divini indispensabilis a papa?" (Is there such a prohibition in the divine law against a man's marrying the widow of his brother who has died without issue after a marriage consummated between them, as the Pope cannot dispense with?) This question, which was debated by the bishops, prelates, and clergy only, was answered in the affirmative with only nineteen dissentients. Secondly, "An carnalis copula inter illustrissimum principem Arthurum et serenissimam dominam reginam ex propositis exhibitis deductis et allegatis sit sufficienter probata?" (Whether, on the proofs adduced, exhibited, and alleged before the convocation, the marriage between the most illustrious Prince Arthur and the most serene lady Queen Katherine was sufficiently proved to have been consummated?) This question, with only six dissentients, the canonists, who alone were required to answer it, decided in the affirmative. After being continued by adjournment, from time to time, until 5th April 1533, the convocation came to a close, and its decisions were then received by Archbishop Cranmer, who ordered them to be recorded.¹

The ready obedience which the Abbot of Norton had given to the summons he had received to attend this convocation, his attending at its opening and taking part in its deliberations, was very likely afterwards remembered by the king to his advantage.

Thomas Roncorne, one of the canonists who attended with Abbot Barkett, may have been one of the canons of Norton, though there was about the same time a person of his name who was archdeacon of Bangor.²

On the 7th July 1540, he was one of those who sat on the royal commission issued to decide whether the king's marriage with Anne of Cleves had or had not been consummated.³ Goodrich, another of the canonists, had afterwards a share in translating the New Testament, and was made Bishop of Ely. It is remarkable that none of the heads of any of the religious houses in Cheshire, Chester, Vale Royal, Combermere, and Birkenhead, except the Abbot of Norton, attended the convocation in person, the rest contenting themselves with being only represented there by their proxies. It certainly must have required some courage in those days of bad roads, when public conveyances were unknown, for the abbot to saddle his palfrey and set out on so long a journey in winter; and it as certainly required some boldness to give his vote on the question proposed, when obloquy was sure to attend it on whichever side it was given. Let us hope that he had the satisfaction of his own conscience in what he did.

[1] Fiddes' Life of Wolsey, appendix 156; and Froude's History of England, i. 418.
[2] Browne Willis, Bangor, p. 133. [3] Strype's Memorials, i. 577S.

CHAPTER XI.

THERE was now, and there had been for some time past, a general belief that the religious houses, especially those of the smaller sort which had but few inmates, were not so well governed as they should be, that they had suffered their rule to become relaxed, and that a full crop of abuses had been the consequence. The remedy for this was thought to be a general visitation of all religious houses, which, by discovering what was faulty in their actual condition, might suggest and apply the means of correcting it, and so bring back the houses to observe their original rule.

Corruptio optimæ fit pessima, or, according to Sir Philip Sidney's paraphrase, "Whatsoever being rightly used doth most good, being abused doth most harm," is certainly a true axiom, and in proportion to the intrinsic excellence of anything, so should be the corresponding vigilance observed to guard it from abuse. Visitations of the monasteries were no new thing; they had been resorted to before. In 1373 Wykeham, Bishop of Winchester, visited all the monasteries in his diocese, where he found such disorders existing that in the next year he issued a commission for reforming them; but not thinking even that sufficient for the priory at Selborne, a house of Austin canons like Norton, which he found wholly given up to pleasure, he issued special injunctions to be observed in the house. But these canons were incorrigible, and one of Wykeham's successors, Waynflete, in the reign of Henry VI., finding them wearing costly furs and rich dresses, quite contrary to their habit, pursuing the pleasures of the chase like laymen, and neglecting their church services, finally suppressed the house. In 1492, Smith, Bishop of Lichfield and Coventry, had visited all those within his diocese,[1] but instead of being frequent, the visitations had been but few and far between, and when they were made they often proved more superficial than real, like that which Mapes says the abbot made of his granges :—

Tota de temporalibus
Est patria inquisitio,

---

[1] Hist. Lanc. iii. 724.

> Quasi nulla de moribus
> Habetur ibi quæstio.
>
> The holy father only makes
> Of temporals his quest,
> And neither thought nor care he takes
> Of morals, or the rest.

The monasteries had always their official visitors, but it was the natural tendency of these visitors to hold the reins with a slack hand, and so discipline became relaxed ; and as

> Neglectis urenda filix innascitur agris,

so it happened that old abuses appeared again and again with renewed virulence. Soon after the accession of Henry V. he was urged by parliament, to whom he had applied for a subsidy, to seize the revenues of the church and convert them to his own use—a subject of which Shakspeare has taken notice in his opening scene of the drama of Henry V., where Chicheley, the Archbishop of Canterbury, is introduced, telling the Bishop of Ely in some alarm at the proposal

> I have made an offer to His Majesty,—
> Upon a spiritual convocation ;
> And in regard of causes now in hand,
> Which I have opened to His Grace at large,
> As touching France,—to give a greater sum
> Than ever at one time the clergy yet
> Did to his predecessors part withal !

The archbishop was successful in persuading the king to spare the church, and, as a compromise, he either suggested or supported that visitation of the Alien priories, which soon afterwards took place, and led to the abolition of more than a hundred of them, and the giving up of the proceeds to the king. Wolsey also, at a later period, with the Pope's full consent, had visited and suppressed a considerable number of the smaller religious houses, and had devoted their revenues to the support of those two great foundations, " which witnessed for him" at Oxford and Ipswich. On this suppression Sir William Barlowe says, "I let pass my Lord Cardinal's act in pulling down and suppressing religious places. Our Lord assoil his soul ! I wrestle with no souls. He knoweth by this time whether he did well or evil, but this dare I be bold to say, that the counties where they stood found such lack of them that they would he had let them stand."[1]

[1] Sir William Barlowe's Dialogue.

In the year 1533, however, the outcry for a general visitation of all these religious houses had become so great, that Cromwell, by the king's authority and with the general approbation of the country, appointed commissioners to go through the kingdom and report upon the state of these houses. Drs. Lee, Layton, Ap Rice, and others who were selected for the work, set about it with such promptness and goodwill that the very alarm of their coming induced the heads of some monasteries to surrender them into the king's hands without waiting for the arrival of the commissioners.

Meanwhile men's minds were disturbed, and no man knew what was to happen, as this story, one of many that might be adduced, may serve to show. Richard Sumner and John Clayton, two Lancashire men, came forward and deposed that, falling in with James Harrison, a priest, they heard him say, "This is a marvellous world: the king will put down the order of priests and destroy the sacrament, but he cannot reign long, for Yorkshire will be in London hastily."[1]

It was not long before the commissioners completed their visitation and gave in their report, which contained so very dark a catalogue of the disorders they had found, that when Queen Mary, to whom the report was especially hateful, came to the throne, she commanded her favourite Bishop Bonner to search out and destroy all the copies of it—a work he did so effectually that it is believed no single copy of it was spared, and with the report he is thought also to have destroyed many other kindred documents of the time. The surrender of Norton, which is well known to have been made, and which is mentioned in the grant to Sir Richard Brooke afterwards, but which is not now in existence, may possibly have been one of the documents which thus perished under Bonner's hands. The bishop, who had a bar in his escutcheon, was descended from the Savages, who were near neighbours of Norton, and he may have had special reasons for destroying the surrender of that house, as a means of reinstating that ancient house on some future favourable turn in fortune's wheel.

The report of the commissioners had prepared the public for seeing some decided step taken against the religious houses, and accordingly an Act passed in the month of April 1536 which absolutely gave up to the king's use all the lands of all such monasteries or religious houses as had fewer than 12 inmates on their foundation or had a less income than £200

[1] Ellis' letters, 1st Series, p. 43.

a year, and the same Act also gave up to the king's use all their churches, houses, plate, furniture, and goods of all kinds. Norton, which had an annual income of only £180 : 7s., was one of the houses which were by this summary sentence thus doomed to destruction.

The smaller houses having been thus disposed of, the king lost no time in sending his commissioners to make an inventory of their valuables and effects, and to take actual possession both of these and their houses and lands in the king's name and for his use. The two commissioners who came into Cheshire on this errand were Mr. Combes and Mr. Bolles, of whom little has occurred before or has been found elsewhere in connection with these proceedings, though the former occurs afterwards, when he is called auditor.

In the meantime the people of these northern parts, who thought the work of monastic destruction was proceeding too rapidly, began to feel uneasy at what was being done. The suppression of the minor houses, they feared, was but the opening of a flood-gate to a wider measure, on which they could not look with calmness and indifference. The wiser part, too, thought as Latimer did at a later period when he gave his wholesome advice that "some two or three convents should be preserved in each county, not for the purpose of perpetuating monachism, but with the view of promoting the twofold object of religious instruction, and keeping up and maintaining the exercise of hospitality." But with these there were great numbers of others who were more impulsive and not so wise. The commons of Yorkshire, under the leading of Dr. Mackerel, the Prior of Barlings, who assumed the name of Captain Cobler, were the first to take up arms in the cause of the religious houses. Dr. Mackerel and his army of followers had, but not without difficulty, been confronted and kept in check by the Duke of Norfolk, when that greater insurrection known as the Pilgrimage of Grace, which it required both policy and force to repress, broke out in Lincolnshire. If the satirist speaks truly when he says of the religious houses thus :—

> There be no tidings nor novelties in war,
> Nor any wonders done in any strange land,
> Whatsoever they be, and come they never so far,
> The priests in the quire have them first in hand—[1]

it was not likely that the tidings of one or both of these risings had not

[1] Barclay's Ship of Fools, 182-3.

reached Cheshire, and kindled some sympathies with their object in the neighbourhood of Norton, if not even in the house itself. Sir Piers Dutton, whose conduct was not wholly disinterested, since the King had granted, and by Act of Parliament in the year 1535 had confirmed to him, the advowson of Poosey Chapel and some other of the abbey possessions,[1] in his over zeal to prevent Cheshire catching the infection of insurrection, secured the person of the Abbot of Norton and some of his canons, and then wrote the following letter to Cromwell announcing what he had done:—

"Please it your gud mastership, my duetie remembert, thes be to advertise you that I have taken the boddies of th'abbot of Norton, Robert Jannyns, and the straunger, a connyng smythe, two of the seid abbottes servantes, also Rondull Brerctone, baron of the Kynge's Excheqer of Chestre, and John Hale of Chestre, merchant, and have theym in my custody and kepyng. And the rest I entende to have as spedely as I can, and to be with you with theym, God willyng, in all convenyent spede as I possible may. Moreover I have causet Dan Rondull Wylmyslow, the moncke of the valle Royall, to cum up to you, for whom I spake unto your good mastership whiche is a gud religious man, discrete, and well groundet in lernyng, and hathe many gud qualities most apte to be a master of a religious howse than any other moncke of that howse. Wherfour it may please your gud mastership to be his gud master toward his preferrement, that he may be admitted master of the same, and that I did promyse your mastership this seid moncke will accomplishe accordyngly, wherefour I beseche your mastership that this berer and the seid moncke may resorte unto you from tyme to tyme, to knowe your pleasure therein, ensuryng you what ye do for me or for my frynde, all is your owne, as knowithe our Lord God, who mercifully you preserve. At Dutton, the iijde day of Auguste.

" By youres assured
" Perus Dutton, Knt.

"To the right honorable and his especiall gud master
"Maister Cromwell, secretary unto our sovereign lord the Kynge."[2]

---

[1] Notitia Cest. Chet. Soc. 357.
[2] Letters relating to the Suppression of Monasteries, by Camd. Soc. p. 52.

CHAPTER XII.

NOTHING seems to have come of the arrest of the abbot, or of Sir Piers' letter to Cromwell, and the abbot and his fellow prisoners must have been soon afterwards released, for it was not until the 10th October—more than two months later—that news reached Norton that Mr. Combes and Mr. Bolles, the king's two commissioners, were on their way to the abbey, and might be expected to arrive there that day. We may imagine the doomed inmates of the abbey anxiously looking for their arrival, and singing their last *miserere*, and while its lingering echoes still floated through the aisles and cloisters, hearing the announcement that the expected visitors, with some servants and sumpter mules, had been seen winding their way through the woody glades of the park and demesne, and would shortly knock at the abbey gates, where the porter was waiting their approach. The abbot and canons had no doubt heard how the commissioners had proceeded elsewhere, and the news was not calculated to allay their apprehensions; and though the report made to Cromwell, so far as we know, had not stated that there had been any departure from the rule, or any want of discipline at Norton, the feelings of the abbot and his canons must have been in sympathy with the gloomy sky, as on that autumnal evening, standing in cowl and hood, they awaited in the chapter-house the entrance of the dreaded visitors. The hour when they arrived was late, and little more business beyond showing their commission and going through some other matters of form, was transacted on that evening; but on the morrow they addressed themselves in earnest to their work, and had finished the inventory of the Norton valuables, had commenced packing them up, and were already thinking of their departure, when a great crowd of people, making threatening outcries and clamour, surrounded the abbey, and not a little daunted the courage of the commissioners; but what further occurred may be best told in the words of a distinguished modern historian. "Here," he says, "is a small spark of English life, lighted by a stray letter from an English gentleman (the Sheriff) of

Cheshire. The Lord Chancellor was informed by Sir Piers Dutton, a justice of the peace, that the visitors having come to Norton Abbey, and having concluded their inspection, had packed up such jewels and plate as they intended to remove, and were going away, when, the day being late and the weather foul, they changed their minds, and resolved to spend the night where they were. In the evening," says Sir Piers, " the abbot gathered together a great company, to the number of two or three hundred persons, so that the Commissioners were in fear of their lives, and were fain to take a tower (which was possibly the tower of the abbey church) there; and thereupon sent a letter unto me, ascertaining me what danger they were in, and desiring me to come and assist them, or they were never likely to come thence, which letter came to me about nine of the clock; and about two o'clock on the same night I came there with such of my tenants as I had near about me, and found divers fires made as well within the gates as without; and the said abbot had caused an ox to be killed, with other victuals, and prepared for such of his company as he had there. I used some policy, and came suddenly upon them. Some of them took to the pools and water, and it was so dark that I could not find them. Howbeit I took the abbot and three of his canons, and brought them to King's Castle of Halton."[1]

The sheriff, who at first conveyed his prisoners to the neighbouring stronghold, the castle of Halton, afterwards conducted them to Chester Castle as a place of more security, and then wrote the following letter to Sir Thomas Audley, the lord chancellor, explaining what he had done, and asking for the king's directions :—

"Pleasethe it yor good lordshipe to be advertesed Mr. Combes and Mr. Bolles the kynges comisayoners w'thin the county fer the suppressyng of the abbey theare, and when they had packed uppe such juelles and other stuffe as they had theare and thought upon the morrowe after to departe them th' abbot gaderid a grete comppany togedere to the number of towe or thre hondred persones, so that the said comissyoners weare in feare of their lyves and weare fayne to take a tower theare, and thereuppon sent a lettore unto me asserteninge what danger they wear in and desyred me to com to assyst them, or else they wear never lyke to come thence ; wich lettore came to me abovt 9 of the clock in the same night, I came thether w'th suche of my lovers and tenants as I had neare about me and found diverse fyeres made theare as well w'thin the gates as without. And the said abbot had an oxe and other vittalles to be killed and prepared fer suche his company as he had then theare, and it was thoughte in the morrowe after he had come forthe to have had a great number moare, notwithstanding I used pollesy and cam suddenly upon them so that the company that weare thear fledd and some of them took pooles and watere, and it was so darke that I could not fynde them, and it was thought yf

---

[1] Froude's Hist. Eng. ii. 424, who, however, places the event a year too early.

the matter had not byn quikly handled, it would have growne to further inconvenience, to what danger God knoweth; howbeit, I took the abbot and thre of the channones and brought them to the king's Castell of Halton, and thear comytted them to ward to the constable, to be kept as the king's rebellious, upon payne of a thousand pounds; and afterwards saw the sayd comyssioners with their stuffe convayed thence, and William Parker, the kyng's servant, who is appoynted to be the king's fermore their, to be restored to his possession, wherfoare it may like your good lordshipe that the king's grace may have knowledge hearof, and that his pleasure mayo be further knowne therin, which I shall be always rely and glad to accomplishe to the uttermost of my powere, as knowethe our Lord God, who ever preserve your good Lordshipe with much honor. At Dutton, the xii. of Octobre, anno 1536, by your assured, PERES DUTTON, KT.

 To the rt. honorable and very singular
  good lord Sir Thomas Audley, Knight,
   lord chanseler of England, thes be delivered."[1]

The family of Brereton, who appear here in connection with Norton, appear also at this time in a variety of characters in connection with the place. Sir William Brereton of Brereton, of whom we shall shortly have to speak, was vice-chamberlain of Chester. Randle Brereton, one of the prisoners arrested by the sheriff, was baron of the Exchequer at Chester, and William the *parker*, to whose care the sheriff gave up the abbey after he had released the commissioners, was another William Brereton, who was then seneschal and park-keeper of Halton. Sir Piers Dutton, the sheriff, notwithstanding that Norton was the burial-place of his ancestors, bore no kindly feeling towards it; and though his own life and character were not free from reproach, and though he soon afterwards fell into trouble on his own account, he was evidently at this time not inclined to extenuate the abbot's offence, or to regret that the commissioners had required his services.

Being released from their danger, the commissioners packed up the abbey valuables, and amongst them, we suppose, its books[2] (a catalogue of which would be a great curiosity now), and when all the movables were packed, the commissioners made the following list of all the abbey possessions:—

ABBATIA DE NORTON.

Scit. nup abbatiæ cũ ter. dominical .			42	16	0
Firma prat. et pastur. quondam de terris dominicalibus		3	12	0
Reddit. et firm. in Norton	.	.	22	3	4½
Aston redd. et firm.	.	.	.	12	5	4
Aston juxta Sutton reddit assis.	.	.	.	0	2	0

[1] Hist. Ches. i. 502-11.

[2] The inventories taken at Whalley and Stanlaw, however, contain not a single book (Liverpool Hist. Soc. Proceedings, 1866-7 and 1871-2, where these inventories are printed). The destruction of the books in the monasteries is said to have caused Leland, the royal antiquary, to lose his reason.

Haltou reddit. et firm.	2	8	0
More redd. et firm.	1	13	6
Preston un. tenementum	0	7	0
Gyldon Sutton redd. &c.	20	15	8
Civitas Cest. reddit. assis.	0	15	8
Walton molend. aquat.	1	0	0
Newton. terr. tenem. &c.	1	19	0
Deresbury feod. firm. terr. &c.	0	9	0
Kekewyke redd. ab antiquâ con. ad inveniend. lampad. in dicto mon. de Norton	0	4	0
Stokeome redd. 7, tenement.	0	19	1
Runcorne abbatis tenement. &c.	3	1	4
Northwich salin. &c.	3	5	8
Lachedenys terr.	2	0	0
Nether Pever	0	6	0
Budworth, Comberbach, Surlach, and Barneton diversa premissa	17	2	8
Landecan redd.	0	10	0
Frodesham redd.	0	18	4
Rowsthorne uñ. mes.	0	16	0
Myllington uñ. molend.	1	0	0
Wyntonley un. mes	1	10	0
Weryngton redd. ass.	0	4	4
Bold, Penkcrich et Rowsiche	0	1	0
Torbok redd. terr.	0	6	8
Stotfield Shawe redd. terr.	0	4	0
[1] Oldgreve juxta Lymne redd. terr.	0	3	4
Swarby elemosina	1	10	0
Runcorne rectoria	50	15	0
Budwerth rectoria	82	2	8
Porco decim. garb. de Gyldin Sutton	2	0	0
Decim. garb. de Halfield et Sutton ultra Mersey Lan.	2	0	0
Halton mede Halfeld and Astmorfeld decim.	0	5	0
Pyrton Oxon. rectoria	26	0	0
Donyngton Linc. rectoria	20	0	0
Burton Stather Linc. rectoria	6	0	0
Penc' ones	1	2	0
Vend. bosc. null.			
Pexquis. cur. null.			
Sum̃a total. recept.	343	13	7¼ [2]

When this work was ended the commissioners dismissed the sorrowing inmates of the abbey, who left their beautiful home with heavy hearts,

---

[1] This place was probably Wilgrave near Thelwall, but on the opposite side of the Mersey, but no mention is made of Thelwall, which was certainly in Runcorne parish, and of which Webb thus speaks: "We turn with the Mersey to Thelwall, a chapelry and goodly lordship having belonged to the abbey of Norton, which place with many others may show unto men the variations and mutabilities of all earthly structures" (Hist. Ches. i. 320).

[2] Ministers' accounts in the Augmentation Office, 28 Hen. VIII.

and departed hardly knowing whither to direct their steps. One of them, who was probably an official, carried his seal away with him, and, as if it could be of no further use, dropped it near one of the outlets from the park, where, after lying hid for more than three centuries, it was discovered in 1863.

It only remained for the commissioners to thank the sheriff for his valuable services, and to take their departure after giving the abbey into the care of the parker.

The letter of Sir Piers Dutton to the Chancellor, though written on the 12th October, did not probably reach its destination for five or more days, and another day or two were probably consumed before the Chancellor could consult the king and receive his commands upon it. On the twentieth of that month, however, just eight days after the date of Sir Piers's letter, the king, rather like an Amurath than an English sovereign, issued a peremptory order to Sir Piers Dutton and Sir William Brereton of Brereton, then vice-chamberlain of Chester, to have the prisoners executed without delay. His letter for that purpose ran as follows:—

"Trusty and welbeloved we greete ye well, and have as well seene the letters written from you, Sir Pearce Dutton, to our right trusty and well-beloved counselore Sir Thomas Audley, knight, declaring the treatorous demeanore of the late abbot and chanones of the monastery of Norton, used at the being there of our comysioners after the suppressyon thereof, and your wisdom, pollecsy and good endeavore used for the apprehensyon of the same, for which we give unto you our right harty thanks and shall undoubtedly consider your faithful service to your singular reving and comfort hereaftere, as other letters written from your Sir William Drearton to our right trusty and well-beloved counselere the Lord Cromwelle, keeper of our privie seall, touching the same mattere, for your good endevores also therein, and we give unto you our right harty thanks, for answere whereunto ye shall understand that for as muche as it appereth that the said late abbot and channones have most traitorously used themselves agaynst us and our relme, our pleasure and commandmente is that yf this shall fully appeare to yo' to be true that then yo' shall emediately, upon the r'ght hearof, withoute any manor further delaye, cause them to be hanged as most arrant traitores in suche sundry places as ye shall thinke requisete for the terible example of all otheres herafter, and herein fayllo ye not travillo w'th such dexterety as this matere mayo be finished w'th all possible dilligense. Gevene under oure sygnete at our castle of Wyndesore the xxth of October the xxviith yeare of our reyne, 1536.

To our trusty and welbeloved servt. Sir Pearse Dutton and Sir William Brereton, knights, and to every of them." [1]

Before, however, the king's commands to execute the prisoners could be carried out, Sir Piers had received a letter from the Earl of Derby, which enclosed one from the Earl of Shrewsbury, the king's lieutenant, and others, informing him that the rebels in Yorkshire were sparpeled (what-

[1] Hist. Ches. i. 503.

ever that may mean), and had retired to their homes, and therefore
charging Sir Piers to do no hurt or molestation to the commons. This
letter, which was meant as a sort of supersedeas of the royal warrant to
Sir Piers and his colleague, was as follows :—

"I co'mend to y'u, and have receaved a lettere from the Erle of Shrewsbury, the kyng's
leftenante, the Erle of Rutland, and the Erle of Huntyngdon, by the hands of one Barwick,
herald, in thes words: My very good lord—We hartely re'commend us unto yo'r good lordshipe, and whear my Lord of Norfolke, and we that be hearc, have stayed the com'ones of
Yorkshire, so that every man is *sparpeled* and retired whom unto their houses, and my sayd
Lorde of Norfolke departed unto the king's grace, and as we be informed from my Lorde Darcy,
yo'r Lordshipe, w'th yo'r retenewe, hath appoynted uppon Monday next coming to be at Whalley
abbey, my lord, the premises considered that al thyng is well stayed, we desire and pray of you,
and nevertheless in the king's name charge yo', that ye *sparpele* yo' company without doing any
hurte or molestacion to the sayd com'ones, or any of them, and that ye fayle not hearof, as yo'
will answer to the king's highness at yo'r perrell, and oure lord have yo'r lordshipe in his
governaunce. Written at Donkestore, the 28 of October. Wherefore ye w'th yo'r companyes
may departe whom to yo'r owne howses, and to be redy to serve the king when ye shall be
com'aunded, and I shall be a meane to the kynge's grace to consyder yo'r paynes, costs, and
good myude that ye have byn at to serve his grace. Written at Preston the xx*th* daye of
October 1536.—Yo'r lovinge frend, E. DERBY.
  To my righte wellbeloved
    Syr Perse Dutton, knight, sherrefe of Cheshire.'

After receiving this letter Sir Piers was left in a state of uncertainty,
as his colleague, Sir William Brereton, not only did not reply to his
letter, but persisted in maintaining an obstinate silence ; and to have
acted without his concurrence in putting the prisoners to death would
have been an act *extra vires*, which might have endangered his own life.

Perhaps his colleague, a near relation of one of the prisoners, had his
own reasons for not promptly obeying the king's orders, and was making
interest with some friend at court to plead for, and if possible obtain his
relative's pardon, and, in the meantime, his silence served to obstruct the
execution of the fatal sentence. Sir Piers, in his perplexity, therefore, addressed the following letter to Cromwell, the lord privy seal requesting his
directions how he was to act :—

" My duty loely remembered, thes to advertes yo'r good lordshipe when I heartofore receaved
the king's most drend letteres of com'aundement and high pleasure to me and S'r William
Brearton, knighte, in thes partes deputy chamberlayne, directed of and concerning the tretorous
demeanore of the late abbot and chanones of the monastery of Norton, by them used at their
late being theare of his grace's comysioners after the suppresyon thereof, as more at large may
appeare unto yo'r good lordshipe by a coppy of the same his gracious com'aundant heare enclosed,
and by virtue thereof incontinently after we had receaved his sayd grace's com'aundement we
appoynted a shorte daye then ensluinge for the execuyon of the same his grace's com'aundement,

according to the contents thereof to have been done, albeit imediatly after and before the sayd daye assygued we receaved somdrey letteres to us directed from the Earle of Derby, mencioning in effect a lettere from the Earle of Shrewsbury, leefetenant unto the kyng's grace, the Earles of Rutland and Huntyngdon, touching that the Duke of Norfolke and they had stayed the comones of Yorkshire, charging the said Earle of Derby in the king's gracious name to sjurjolle his company w'thout doing any hurte or molestacion to the sayd comones or any of them, as more at large shall appeare unto yo'r good lordshipe by the coppyes of one of the same letteres to me, directed herein also enclosed ; and thenruppon in consideracion of the same, their doing we contynued and respeted the accomplishmente of the king's sayd gracious com'aundemente untill his most gracious forther pleasure to us therein were known, determinyng ourselves to certify his grace of the promesyes, and made our lettores certifycate accordingly with my hand and thereunto subscribed, having the sayd eveldoers and offenders in strait endurance of imprisonment within his Castell of Chestore, there shurely to be kept to abide his grace's pleasure ; and afterwards the sayd Sir William Brearton denyed that to certefye and I was allways ready to execute the same according to the purport thereof ; what cause or meaninge he had so to refuse I know not, and for that the king's said com'aundement was to us both joyntly directed to execute the same. I w'thout him in no wise could, nor yet cane execute the same, wherefore I would be glad to have knolledge of his most gracious further pleasure therein, that I may follow the same as to my dutye appertayneth, most meeklye beseechinge your good lordshipe that I may be ascertened thereof, and I shall praye to God for his highness and your good lordshipe long to contynew. Atte Dutton, the xxx*th* daye of November 1536.—
By y'r owne assured,   PERUS DUTTON, Knight.

"To the righte honorable, and my singular good lord, my Lord Prevy Seaile."

All this while, shut up within the four walls of their prison, where no news could reach them, the abbot and his fellow-sufferers lay hardly daring to hope, for the absence of all tidings from without aggravated their anxiety and suspense as to their fate, so as to make them fear the worst.

Sir William Brereton of Malpas, the Chamberlain of Chester, had very lately lost his life by the headsman's axe, in consequence of the charges brought against him relating to Queen Anne Boleyn, and, for aught that the abbot and his companions knew, that same "two-handed engine," which had despatched him, might be "waiting at the door" for them. The king's command to Sir Piers and his colleague to do speedy execution on the offenders they probably knew had been peremptory. How then came it to be delayed? Was it because the execution was to be the joint act of the two officials, and that while Sir Piers betrayed an unseemly anxiety to put the prisoners to death, his colleague had his own reasons for deferring it? Either he was grieving over the recent death of his near kinsman, or, entertaining some doubts whether, by the death of the chamberlain, his own office as vice-chamberlain was not ended, and if so, whether, by exceeding his powers, he might not bring danger to his own door. The correspondence, indeed, seems to show that there existed no great cordiality between the two officials, Sir Piers and Sir William, who probably took a very different view of the abbot's share in the Norton outbreak. Comparing the dates of the several events, it seems not improbable that the Yorkshire rising having been settled, and the Lincolnshire one being in a fair way of arrangement, the king felt uncertain whether, through the conduct of the Duke of Norfolk and the other commanders, he was not pledged to grant an amnesty, and being in a relenting mood, might have been led to visit with his anger any of his officials who had precipitated an execution while he was debating of an amnesty. Sir William Brereton may have represented the abbot's share in the outbreak as having been less culpable than it at first appeared, or the act itself may have been rather the work of the people without than of the inmates within the abbey, or, which is not improbable, the king may have been more inclined to clemency by remembering the abbot's former readiness to attend the convocation in person, and the votes which he gave there. As the execution did not take place immediately, it is evident that there must have arrived some respite to delay it. No notice of the execution of the abbot and his fellow prisoners occurs in the Chester annals, and no tradition of it lingers about the house at Norton, where, had it occurred, it would most likely have been found. The very place where the abbot of Whalley was executed is still pointed out at Whalley, and as many years afterwards Robert Jamyns, one of the prisoners, is found living and farming some of the abbey lands of Norton, it is probable that the royal amnesty which had been promised arrived, and brought with it a pardon for the abbot and his fellow prisoners. If so, Mr. Willis and others are probably correct in saying that the last abbot of Norton was not put to death, but that he retired upon a pension of xxiv. li. a year, which still continued to be paid in the year 1556.[1]

We are nowhere told how many canons there were in the house of Norton, either at the foundation or any other time. We know, however, that three of the canons were made prisoners, with the abbot, in the house; we know also that Randle Wilmyston, or Wilmslow, was there. He was a kinsman (Dr. Ormerod thinks) of the Wilmslows, the illegitimate relations of Bonner The visitors, who found him in the house, allowed him to migrate to Vale Royal, and finally, for some expected treachery to his new home it is thought, recommended for a pension " as a good, religious man, discreet, and well grounded in learning, and as having many good

[1] Hist. Ches. i. 503; n. Greswell's Hist. Runcorn, 52.

qualities,"[1] and that William Boyes, another canon, who was pensioned, was also there; and if Runcorn, the canonist, was one of the canons, the house had not less than eight or ten canons on the foundation; and these, with the abbot and a few novices and scholars, and their necessary servants, must have formed a tolerably large household. When the abbey bell had rung out its last knell, the sorrowing inmates quitted the house to seek new homes, and the history of their house, which had stood for four centuries, was ended. As soon as they had left the abbey it was handed over to William Parker, or William "the parker," that William Brereton, the seneschal of Halton, who had directions to dilapidate and pull down the church, and so prevent its former inmates from resuming the possession of it, a danger which, in the case of another abbey—that of Leicester—had already presented itself to one of the visitors, who thus wrote to Cromwell: "Let me know your pleasure as to defacing the church and other superfluous buildings."[2] The church being destroyed, Brereton was to look rigorously after the king's rights. If for that purpose he took up his abode in the dreary and deserted abbey, his ear would be often startled in the night by the hollow echoes which haunted its walls.

After retaining the abbey in his hands for nine years, the king then sold it, for a full and fair consideration, to Sir Richard Brooke, the direct ancestor of the present owner, and never since that time have the provisions of the statutes of 27 Henry VIII., c. 22, and 5 Elizabeth, c. 2, that the owner of the site or precincts and demesne of any late dissolved religious house that was under the value of 200 a year should keep an honest and continual household therein been infringed at Norton.[3] The grant, which bears date 10th December, 37 Henry VIII. (1545), conveys to Sir Richard the manor of Norton, the site and house of the late monastery, with the higher and lower court, the "fermery-orchard," the great garden, the smith's orchard, Enley wood, seven messuages and lands in Stockham, with all the rents from the preceding Lady-day. The names of some of the fields, and a few of such other particulars contained in the grant as seem most worthy to be remembered, are as follow:—

The names of some of the fields were:—
The Mayden's Crime, or the Great Crime.
The Trentam Trental.

[1] Harl. MS. fol. 604, f. 54; Hist. Ches. i. 432 and 502.
[2] Strype's Memorials, i. 407.
[3] Eirenorcha, 471.

The Sely Lowe (or Silly How). In Scotland the women call a film or membrane stretched over the heads of children new born, a sely or silly how, and Sir Thomas Brown says "great conceits are raised of the involution of membranous covering commonly called the *silly how* that is sometimes found about the heads of children upon their birth, and is therefore preserved with great care, not only as medical in diseases, but effectual in success concerning the infant and others, which is surely no more than a continued superstition."[1] How came the field to obtain this singular name?

The Great Orchard Field.
The Church Fields.
The Hemp Yardes.
The Shepe House.
The Kale Yards.
The Dame Savage Meadow (which had probably been given by her)..
The Wholrow or Wholroe (a strange provincial corruption of the word Warren).
The Fowle Acre.
The Cellarer's Medowe (which had probably been attached to that officer's office).
The Pikel.
The Abbey Park.

Beside the Abbey there is only one house mentioned as being in Norton, and this is said to be in the occupation of Robert Janyns and Margaret his wife, who also held other lands there. The other tenants were as follow:—

William Rede.	Radulph Glydale.
Robert Chesshyre.	Richard Okehyle.
John Houghe.	Matilda Dutton.
John Byrkehode (some connection of the Abbot's, who, like him, was afterwards pensioned).	Robert Haton.
	Hugh Sankey.
	Robert Lee.
Richard Hueghson.	Hugh Jackson.
Hamonde Rider.	William Heyward.
Ranulph Hale.	Katherine Coppoche.
Thomas Jakeson.	Thomas Toppoche.
Richard Johnson.	Richard Crosse.
Robert Hunte.	Thomas Jackson senior.

[1] Vulgar Errors, b. v. c. xi. s. 17.

Cristofer Myddleburste.	Thomas Bolton.
Thomas Barlowe.	Thomas Yate.
John Hylton.	Thomas Houghe.
Henry Johnson.	

There was one water-mill, one windmill, and one fulling-mill, in Norton.

In Stokecombe seven houses are mentioned, which are said to be in the possession of—

Marion Norcote.	Richard Aishton.
Jacob Alcocke.	Roger Broxton.
Thomas Lydyate.	Robert Goldyng.
Richard Yerle.	

The price paid by Sir Richard Brooke for his purchase was £1512 : 1 : 9, and a yearly reserved rent of £7 : 18s., which altogether was about equivalent to twenty-two years' purchase upon £78 : 19 : 7¼, the sum which, with extreme particularity, is stated to be the annual rent of the property, not deducting the one-tenth (*decimâ non deductâ*) which, as the law then stood, was always to be reserved on the sale of Crown lands. According to the original agreement, one-half the purchase money was to be paid in land, and the remainder in two years, and at any time within that date the king might take the land back—a strange provision. But, besides the monastery and its lands, the letters-patent expressly granted the purchaser "all male and female neifs and villeins with their issue" (*omnes nativos, nativas, villanos cum eorum sequelis*). This last grant, which will require some explanation, shows that the purchaser of Norton was to have and hold with it a number of his fellow creatures, who were not only not free, but were bondmen, as were all the children born or to be born of them. The canons, therefore, like many of the laity, had some such persons on their domain, who were capable of being transferred with it like the cattle feeding upon it. But we may explain a little more fully what these serfs or villeins were, and show the distinction which the *religious* made between holding serfs of this kind themselves and suffering the laity to hold them. "A villein then could acquire no property, either in lands or goods; and if he claimed to have acquired any, the lord might seize them to his own use. He might not marry his daughter without the lord's consent; and if he did so, the lord might bring his action against the husband for purloining his property. The children of villeins were in the same state of bondage with their parents, whence they were called in Latin *nativi*, which gave rise to the female appellation of a villein, who was called *nativa*—a neife. It was no wonder, therefore, that the holy fathers, monks, and friars, in their confessions, and especially in their extremest deadly sickness, from time to time convinced the laity how dangerous a practice it was for one Christian man to hold another in bondage, so that temporal men by little and little, by reason of that terror in their consciences, were glad to manumit all their villeins. The holy fathers, abbots, and priors, however, were in no haste to do the same by theirs, for they had a conscientious scruple against impoverishing or despoiling the church so much as to manumit the villeins who were bound to them, or their churches, or to the manors which the church had gotten, and so they kept their villeins still."[1]

There were a fulling-mill and several other mills on the property, the pasture land of which let for 2s. and the meadow at 4s. the acre.

From the grant to Sir Richard, however, there were excepted "all and singular the bells and bell metal, and all manner of lead of, in, or upon any of the buildings of the late monastery, except all lead gutters, and all lead in the windows, and also except all stones, wood, iron, and glass, being in or upon any houses, edifices, and buildings within the said site (exceptis omnibus et singulis campanis et campanarum metallis ac toto et omnimodo plumbo de et in vel super quibuscunque ædificiis dicti nuper monasterii existentibus præter gutturas plumbeas et plumbum in fenestris, ac etiam exceptis omnibus lapidibus, mæremio, ferro et vitro existentibus in vel super quibuscunque hujusmodi domibus ædificiis et structuris infra dictum scitum quæ quidem domus, ædificia, structuræ firmario ejusdem scitus minime assignantur vel appunctuantur)," which seems to show that the church and its attendant buildings had already been laid in ruins. Some of the stalls, however, and a few fragments of the glass and tiles which have been preserved, are still remaining at Norton.

No legend like that of the Combermere bells, which is told in the following verses, occurs at Norton, whereas at Norton, as at Combermere, there was water to drown them, which might have helped the story:—

> The sun shone clear on the broad bright mere,
> And the menials thronged its shore;
> They sought to guide from the deep flood tide
> The Bells of the Monks of yore.

---

[1] Blackstone's Commentaries, ii. 96, quoting Sir Thomas Smith.

When lo! from the mere, these words of fear
Struck awe to the list'ners round ;
It seemed from the wave some spirit gave
That supernatural sound.

Let none who would sweep these bells from the deep
One word unholy use ;
Or his strength will be vain, and never again
Shall they rise from their watery ooze.

And deep 'mid the wave, shall be his grave
An undiscovered tomb ;
And this smiling shore shall shine no more,
Till the fated blast of doom.

With awe and fear the menials steer,
The last Bell to the side ;
Till it rests on land, and with eager hand,
One grasped its rim, and cried,

" Though earth, and air, and the waters there
Conspire with the massive Bell ;
In spite of them all, it no more shall fall,
I swear by the fiends of hell ! "

Scarce had he spoke, when with thundering stroke,
The crumbling earth gave way ;
And the waters close o'er the holy Bell,
And the sinful child of clay.

They dragged the mere both far and near,
But their comrade never found ;
And their sons still tell of the holy Bell
That the impious Scorner drowned.

For some purpose, probably connected with Sir Richard Brooke's purchase, another valuation was made of Norton, which is preserved in the Augmentation Office. This paper, which is valuable as showing the then rental value of lands in Norton, is as follows :—

The Abbey of Norton, in the county of Chester.

MEADOW.

	£	s.	d.
First 64 acres of mead lying about the abbey; price the acre, 4s.	12	16	0

PASTURE.

		£	s.	d.
Item, 72 acres lying about the abbey ; price the acre, 2s.	104s.			
Item, 6 acres lying in Middleton ; price the acre, 18d.	12s.			
Item, Barlowe and Mosse Moor be worth by the year	33s. 4d.			
Item, the Oxmoor with the appurts. is worth by the year	40s.	12	3	8
Item, a pasture called Sondewall Moor, by the year	33s. 4d.			
Item, the park is worth by the year to be letten	13s. 4d.			
Item, the Lower Swyne park is worth by the year	2s. 8d.			
Item, the yards at the Sheephouse be worth by the year	5s.			

LEY.

		£	s.	d.
Item, 24 acres in Saunders field; price the acre, 8d.	16s.			
Item, 16 acres in crop field; price the acre, 8d.	10s. 8d.	2	6	8

ARABLE LAND.

		£	s.	d.
Item, 10 acres in Horselownes; price the acre, 2s.	20s.			
Item, the cryme 6 acres; price the acre, 2s.	12s.			
Item, 16 acres lying in two orchard fields, price the acre, 22d.	29s. 4d.			
Item, 5 acres lying in Morley crofts; price the acre, 20d.	8s. 4d.			
Item, 7 acres in Churchfield; price the acre, 18d.	10s. 6d.	7	9	8
Item, 17 acres lying in Middleton; price the acre, 2s.	34s.			
Item, 10 acres in Radford field; price the acre, 8d.	6s. 8d.			
Item, 14 acres in the Weldmare Flatts; price the acre, 8d.	9s. 4d.			
Item, 13 acres of barley stubble; price the acre, 18d.	19s. 6d.			
Item, the scite of the monastery there by year	20s.			
Item, the Water Mill there by year	20s.			
Item, the Windmill there by year	20s.	9	0	0
Item, the herbage of the Warth and the Moss, where the tenants get their turf, is worth by the year	100s.			
Item, the fishing in Mersey is worth by the year	20s.			
Sum		42	16	0

By THOMAS COMBES, Auditor.

Of the abbey as it was when it passed into the hands of its new owner, no contemporary account has come down to us, but these particulars given of the house at a later period may help us to form some idea of what it was when the canons quitted it. The particulars are as follow:—The chamber at the end of the *hall* in which Sir Richard Brooke lay; the inner chamber, the closet above the nursery, the maids' chamber, the *Leighes* chamber, Carew's chamber, Brooke's chamber, the higher *turret's* chamber, the middle *turret*, the green chamber, the lowmost *turret*, the two ground chambers, the two *outshalls buttery* out of that end of the house, the lower *gallery*, and the entry with three chambers at the side thereof, for servants, the closet over the *porch*, with the passages through the hall, as they were then accustomed, the kitchen, the dry and wet larders, the brewhouse, *boulting house*, with their passages, the *dayrie house*, the *dayrie* vault, and little storehouse, the *kiln*, the *malt lofts*, the *hack* house, the stable and *slaughter* house at the end thereof, and the vast room at the end thereof, the nearer barn, the cow-house, the outbuildings for swine and *pullen*, the garden house, the new buildings at the east end of the cow-house, the lower garner, with free egress and regress for horse, coach, or carriage through the gates.[1]

Of the former inmates of the abbey after the dissolution, the notices are very few. Canon Randle Wilmslow, who was so strongly recommended by the Commissioners, and was allowed to migrate to Vale Royal, as Dr. Ormerod thinks, for some treachery to his order, has been already mentioned. But there occurs a strange notice, in connection with Norton, in the rental of Cockersand Abbey, where it is said that one Agnes Schepte retired from Norton Abbey, to live an anchoress at Pilling.[2] Dr. Whitaker, in his History of Whalley (p. 76), gives an account of several such anchoresses, and in particular of one who retired to the hermit house at Whalley, and there broke the vows which she had taken, upon which Henry VI. dissolved the house. But even Agnes Schepte's retirement is less startling than the story told in the Smyth pedigree, where Anne Smyth, the Bishop of Lincoln's niece, is expressly stated to have been Abbess of Norton Priory.[3]

The only other notices of the inmates and officers of Norton occur in this account of the pensions paid to the survivors in 1556.

PENSIONS OF THE DISSOLVED ABBEY OF NORTON, IN THE COUNTY OF CHESTER.

The fees of the most noble Edward, Earl of Derby, chief seneschal of all the possessions late belonging to the said monastery yearly, £3.

ANNUITIES.

John Berkenhed, yearly	£1	6	8
William Boyes, yearly	5	0	0
Thomas Bricket, yearly	24	0	0[4]

The patronage and right of presentation to the churches of Runcorn and Great Budworth, which belonged to Norton Abbey, with the tithes of those parishes, were granted to Wolsey's College of Christ Church, Oxford, which the king had refounded. The grant to the college of the patronage of those livings, which was made subsequently to Sir Richard

---

[1] From the Inq. P. M. of Sir Richard Brooke III., who died 10th April, 8 Car. I. (1612).
[2] Rental of Cockersand, Chetham Miscellanies, iii. pp. 29, 30.
[3] Gregson's Fragments, p. 179.   [4] Augmentation Office.

Brooke's purchase, bears date only a short time before the monarch's death, when with him "terror had begun to assume devotion's mien." The college, however, were not called upon to exercise their right of presentation to Runcorn until the 25th January 1549, when Richard Coxe, the Dean of Christ Church, presented Thomas Boswell to that vicarage. Dean Coxe, who had been one of Edward VI.'s three tutors, was a man of many preferments, having been at different times Canon of Windsor, Dean of Westminster, and finally Bishop of Ely, and he is honoured with having his portrait hung in the library of Trinity Hall, Cambridge.[1]

No presentation to Great Budworth, however, took place until the 25th September 1580, forty-three years after the dissolution of Norton Abbey, when the Dean of Christ Church presented Robert Dobbes to that living.

Having now brought this history of the priory or abbey of Norton to a termination, it only remains that we add a few remarks by way of conclusion. In the long calendar of the heads of the house of Norton we have failed to discover any one who has left his name on the rolls of learning, and almost the same lack of information meets us with respect to the canons. We should be glad to find if we could, and the fact is not improbable, that William, an ecclesiastic who, in 1186, under the patronage of John fitz Richard, Baron of Halton, became an excellent astronomer or astrologer (for the terms were then convertible), and who wrote an able work on the planetary conjunctions[2] was one of the early canons of Norton, and that the learned canonist Runcorn was another. Roger de Mamecestre, the ninth prior, came of a learned family, and he may have written something which has not come down to us, but we have the express testimony of the visitors that Randal Wylmslow, whom they found a canon of the house, was "a good religous man, discreet, and well grounded in learning, and had many good qualities."[3] It was this canon who, in pursuance of that direction contained in the Act for dissolving the lesser monasteries, that the inmates should be distributed among the greater abbeys or be dismissed,[4] was allowed by the visitors on the dissolution of Norton to migrate to the abbey of Vale Royal.[5] Barkett, the last abbot, would hardly have ventured to attend in person the convocation in which the

[1] Stanley's Westminster Abbey, 420.   [2] Hist. Ches. i. 510.
[3] Harl. MS. fol. 604, f. 54.   [4] Froude's Hist. Eng. ii. 443.   [5] Hist. Ches. i. 502.

question of the king's marriage was debated, if he had not been a man of some learning, and it was this circumstance, and the readiness he had formerly shown to obey the king's summons to the convocation, which perhaps saved him from the fate that overtook some other refractory abbots, and which once threatened even him. He would seem to have survived the dissolution of his house, and to have died an old man in the reign of Queen Mary. In his old age we may imagine him.

> "a meagre man
> In humble garb, who rested with raised hand
> On a long staff, bending his head like one
> Who, when he hears the distant vesper bell,
> Halts by the way, and, all unseen of man,
> Offers his homage in the eye of heaven."[1]

If these are the only records of the literature of Norton, we shall hardly think, with Oldbuck in the "Antiquary," that the religious "spent their time in investigating points of remote antiquity, transcribing manuscripts, and composing new works for the information of posterity." Let us hope, since no report has reached us to the contrary, that no such disorders as were reported to prevail elsewhere were found in the house at Norton, and that its inmates employed themselves in those sacred duties for which the house was founded. It had stood for 400 years before it fell, and it had helped to keep the lamp of religion burning in dark times; but long before its end came, a period of decrepitude had crept over it; religion was languishing, and the house gave way before the demands of an advancing age. Though its end could scarcely be called peaceful, some regrets undoubtedly followed its fall, as they do everything that is old. Its possessions, however, did not, like those of many other of the religious houses, pass into the hands of a needy courtier as the reward of his interested zeal, but were purchased for an adequate price by the ancestor of the present owner. Since the purchase the estate has gone on steadily improving under careful management, and all regret that it has changed hands, and is no longer in *mortmain*, has long since ceased.

[1] Southey's Roderick.

INDEX.

A

APPLETON smiths, when the castle fell, became tool and watch movement makers, 121
Appleton, William, appointed serjeant at Halton, 71
Aston, Thomas, sues Thomas Butler for trespass, 97

B

BARRETT or Birkenhead, 19th abbot, presents a clerk to Budworth, 183; attends the convocation at Westminster, 184; answers the questions there, *ib.*; arrested, 191, 193; his canons dismissed, 198; is pensioned, 206
Barrymore, Elizabeth, countess of, succeeds to Rock Savage, 135; is succeeded by her daughter, *ib.*
Beeston Castle ordered to be dismantled, 119; its gateway mentioned, x
Bernard, Robert (12th prior), sells land to the Bishop of Lincoln, and has the king's licence, 172; presents a clerk to Runcorn, *ib.*; the king asks a loan of two sacks of wool, *ib.*
Bolingbroke, Henry of, afterwards Henry IV. (15th baron), made a knight, 79; character given of his mother, 80; marries, *ib.*; travels into Prussia, etc., *ib.*; goes on pilgrimage to Jerusalem, etc., 81; created Duke of Hereford, *ib.*; removes all obstructions in the Dee, *ib.*; charges Norfolk with treason, *ib.*; sentenced to banishment, 82; his departure a triumph, *ib.*; lands at Ravenspurg, and marches with his retainers, 83; puts to death the king's favourites, 84; takes the king prisoner, and conducts him to London, 85; makes his will, 86; dies, 87
Booth, Sir George, issues a manifesto before rising to restore the king, 124; is defeated at Winnington, 125; is set at liberty, *ib.*

Brereton, William, prosecutes two persons for trespassing on the Halton fishery, 97
Brooke, Colonel Henry, seneschal of Halton, 121; purchases the honour of Halton, *ib.*
Brooke, Sir Richard, purchaser of Norton, a knight of Rhodes, xi; short account of the Brooke family, xvi to xxvii
Bruche, Henry del, receiver at Halton, 36
Burscough priory founded, 157
Butler, Thomas, Esquire, sues Thomas Aston, for trespass in Halton Park, 97

C

CARINTON, Adam de, his grant of half of Sala, 159
Chesshyre, Sir John, some account of him, 136; his portrait painted, 137; confines his practice to the Common Pleas, *ib.*; in favour with the great, *ib.*; founds a library at Halton, 138; his monument at Runcorn, *ib.*
Cholmondeley, Hon. James, marries the heiress of Rock Savage, 135; distinguished as a soldier, *ib.*;
Cholmondeley, George James, marquis of, succeeds to the Rock Savage estates, 140
Cholmoudeley, General, dies at Rock Savage, 140
Christopher, Saint, his figure at Norton, 159; his legend, 160; the merits of his effigy, *ib.*;
Clinton, Sir William, afterwards Earl of Huntingdon, has a grant of Halton, 46; marches to Scotland, *ib.*
Cock fights abolished by the Protector, 124
Colchester, Lord, is the first to join the Prince of Orange, 128; dies, 129
Collar of S.S., origin of, 77
Congleton, cock-fights and bear-baiting there, 104
Cromwell's death, 124; his son Richard succeeds, but is too weak to wield the sceptre, *ib.*

Index

D

DANISH and other incursions, 2

Daresbury Church first mentioned, 154; its architecture, 155; arms in, ib.; called the White Church, ib.

Derby, the Earl of, visits Chester, and hears the Halton ballad, 99

Drinking tastes, change in, 109; sack substituted for ale, ib.

Dutton, Hugh de, made seneschal of Halton, 43; his death, 45

Dutton, Lawrence de, desires to be buried at Norton, 183

Dutton, Sir Piers, holds a halmote at Norton, 98

Dutton, Sir Thomas de, obtains a grant of a chantry, 168

E

EDWARD II. visits Halton, 39; has minstrels to sing before him, 40; comes to Norton and Vale Royal, 170

Egidius (4th prior), witnesses Earl Roger's confirmation of the Warburton charter, 162

Elfleda governs Mercia, 145; built a castle at Runcorn, 3; her character and epitaph, 4, 5

Elizabeth (Queen) orders a survey to be made of Halton, and calls herself Duchess of Lancaster, 92, 93

Eustace fitz John (4th baron) marries, and has the barony confirmed to him, 11; succeeds to Serlo de Burgh, ib.; his possessions, ib.; gives land to the builder of Norton church, ib.; founds Alnwick and Malton abbeys, ib.; dies, ib.; his arms, 12

F

FERDINAND, master of the military order of St. James, goes to Spain, 71

Free, Dr. John, vicar of Runcorn, an account of, 139; the inscription put up by him on Runcorn hill, 140

G

GARTER, order of, instituted, 54

Gaunt, John of (14th baron), born at Ghent, 60; created Earl of Richmond, ib.; his nurse, 61; precocious, ib.; joined in a commission to instruct the ambassadors to the Pope, ib.; marries, ib.

H

HALL, Roger or Robert (7th abbot), an executor of Robert Hedish's will, 182; mentioned in the Budworth windows, ib.

Halmote at Halton levy the land-tax by a mise, 130; regulate the causeways, ib.; interfere with the poor-laws, 132, 135; make rules as to the commons, 135; prohibit persons gathering boulders at the Hempstones, 139; interfere about settlements, ib.

Halton compared with scenes on the Rhine, 1

Halton, its name, and its castle, 6, 7; Webb's account of it, 123; chapel rebuilt, 127; assize of bread and beer there, 128; the halmote there, 128; its castle besieged and taken, 116; falls a second time, 117, 118; short account of its barons, 88; its chapel, some account of, 111; its courthouse rebuilt, 139; its court of pie powder, 123; its aleconners mentioned, 100; the castle a prison for recusants, 101; and other offenders, 103; its court claims an exclusive jurisdiction, 91

Harrington, William, seneschal of Halton, 94; ordered to give an oak to Farnworth church, ib.

Henry IV., on attaining the crown, took steps to secure his old inheritance, 90; makes the Prince of Wales Duke of Lancaster, ib.

Henry V. makes his will, and limits Halton to his brother John, Duke of Bedford, 90; his officers at Halton, 91

Henry VII. settles Halton on himself and his heirs, 92

Holland, Sir Robert de, slain, 45

Huxley, William de, breaks into Halton Castle, 36; pleads his clergy, 37

I

IRELAND, Thomas, succeeds Sir Thomas Holcroft as bailiff of Halton, 105; bailiff sergeant, ib.

J

JAMES I. visits Rock Savage, 109; kills a buck in Halton Park, ib.

John (6th abbot) obtains a charter of exemption from the earl, 164; in defiance of the law presents one of his canons to Runcorn, 182; pleads to a quo warranto, ib.; presents a clerk to Budworth, ib.

John fitz Richard (16th baron) gives Clifton to Geoffrey de Dutton, 14; keeps an astronomer, ib.; gives land to Adam de Dutton, ib.; the same to Punterling, 15; founds Stanlaw, ib.; founds the ferry, ib.; sent to Ireland, 16; dies, ib.

John Lacy (8th baron) gives Hugh de Dutton the right to license minstrels, 23; joins the nobles against King John, ib.

K

KING, reverend John, his and his wife's legacies to Halton, 113

L

LACY, Edmund (9th baron), his education and marriage, 25; the king present, ib.; alienates Thelwall, 26; goes to Bordeaux, ib.; his death, ib.

Lacy, Henry de (10th baron), his rule a busy one, 27; introduces the maiden, ib.; is in favour with Edward I., ib.; at the siege of Chartley, 28; founder of Whalley, ib.; governor of Denbigh, 29; has a commission to reform the law, 30; repairs Halton, 31; ambassador to France, ib.; settles his lands, ib.; goes to Bellegarde, 32; fights at Falkirk, ib.; attends the Parliament at Carlisle, 33; marries first Margaret Longespee, 2d, Joan Martin, ib.; dies, and is buried in London, ib.; his seals, ib.; his inquisitions *post mortem*, 34

Lacy, John, has a grant of lands from King Henry III., 23; gives lands to Stanlaw, ib.; marries twice, 24; obtains the earldom of Lincoln, ib.; attends the king's marriage, and carries the curtein, ib.

Lancaster, Henry of (12th baron), marries Maud, daughter of Sir Patric Chaworth of Kidwelly, 47; inquisitions on his death, 47-8; serves in Scotland, 44; attends the king at Dover, 44; joins the queen's party against the Spencers, ib.; has the king in his custody, 45; knights the young king, ib.; has a grant of *jura regalia*, 47

Lancaster, Henry, duke of (13th baron), has a grant of Kidwelly, 48; accompanies the king to Scotland, ib.; captain-general of the army, ib.; has a grant of 1000 marks to support his title, ib.; called "The soldier's father," 49;

sails with the king to Cadsand, 49; an admiral, ib.; is left by the king as a pledge for payment of his debts, 50; ambassador to the Pope, ib.; a great pageant in which Lord Beaumont was slain, 51; governor of Aquitaine, ib.; lieutenant of Gascony, ib.; goes to Guienne, ib.; his successes, ib.; gives the booty to the soldiers, 52; commanded to bring forces to the king, 52; appointed to judge causes of arms, 53; has a grant of Bergerac, ib.; a renewed grant of *jura regalia*, 53; has a grant of the earldom of Lincoln, ib.; created a duke, 54; serves with the Teutonic Knights, ib.; attends the judges at Chester, ib.; goes to the Pope at Avignon, 55; is seized and put to ransom, ib.; challenges the Duke of Brunswick, ib.; appointed lieutenant of Brittany, 55; leads a reinforcement into Normandy, ib.; is near to Poictiers at the time of the battle, 56; invests Rennes, ib.; goes to France, ib.; pleads to a *quo warranto*, ib.; claimed not to serve in Wales beyond the Clwyd, 57; the extent of his rights at Halton, ib.; marries Isabel Beaumont, 58; his gifts to the religious, ib.; his will, ib.; dies of the plague, ib.; his character, ib.; writes a book, ib.; called the "Good Duke," 59

Lancaster, Thomas, of Lancaster (11th baron), takes part in the Scottish wars, 35; marries Alice, the daughter of Henry de Lacy, ib.; she marries after his death, ib.; has a dispute with the chapter of St. Asaph, 36; a privy councillor, ib.; confronts the king at Burton, 37; is defeated and put to death, 38; his household book, 39; his estates seized, ib.; is esteemed a saint, 40; the king seizes his possessions, 42; his arms, 43; his attainder reversed, 45

Lancaster, John, duke of, retained to serve the king, 65; lands at Harfleur, but is unsuccessful, ib.; goes to Gascony, ib.; impales the arms of Castile, ib.; retains some Lancashire men, 66; makes Halton his hunting seat, ib.; the castle architecture, ib.; crosses the sea with the king, 67; returns from France, ib.; appointed a commissioner for the truce, ib.; levies an aid to marry his daughter, 68; has a grant of a county palatine, ib.; incurs popular odium, ib.; protects Wycliffe; ib.;

takes 14 merchant vessels, 68; settles the coronation of Richard II., *ib.*; leads an army into Brittany, 69; levies an aid to make his son a knight, *ib.*; sails to St. Malo, *ib.*; his conduct to the captors of Count Denia, 70; goes to Spain, 72; marries his two daughters there, *ib.*; created Duke of Aquitaine, *ib.*; is a commissioner to treat of peace, *ib.*; made lieutenant of Picardy, *ib.*; marries Catherine Swinford, 73; concurs in the seizure of the Duke of Gloucester, *ib.*; has a renewal of the office of constable of Cheshire, *ib.*; introduced in "Richard II.," 73; his son banished, 74; dies, and is buried in St. Paul's, *ib.*; founder of St. Nicholas's chapel at Liverpool, 75; loses the favour of the clergy, *ib.*; his character, *ib.*; commemorated by Chaucer, 76

Leftwich, Robert (4th abbot), settles the disputes about Aston, 181; presents a clerk to Runcorn, *ib.*

Lincoln, Roger de (10th prior), agrees with the abbot of Vale Royal as to Aston chapel, 166

Lyon, William, the sailor bishop, 105

M

Malborn, John (5th abbot), an arbitrator in a dispute about lands, 182

Malborn, Richard (5th abbot), of the yeoman family at Walton, 182

Mamecestre, Roger de (9th prior), account of, and of others of his name, 163; grants Geoffrey de Dutton a license for divine offices at Sutton, 166

Monasteries, the royal visitors at Norton, 97; the peril they were in, and their rescue by Sir Piers Dutton, 98

More, Richard de la, his charter about the ferry, 157; receives a grant of lands subject to paying a sum towards the ferry, *ib.*; witness to an important charter, 158

N

Navarete, battle of, 65

Nigel, first baron of Halton, 1

Norton Priory, some other religious houses of the same name, 143; dress of the canons, 144; the order of canons reformed, *ib.*; their rule, *ib.*; their houses numerous, 145; the Norton house first placed at Runcorn, *ib.* its architecture, 150; its priors and abbots met in the earl's palatine parliament, 152; its church consecrated, 153; its site, *ib.*; sepulchral slabs in it, *ib.*; its possessions, 194; sold to Sir Richard Brooke, 200

Norton, amount paid for the purchase, 202; villeins there, *ib.*; mills there, 203; bells excepted, 203; no legend about them there, *ib.*; valuation of Norton, 204-5; account of the abbey, 206; conclusion, 207

Norton Priory attacked by the king's forces, 115

O

Olton, John de (11th prior), has a license to acquire land in Newton, 169; presents a clerk to Grappenhall, *ib.*; is cited before the bishops' commissaries, *ib.*; appoints a clerk to Runcorn, 170; obtains grants, 171

P

Pilkington, Thomas, appointed park-keeper, 71

Plemouth, Roger (3d abbot), sells the advowson of Grappenhall, 181

Preyeres, seneschal of Halton, 36

R

Regulars not to be presented to livings, 168

Religious houses required visiting, 187; a general outcry for it, 189; visitors appointed, *ib.*; visitation made, *ib.*

Religious houses, the smaller dissolved, 190; the dissolution opposed in the north, 191; Sir Piers Dutton's letter, *ib.*

Restoration of Charles II.—the king's arms set up, and the prisoners released, 126

Richard (1st prior of Norton), 147; settles the dispute with Adam de Dutton, 151; and obtains the king's confirmation of the priory charter, 152

Richard (15th prior), has John of Gaunt's confirmation of his tithes, 175; lets his corn tithes in Appleton, *ib.*; presents a clerk to Grappenhall, *ib.*; is present at the founding of the Dutton chantry, 175; leases the tithes of Appleton, 176; has a burgage in Warrington, *ib.*; presents a clerk to Budworth, *ib.*; services at Aston intermitted, 177

Richard the leprous brother of Roger, 18; notice of lepers and leper-houses, 19; dies and is buried at Norton, 22

Richard fitz Eustace (5th baron), marries Albreda, sister of Robert de Lacy, 12 ; a curious charter made in his court, *ib.* ; dies, 13 ; his arms, *ib.*

Rivers, Earl, joins the nobles who engage to find forces for the king, and is abused by the writers of the other side, 113 ; he and the Brookes take opposite sides, 114 ; his castle burnt, 119 ; excepted from Essex's pardon, 120

Rivers, Richard, Earl, active in public affairs, 129 ; probably favours the land-tax, *ib.* ; introduces the Duke of Argyle in the House, 130 ; is sent to Spain, *ib.* ; resigns his command 131 ; sent to Hanover, *ib.* ; made Master of the Ordnance, *ib.* ; father of Savage the poet, 133

Rivers, Thomas, Earl, a favourer of William III., dies in 1694, 129 ; the epitaphs on his daughter and son-in-law, *ib.*

Robin Hood, some account of him, 41

Rock Savage, built, 107 ; the place deserted, *ib.*

Roger (7th baron), his character, 17 ; takes the name of Lacy, *ib.* ; rescues the Earl of Chester, *ib.* ; has a grant of the right to license minstrels, *ib.* ; takes the cross, 20 ; is present at the storming of Acre, *ib.* ; goes to conduct the King of Scotland to Lincoln, *ib.* ; goes to Normandy, *ib.* ; commanded to let William Earl of Pembroke have six wains of wine, toll free, 21 ; besieged in Saucy Castle, *ib.* ; receives money for fortifying Carlisle, *ib.* ; acquires Penwortham, 22 ; gives land to Stanlaw, *ib.* ; marries Maude de Clare, dies and is buried at Stanlaw, *ib.*

Runcorn, origin of the name, 146 ; the priory removed from there to Norton, 148 ; castle built there, 4

Runcorn church, a sort of sanctuary, 176

Runcorn ships not to sail thence with cargoes direct for Dublin, by an order of 21 Ed. IV., 95

Rupert, Prince, arrives in Cheshire, 117

S

Savages, a short account of the family, 106 ; two of them charged with slaying John Pouncefote, *ib.* ; Bishop Bonner and Richard Savage of the family, 107 ; obtain a lease of the honour of Halton, 108

Savage, John, murdered by Ralf Bathurst, who, refusing to plead, was condemned to the *peine forte et dure*, and pressed to death, 105

Savage, Sir John (the 1st), seneschal of Halton, ordered to receive certain prisoners from the sheriff, 94

Savage, Sir John, seneschal of Halton, in the time of Philip and Mary, 99 ; dies, 103

Savage, Sir John (2d) seneschal and constable, 103 ; attends a cock-fight, *ib.* ; reports on the records, 104 ; erects a beacon, 105 ; dies, 106

Savage, Thomas, Viscount, has a present from Congleton, 111 ; dies, 112

Savage, John, Viscount, succeeds his father, 112 ; the times are low'ring and threatening, *ib.*

Savage, Viscount, Thomas, appoints officers at Halton, 127 ; joins the exclusionists, *ib.* ; receives Monmouth at Rock Savage, 128

Savage, John, Earl Rivers, declines the title, 134 ; the title extinct on his death, *ib.*

Savage, Richard, the poet, notice of, 134

Saxon coins struck at Runcorn, 5

Sely How, explanation of the term, 201 ; a field so named, *ib.*

Sequestrations at Halton and the neighbourhood, 119.

Southworth, Henry, yeoman of the crown, born in Halton Castle, 96

Southworth, Sir John, confined at Halton, 101 ; removed to the New Fleet, Manchester, 102

Stafford, Humphrey, Earl of Buckingham, seneschal of Halton, 95

Sutton, John (1st abbot), presents a clerk to Grappenhall, 177 ; presents clerks to Runcorn, *ib.* ; makes a lease of Pulsaye, 178 ; presents a clerk to Budworth, *ib.* ; arbitrator in a dispute, 179

Swinford, Catherine, buried at Lincoln, 73

T

Tarlton, Forget-not, the actor, anecdote of, 100

Tyler, Wat's, rebellion, the Duke of Lancaster's palace burned, 71

V

Venables, Sir Hugh, appointed seneschal of Halton, 46 ; an inquisition taken, *ib.*

Visitors besieged at Norton, 193 ; rescued by Sir Piers Dutton, *ib.*

W

WALTER de Vernon, bailiff at Halton, 33
Warburton, Sir Geoffrey, deputy seneschal of Halton, 95
Warburton, Sir Geoffrey, buried at Norton, 150
Warburton, Piers, called "the Wise," succeeds his father, and is ultimately chief seneschal of Halton, 96; rebuilds the house at Arley, *ib.*
Warburton, Sir John, is made constable and seneschal of Halton, 96; receives into his custody William Pull or Poole, *ib.*
Warrington besieged, 116
Westbury, Thomas (2d abbot), appears to a *quo warranto*, 180; is thought to have helped the Countess of Richmond, 181; distrained for his relief, and shows his exemption, 92
Wevirham, John de (13th prior), appears to a *quo warranto*, 173; has a dispute about the Aston corody, *ib.*; presents a clerk to Budworth, 174; requires a rent, *ib.*
William fitz Nigel (2d baron), 8; rescues the earl his master, 9; gives Daresbury to Norton, *ib.*; visits Hugh fitz Oslant, *ib.*
William fitz William (3d baron), removes the canons from Runcorn to Norton, 10; gives them the tithes of Thelwall, *ib.*; gives land to Shrewsbury abbey, *ib.*; and to St. Werburgh's, 11; dies, *ib.*

THE END.

Printed by R. & R. CLARK, *Edinburgh*.

www.ingramcontent.com/pod-product-compliance
Lightning Source LLC
Chambersburg PA
CBHW031347230426
43670CB00006B/463